Praise for
SELECTED POEMS 196

Reading through the still incredible work collected in this exemplary *Selected Poems*, I marvel all over again at the force of even the "smallest" of Clark Coolidge's poems. Coolidge's sonic expertise has often been noted, and music—especially bebop and what has followed it—clearly has suggested to him ways to generate rhythmic clusters, to ride accelerations, to invent scales. No other poet ever has so exquisitely, and sometimes also turbulently, written sheer sonic wonder into poetry. But painting and sculpture, too—from Quattrocento Italy to the New York School and after—has been an aesthetic source, suggesting ways to work against time-driven linearity so as to produce verbal fields and signifying word masses, raw thought matter, formal flicker. But that flicker is indigenous to film too, of course; it passes along stills, binding what's framed into sequences: "everything seeming to say clad aside clad" (*Polaroid*). What's in this beautifully edited volume is, for me, the manifestation of art's ultimate achievement. Clark Coolidge writes a whole art, an all-moment of being somewhere and thinking it.

—Lyn Hejinian

The precision of the ear (count consonant clusters, hard as carbon), the scope of the imagination (why pause just because no one's ever pushed over *this* horizon?), the fearlessness of a spelunker (*everywhere!*)—Clark Coolidge's early poems looked & sounded like nothing anyone had ever seen before, imagined before, and they changed poetry, at once and completely. But what persuaded me, and persuades me still almost half a century later, is the fine wry wit with its winking nods to such masters as Jonathan Williams or Philip Whalen. This is work as American as a Gee's Bend quilt, as polished as a Donald Judd sculpture, oh but with such syncopation—*read these aloud!*

—Ron Silliman

SELECTED POEMS 1962–1985

CLARK COOLIDGE

EDITED BY LARRY FAGIN AND CLARK COOLIDGE

INTRODUCTION BY BILL BERKSON

Station Hill
of Barrytown

Published by Station Hill of Barrytown, the publishing project of the Institute for Publishing Arts, Inc., 120 Station Hill Road, Barrytown, NY 12507, New York, a not-for-profit, tax-exempt organization [501(c)(3)].

Online catalogue: www.stationhill.org
e-mail: publishers@stationhill.org

 This publication is supported in part by grants from the New York State Council on the Arts, a state agency.

Cover and interior design by Larry Fagin.

Cover image: "Clark at a Serpent Power rehearsal, sitting on a suitcase, wailing away" (1967), Susan Coolidge.

The author thanks Bill Berkson, Miles Champion, Susan Coolidge, Mathew Gonzalez, Susan Quasha and Sam Truitt.

Library of Congress Cataloging-in-Publication Data

Names: Coolidge, Clark, 1939- author, editor. | Fagin, Larry, editor.
Title: Selected poems 1962-1986 / Clark Coolidge ; edited by Clark Coolidge
    and Larry Fagin.
Description: Barrytown, NY : Station Hill Of Barrytown, 2016.
Identifiers: LCCN 2015041883 | ISBN 9781581771497
Classification: LCC PS3553.O57 A6 2016 | DDC 811/.54—dc23
LC record available at http://lccn.loc.gov/2015041883

Manufactured in the United States of America

for Michael Palmer
first friend of the poem

Contents

INTRODUCTION: THE SPOOLS OF COOLIDGE, BY BILL BERKSON   xv

POEMS (1962)
Meditation in the White Mountains   1

MOTOR GROWERS 'PEDIA (1963–65)
Noon Shed   2
Noon Print   3
Pinks   4
The Past Wrestler   5

FLAG FLUTTER & U.S. ELECTRIC (1964–66)
The Death of Floyd Collins   7

SPACE (1965–69)
Machinations Calcite   9
The Tab   10
Soda Gong   11
Crisp Loss   12
The So (Part 2)   13
Gobi   14
Brill   15
Rights   16
Red Size   18
Bee Elk   20
Styro   21
"clip"   22
"contact back"   23
"prune acrylic whose"   24
"agape model serene"   25
"ounce code orange"   26
"dial urn"   27
"of   about"   28
"listene"   29

DIAMONDS (1966)
  "ace"   30
  "gee"   31
  "pro"   32
  "for"   33
  "mat"   34
  "non"   35
  "one"   36

UNREAD & UNLOVED (1966)
  Hey! You Look Like a Girl!   37
  West   39

THE SO (1966–67)
  Vegetable Inlet   41
  A Glitter Shoals   42
  Mangrove in Chrome   43
  The So   44
  The Agate Ace   46
  High Pitched Whale   47
  Movies   48
  Sum Sun Elbow   49

STRETCHER (1966–67)
  Mount Notes   51
  The Blue Pomade   53

TOOLS, MODELS, SPECIFICATIONS (1966–68)
  to ea ut ue ir   p   es   de   he   in   ss   56

SUITE V (1967)   57

POEMS (1967–69)
  Drummers   95
  While   98

AS IF IT (1968–69)

The　Ments   100

By　of　Much   104

Among　the　Newbegins   106

Size   111

AMOUNT (1968–69)

Simmer   114

"moon silent mike breasts"   116

Scrip Ant   117

"tam moil"   118

Dharma Snow   119

Pontoon Bonita   120

"permission douse a taint blunt"   121

"rice"   122

WHOLES (1968–69)

"A"   123

"in yet"   123

"flow"   124

"flat"   124

THE WHICH WAYS, PT. I (1969–71)

All Talk   125

Sonnets: The Blanks   126

The Arp   129

Deem   131

Made Thought   132

A Tanguy   133

Color Slides   135

Horizon   136

Moroccan Variations   137

PAGES FROM THE PORTER HOUSE (1970)

A Satie   139

THE WHICH WAYS, PT. II (1970–73)

    Pin Elegance   140

    Dumb Ague in Ouray   141

    The Basal Strings   142

    As Apt as Squares as Pounds   143

    The Skippers   148

    Basil Rathbone's Bathrobe   150

    Soup Tends   155

    The Lead Chamber   156

    The Beelines   164

from THE MAINTAINS (1971–72)   168

from QUARTZ HEARTS (1972–73)   184

from POLAROID (1972–73)   191

AS IS (1973)   202

OWN FACE (1973–78)

    Of Tanguy   206

    There Is a Caterpillar that Makes a Very Complicated Hammock   209

    Rhymes with Monk   212

    Album—A Runthru   214

    A Note   217

    By the Island   218

    The Cave Remain   219

    Cavemen   223

    Between You and Me and the Lamp Post   224

    Our Nature's Future   225

    Connie's Scared   227

    At the Poem   230

from A BOOK BEGINNING WHAT AND ENDING AWAY
(1973–78, 1981)   231

MIDDLE BORDERS (1973–85)

    At Sphynx Edge   250

    Middle Borders 1 & 4   256

    Chondrules   260

    Moon Down   264

    Head Broken Open It Seemed like an Egg with a Can Opener   265

    At the Point Let's Have Us a Tune   266

    New Old City Chimes   267

    Over Time   272

    Leads from Somebody Else's Notebook   273

    A Monologue   274

    Monk, a Head   280

from SMITHSONIAN DEPOSITIONS (1974)   283

from SUBJECT TO A FILM (1974–75)   291

AMERICAN ONES (1977)

    III   298

    IV   300

    IX   301

SEER'S ROW (1977–81)

    To the Capital   303

MELENCOLIA (1978)

    Part I   317

SOLUTION PASSAGE: POEMS (1978–81)

    On Induction of the Hand   320

    One of Essence's Entrances   322

    HPL   323

    Darkling Thrums   324

    Brass Land I Live In   325

    Out to Business   326

    What Saw?   327

    Forth Poem   328

A Walk 329

Homage to Melville 330

Noon Point 332

The End 333

Radiational Bowling 334

A Dalliance with Salt Sides 335

Sun Shine on a Fog Horn 337

The Man in the Light of the Con Ed Tower 338

Peru Eye 339

Gab Shift 345

Of What   The Music to Me 348

Homage 356

MINE: THE ONE THAT ENTERS THE STORIES (1979–80)

I 357

VI 368

VIII 372

from RESEARCH (1981) 377

from THE CRYSTAL TEXT (1982–83) 380

SOUND AS THOUGHT (1982–84)

The Great 389

The Once Held 391

Two or Three Things 393

On the Road 407

Back Aways 408

Hommage à Ron Padgett 416

For Larry Fagin, as He Passes Me Unknowing 417

"There's Roller." 418

Motel 419

Mammoth Night 420

The Sixth and After, Nothing Easier 421

Homage to Ballard 423

"He walked around and couldn't think of anything" 424

MESH (1984)

 Movement on a Dream   425

from ROME NOTEBOOK (1984)   430

ODES OF ROBA (1984–85)

 L.A. in Time   440
 Rome Passage   442
 Rome Once Alone   444
 Glance in White Space   445
 In Cell   446
 Somehow to Be Able to Say   448
 The Saints   449
 Ashbery Explains   451
 Cats Mounted on Cots   454
 Attention   458
 Godard and the Rhapsody of Mention   459

  ACKNOWLEDGMENTS   463
  ABOUT THE AUTHOR   464

Introduction: The Spools of Coolidge

What did Clark Coolidge say then?
                    —Philip Whalen, "The Task Rejected," 1965

By some fine coincidence, Clark Coolidge and I were students together at Brown University during four semesters in 1957–58. Even though we had one or two friends and many interests in common, we were unaware of each other at the time and didn't meet until much later, in New York. In the late 1960s, our friendship solidified over my acting as an intermediary in asking Philip Guston to make a cover drawing—it ended up being two drawings, front and back—for Clark's book *Ing* (1968), which was also how Clark and Guston first met, and soon began collaborating, and how the series of poem pictures Guston made with assorted younger poets' poems over the next ten years began, as well.

While Clark comes from a New England intellectual and artistic family, both my parents had come to New York from modest, and modestly acculturated, circumstances in the Midwest. Fine-boned, tall, and slender, Clark resembles the upright patriarchal figures from Colonial portraiture. With his boyhood passions for rock collecting and spelunking and for fantasy writers like H. P. Lovecraft, Clark seems to have initiated himself early on into a private sacred world. Granted that the glittery New York of my youth was a fantasy realm in itself, I had as a child no such thing, just the usual romantic daydreams engendered by movies and popular songs. Allowing for our differences in background and temperament, the tallies of events that either of us took as important news, literary and otherwise, in those years when virtually everything was a discovery, are strikingly similar. By extension, such listings would define the changes experienced—like so many doors and windows radically opened wide—by many poets of like persuasion then starting out.

The son of the chairman of the Music Department at Brown, Clark came to writing by way of music; although an avid reader as a child, he speaks of having taken only one course in literature at Brown while majoring in geology and doubling as a jazz drummer. Having entered a year before me, in the fall of 1956, he quit his college studies altogether at the end of his second year and, inspired by reading Jack Kerouac's *On the Road*, hitchhiked across the country to Los Angeles. Soon afterward, he lived for a time in an apartment on Horatio Street, in Greenwich Village, and wrote. Having to start somewhere, with an idiosyncratic feeling for prosody prepared by his musical training, he began by imitating, along with Kerouac, Allen Ginsberg, Gregory Corso, and Philip Whalen.

During Thanksgiving vacation that same fall, I flew to San Francisco in search of, as I rather fuzzily thought of it then, the Beat Generation. The bartender at The Place quickly confided that the writers I was hoping to find there were "all in New York, man." A few months earlier, in Paris, I had caught a glimpse of Gregory Corso berating a man in a bar. In early 1959, I too left Brown and returned full-time to New York. The following summer, again in Paris, I met William Burroughs and at George Whitman's bookstore heard a tape recording of him reading from *Naked Lunch*. (It had been announced that Burroughs himself would read, but instead there was only the cassette player on a small table in the middle of the upstairs room, *el hombre invisible* nowhere in sight.) That fall, when I accompanied Kenneth Koch to his reading at Brown, in the same auditorium sat or stood both Clark and Ted Berrigan, fateful company unbeknownst to any of the three of us, but there we were. Looking back, it seems both Clark and I took Kerouac's books as manuals for how to live (natural-born existentialists that we were) as well as how to write; at first the two seemed inextricable, and it took a while to learn which was which. For Clark, *Doctor Sax* was the book that resonated with the dark side of his New England childhood imaginings; for me, it was *The Subterraneans*, starting with the message on page one, a loud-and-clear corrective, which probably stood out for Clark, as well:

They are hip without being slick, they are intelligent without being corny, they are intellectual as hell and know all about Pound without being pretentious or talking too much about it . . .

Events in music between 1957 and '59 that we responded to, and took as artistic models in our separate ways, included John Cage's *Indeterminacy*, Ornette Coleman, Thelonious Monk's stints at the Five Spot and his Riverside recordings of that period, Cecil Taylor, Robert Craft's Complete Anton Webern and the *New Directions in Music 2/ Morton Feldman* LP (liner notes by Frank O'Hara and cover drawing by Philip Guston). What was going on in the visual arts—the work of Guston, de Kooning, Pollock, Rauschenberg, Johns, and others—figured in there, too, as did the films of the burgeoning New Wave and Underground Cinema, but the analogous impact of all that was realized slightly later.

In those days it became a revelation to write poems primarily influenced by John Ashbery's "Europe" once it appeared in *Big Table* (1960), with the sense—shared partly, as I learned later, by Ashbery himself—of different frequencies interrupting one another as in Cage and with spatial silences between words, phrases, or whole lines on the white page like intervals in Webern. As Clark said during an exchange with Allen Ginsberg at Naropa in the '70s, "'Europe' was absolutely the poem that turned me on and mystified me." In turn, John Ashbery once told me that Coolidge's work as it developed early on in the '60s was the best extension he could imagine of what he had been doing in that crucial poem.

What we shared then, and talked about only later, was a need and readiness for a mode of writing other than what Coolidge has called "frozen literature," a feeling that words, and the sentences they came all-too-neatly wrapped in, required refreshing via intensive disruption and rearrangement. It seemed urgent for the language we had been taught and that was all around us to be short-circuited and aired out in order to give words more breathing space and physicality, away from their preauthorized, anticipated meanings, so they could exist and mean more in themselves, as their own mutable occasions—in effect, what William Burroughs called "breakthrough in the grey room."

The varieties of "pulverized" or shredded syntax of *The Tennis Court Oath* and Burroughs's *The Soft Machine* were exemplary, but for me—and I think for Clark, too—rather than relying on collage or cut-up or any other mechanical procedure for taking language apart and reordering it, there was a readymade cut-up or scanning device accessible in one's own mind; once you found the dial, you had only to turn it. Only in retrospect did this technicality seem to mark a change in sensibility, the previous generation's relation to conventional syntax being fairly compliant albeit aslant with irony (every quivering word or phrase bearing quotation marks around it), whereas ours more frontally resisted the rules altogether. We had been schooled to read poems and almost everything else as cluttered terrains of dangling symbolism. The words thereby felt ruinously overdetermined and stuffed. We existed in a plethora of language, our own ironies augmented by sarcasm, with only very slippery syntax, if any. Lacking meaningful forms to proceed with, one had recourse to format, or what William Carlos Williams and Frank O'Hara both had called "design." Although this was all very new at the time, the idea wasn't to be avant-garde but to get real. If any form were possible, it would be the one Clark regularly invokes in interviews, talks, and such, coming from Beckett: "a form to accommodate the mess."

The word book . . . *What has that got to do with an actual book really?*
. . . It's booooook. Like in Krapp's Last Tape, *he takes a spool of tape and he*
says "spoooooool" and he says it over and over again, so it's like an incantation.
—Clark Coolidge in conversation with Philip Guston, 1972

William Carlos Williams once wrote that a poem should constitute an event—or more properly, as he put it, "a revelation"—in the language in which it's written. In a poem of that order every word gets its "aha" moment. Clark's work of the past fifty years, of which this book represents a fair fraction of the first half, can be read as one prolonged event, with plentiful revelations. It is still partial, a clause, as the whole sentence to which it belongs remains an ongoing furtherance of grammar and expanded sense.

"As prolific as Clark Coolidge" is an idiom, wistful as can be, that has entered the conversation; of recent times no poet comes close in sums of page count. The rumor that Clark writes ceaselessly on a daily basis—with no outside occupation, in tidy domestic surroundings (hence the proclamation, "raging in my paradise")—produces an image of still more black spring binders full of works as yet unreleased. In the seemingly boundless lap pool that is his commitment, he waves gingerly at completion, all the while shoving off it for the next turn. To a poet like myself, whose work comes slowly, sometimes with uncomfortable pauses between, the specter of such fluency is bound to be both a wonderment and cause for alarm—an alarm both frightening (the feeling of inevitably lagging behind) and a goad to do more (like O'Hara, Coolidge shows us there is always a poem to be written). Then, too, there is the reminder that keeping at it is not so easy as all that; once when my own work was foundering on an excess of doubt and distraction, he wrote usefully of the need to "sit down solitary and scary and work the words out."

In seminars at the San Francisco Art Institute over the years, I repeatedly brought up what John Cage had made happen and each time realized that, although Cage was right when he said at a certain point that he'd done what he had set to do, to open people's ears to the sounds around them, the job still had to be done again, perhaps every generation or two. Certain kinds of art lead a double life as arcane bedazzlements and primary lessons for any viable commonality. It may be that the culture beyond Coolidge's immediate readership has already absorbed these poems without knowing it and without ever knowing how to assimilate them. Once heard, a single poem can be infectious. Imagine schoolchildren reading *The Maintains* to become intimate with vocabulary and what constitutes any possible sentence structure.

Clark has kept to his own orbit, all the while increasing its depth and breadth. And he has the good sense to please himself first, following from the merest drone or mutter out to where one or another terminus of mental membrane is struck and the reader's low, rumbling chortle segues into an all-out *hrumph*! Commentators on his poems tend to write as if they were witnessing some kind of technological feat, a classroom science project or thought experiment. Their exegeses project an image of the poet's brain pickled in a bell jar telekinetically aligned with standard-issue digits frantically pecking. Such descriptions suffer from overstudiousness; they leave out how playful Clark is and how funny his poems often are, how most every word shows off its risible side. It flourishes, funny and deep, as deep and dark as words can go, allowing for the oddball nature of words in the first place, that there's nothing natural about them and yet they have been part of human consciousness for millennia. Open anywhere, you'll find his humor at home. But turn around, and back on the same page, he's got a case of the willies: "terrible picture of all the words waiting relentless *outside*." "A writer of few satisfactions," as Clark says of Kafka, whose readings of his own work were punctuated by truffles of laughter, not itself a sign of satisfaction.

I work, guided by an inner reptile. —Pierre Soulages as per Coolidge,
"The Blue Pomade: 22 European Painters & Sculptors"

The inarticulate is a closed fist, like a stone; articulation, the release
of splayed fingers. The material life of thought: I recall a hallucinogen-
ic experience of thinking to think, then experiencing, together with
much grinding of teeth, the prolonged drilling of a vein of "thoughts,"
all of them flying off and away like iron flakes.

    Evidently, it is all improvisation: the performative winging-it,
as unplanned as intense, a case of stamina and decisiveness, admitting
of no bluff or cliché, but riding on sustained wonder about whatever's
at hand. Coolidge's titles, small wonders in themselves, come last, as
if by interpretative afterthought (viz. "Basil Rathbone's Bathrobe,"
"Connie's Scared," or "Radiational Bowling"). A continuous present is
transmitted to the reader's mind as what's on the page, in your ear, to
be "read" only by staying with it. The dynamic threatens implosion,
madness—you can get lost in there, in the consciousness of a single
word, that potential maelstrom. Because Coolidge will never guide
you, you take upon yourself the freedom to proceed as you will in the
poem—equally fearful, baffled, and amused—beside him. None of his
attributes, except perhaps a rare type of surplus fixation, seems to have
come naturally. As a graph of a poet's growth, this book shows how
hard he worked, as well as the refusals ("the necessary negatives") im-
plied, in devising his habits, and how to break them.

    "Look at any word long enough . . ." Inspiring how he keeps
pushing, changing, emptying, and then augmenting by writing what's
on next. A kind of manic sincerity therein: normal self-doubt unin-
flected by self-irony; all the major ironies saved up for what impinges
from the uselessness outside. A fluency that denies stopping: "Why
stop?" The chronological shift, for instance, from inventories of words
like collections of things (marbles, fossils, bean jars, the ever-mounting

directory of proper nouns) to what will pass as "gab." (The writer-drummer who has "the gift of gab," but only by figuring it, soliloquizing at his fingertips.) Then another shift, from short, fine-tuned line lengths to poem and extended-prose masses where caesuras are brushed by in the heat of pressing onward. "Just a bunch of words" is not far off. In the early poems, they seem at first to scintillate in space like pieces of a mobile construction, or else you hear the truncated syllables clattering, or else words or parts of words tumbling like numbers out of a bingo cage, brandishing cadenzas en route.

I recall Clark's telling me in the early 1970s that he didn't really like Schoenberg's music, but he appreciated that large parts of it go along without any development. Likewise, around the same time, he mentioned a particular solo of John Coltrane's as proceeding at "exact speed." In the writing, I hear him hearing ahead, in front of and behind the word as it reveals itself, the poem's surface compounding thereby. He himself stands revealed as some kind of visionary, in the sense of turning open a world simultaneously apprehended and there for the making. The passion for and of the activity of writing is the overriding sentiment, within which there are, for Coolidge, endless curiosities to be satisfied or anyway dealt with. As Bernadette Mayer once said, a concordance to his work would be fascinating.

The poems in this book were written over twenty-three years in such places as Providence (1962–66); New York (1966); Providence/Cambridge, Mass. (1966–67); San Francisco (1967–70); Hancock, Mass. (1970–85); and Rome (1984–85). The fact that in many of these towns and cities Clark lived on the top or side of a hill suggests a quality of remove and gazing on things from above. From the heights each poem appears to take its own peculiar plunge. The insistent musings, discriminations, glees, puzzlements, irritability, those sardonic drive-by puns, and philosophic remarks that register almost as stage whispers without claiming any prior authority, all signify a powerful affection for the world as encompassed, and ultimately, Clark's will to articulate that fabled specific infinity he has had his eye on, the "quest to know anything, write everything," the Chapel Perilous of these poems.

—Bill Berkson

SELECTED POEMS

MEDITATION IN THE WHITE MOUNTAINS

Blue sky
few crags, the slopes
are green

air
whistling by
 the granite stopwatch

NOON SHED

this day is grin machine shed
powder red rust over every
thing girl & tree
                        (slow moons

ocher snuff & ideas

I breathe past beauty
kicks?
            (on an armor slat sky

& the mine-disaster printed
on a dark tin wafer

NOON PRINT

morning in lunch
    time bread or
        tobacco birds

watching thc cciling for changes
                  in white
          (or whirl-beasties)

I'm
    never over
         come by prophecy

I stomp down (any
turns)   street town

PINKS

red
night
the bees are working in
the black room

•

the sneeze didn't come
before I wanted to finish writing
the words came

•

it doesn't
echo   the cigarette
smokes

•

the ceiling isn't happy
smoke gets smaller & smaller til finally you can't gets swallow
see it

•

shrill hand of talk
buttons
the cobra's eyes

THE PAST WRESTLER

Apollinaire in a chair . . .
& then one breast . . .
there's nothing to say

the poets union
as for me . . . hmmmmm . . .
from her lips
out of corners
nuts, skin bolts, clanking in his stomach
turn off TV

if nothing else
there   as I am high
to see what happens household mustard is
few wash
with my eyes

there are ways
there have been too many years
try to forget last
night.   broke it up

glancing at me happily
the Baltimore sun said
I am like a mask of jelly in your arms
was once a man who shouted across tables
we can't know
eel grass, tough shells
the sky empty

send this poet to Mexico
his society's gone to pieces in his belly
pillow has turned to stone
as the cock flies

Edgar Allan Poe,
don't worry about growing old
just a minute I'll get a new set of pajamers

THE DEATH OF FLOYD COLLINS

1.

these were contemporaries of the mammoth
looking back up the ridge
on this unfortunate friday morning Floyd
whose stem, extending
no foundation for assuming
sleeps when his temperature is lowest

came upon our first Typhlotriton
gills disappeared and henceforth respiration
any one of which might be the one
to create mystical ideas in the minds
sliding thru their tank
before it ended in a blank wall

because beneath the guano are numerous
time a train rumbled by a whole
to move his powerful leg the rock
led me down a long wooden black space
the north, south, & west surfaces also bore
inch long bugs closely related

2.

neighbors never forgot the cure speleologists do
in a lifetime, he usually he explored alone, with sight
of a boy tramping over cornfields in the middle of winter
he was a stocky boy who would lie down on the thin
mantle of snow & blow into man, muscular
with powerful arms

He spoke little & seldom a breathing hole
in any sense of the word   cold air in summer &
warm air in winter, & at other times night, caves
little concerned him, except as it might hold a
suck in air, just as mysteriously

How baked beans in his pocket — knew risks,
for he had several brushes
a cave was further from home, woods, & the words with death
He-came was a cave, & Floyd knew it

"I'd rather be dead, than down past his head"

MACHINATIONS CALCITE

acetone imprinted
oblique swatch on the skin car barn oil wall
ocarina & mumps
much wet green
I'd leave sole key to this game to my friend, sheet water cat

actor impressed
weaving candle turn on computer cigarette, paper wall
tarheels & balance
a lot of yellow stick neck
He'll have to hurry & carry away, to my blue friend hustling
       bringing his moon & car

agate inked
merry melodies drool on shank of wet lead star tool
crayon & sands
length of granite buck-drill
It's sucking up the strand, his crystal flag, & the eels tube for that,
       their parade swizzle fun

arctic suck
splinter dry-ice spazz luke-ing ace supper at church
hard pinks & sponge breath
many forams drift
Roller window going up on I repeat my offer food list in iron flakes

THE TAB

mica flask moves layout hasty
bunkum geode olive loin candle
mines repeating sky hot dregs, in cast
lank oiler blocks, hats sink
wig pyrite & hasty troll by the rim

myhrr louvres   coinage hovers
the mast glitter planting new bulgers tolling
stained-glass hole of suds, repeater
shaking in salt, mud domes falling
trellis concretion, one green mote

the gas farm on Blue Ledge
pine mist into "darlings" chasten
elevator lap rest to the lead block
chain arrival starting, a silver flight
hunks sharpen up, in the fold of coin

spines bee air tower in azure launch
on steaming hair, slid rock
tipped grind to shelve-cirrus shake-up
pale take-off
shale widens, baking

SODA GONG

box of surinam toad glass hill
pastiche bartender a live teeth
tepid tones — brine

_____

orange
          milk
suction
sentence

_____

do fuck they it's
        is
     you
     filled-in washtub board

_____

gas viper comprende
liar snatch, unh . . .
black snake search
       tops
finger bunt I'll
 flakes
  car ice in bring bong bone flat tints

CRISP LOSS

red eggless drop-closet days
too angle-tuned to be numb
his leg . . .   no, smileless   glass eels
fall-out into the silt lesson, cab-edges
roughen the skin around the lapel, the lemon
hedges & widens, pulling in the direct forcep: the laughter

rod-lead windows of classic farm marshes
eeking in the snub of oil, & tanned sandwiches
roughage at the elbow, but clear neon head   step
up tuba & buckle don't wait around the rims
his vents of the hum passage . . .   no.

eggs on sleeve visions of the pyrite mine, Amen.

yellow days thudding to battery-park,   elms
spreading bacilli & wires, mind drone, cheese melting
lucky rims, in back of the mobile palace,   fleet
turnover in smiler mushrooms, beaks fading
tower of lice & the flag next house, "what ditch?"
"Marry Me" & cheese-graters & the sons of the pioneers

black pits, how can the flame be sunk?

     toe neons & toe neons

THE SO (Part Two)

backed hole, the night rip, the stand sags
so you?   hedge & lance, the right rip
so bound & leaf lance, hedge
hedge the right stand, rip it & sags
smacks lands, cart backed & the hole
right stand so you?   sooner?   melds
the night stander rips & so you sags
echo glancer type & rips? stands so.

patch conning hedge & the right sog lance
rip it? stands. the leaf in night so bound
leaf thru you to right stander spits & sogs, if?
smack lander carting, backed & stand
ing it right you so? lands, hedge & stands so
over caution rip & blend, meld, launch stand & rip

hole the backed rip, stand cart you?   the hole so
type rip & night type blands, smack stands & stander
echo glancer stander lander, if?
night in the right rift, glancing & lanker
soon to meld & echo you, if, rip, sands
the sand so, oh you?   & rightly in the rift
land echos smack midrift, right.
so you sag leaf lip   & the night stand rips so
                          ripe cart the sands
                          echos sooner
                          you if
                                    so if?

GOBI

columnar mufflered huffs   in kelt spit back
top o the morph echo   lifters chaff chapters flue
be Ned 'nd cuff   like mild falls in   clastic mates
and drop and tip it   laughter   mad calfs   lies & nut
false   side mud pliers   monk girl   window
careen & back in car whites & stew   pen   glyphs puff
bare   lights lights   none fell so

                                        good bad

rotten   onion owl & morning   meow   cars & pin home
rat flange   a runner nearing recent sinter   Elba
ovoid of fat block   calcium   wheat   rims
pinch   pints   tile ape ketch   rent or ramp if

on   said   gone   fell   smear   flew
   clear   bell   pawn   fed   true row

BRILL

emotional the
fox at an am   land kept chess   dim after dim
   two things   shrink very barren
        parts of the 6   wind but
act no like   canvas can
   A he up   very least
    or may in that   lonely like part
merely Davis 1956   body very   red soapy
      complexity it   means fees
    it to out   can't ready doing
  scratched up once   in the seemed the in
      life crab   but by so
   cigs or visits   last d   his the
like darkness   past is root   "Woolp-klo"
    wings nohow   planet three speed
  fast like not
      column stood still
sin   sun   wig   coin in what in
        dry   one   tat
  fun   six   not   hell   pall
        new
   tic   way   was   yes   two
        not   bud
 bar   sip   has   day   you
   get   here
pip   now   guy   air   wen   hod   no

RIGHTS

must file down buttons the kickers lob
is kept OK, knowledge be a drop
an of

writhes make it, sell is a right blade
rim of green catch is clog, blattering back
alright was & Kelso too, the loathes

fin guesser, troll ripper, guess
the glass ates, part block patrol wreck
slight deck, on the mauves saps
on right lies chews

pale ant papal rot summer smoothes
of knocks under pin gun, why so
blow fleds, wrought gats, frown tropes
prince light egg grows a must

a ribbon, that's caps too, a free lung
tropics ketchup & rust that, teals
spivened in growlapes lorry
is bucket teems & reds tarry

can it be rights to a be fleds?   (Hut)
cancels brackish in lean organ
stops as float films & goes
grunt stubbles on in echo

a mere sup lofts in Dago, lights
& Christ tongs on rear crush button
sops & it weighs lights, preys on lights
right enough sign sighing in high lee of this
point   (point)

itchy fickles freedom in feldspar, gecko lave
hell bender backs to back, time fray party sample
it's its list & crust soak be slow
bang gravy little its apes a few
the fire on asp street crooning

RED SIZE

kelp poem right flats egg egg egg
placed had case red ain'ts, scape
dials, & bell wrist, nails cap
blacking over saddlers it combs it gongs jowl
the planets, headgear red anoint

glade hind or bar bight, hecklers' rip
be here, rape, & heck bland is naps
peeled, glass or clay, skatekey
number's up is moon, help's mite
hole grand napes, flair construed, tock

blurt flange ape peat
ahead risers, car's fly
rig a sit debut, a leaf
sound very awl hall sob
collect, debunk galoot

is a chubby hard try (is cough)
notch tines cherry gel
is honked is whist it
collapse a (no) collide

or is black be trumps not a bee?
ca-death!   (pall hats) a plate
few ray knock Bach's newel gazes
row ant boat lines tidal cuspy

is not is a block is space a was
very beer, honed wash, almost pounce
glides & tips
shoves
end up airplane so long

BEE ELK

arch film duds
"Cheever"   can aiming laps
dorm sieve

nor black   tugs toward colog
alight paramecium   bloom ice
chigger geer dads
                    block

but a prime buds
Keds nor slam up labs
sham a shatter
                    puree

tins
      clock sauna
Coit ether

till sit mid sides
sign laughter
                    Anthracite

tea lure

STYRO

        quite is high
        quatic
                deliverance rates   dial   3
in ex
            trees palling steins ing
snail of it, acrid, the dumps
                    the "sill row"
  to knees smoke
               sir fins

drub in minnow the elicit of haunt (bite)
crust, stub, crayon, chives
                Galatea dumbing hard
cawl o'wrist it?
           nubs
             (Nile)
an green   and ever attack
                styrene mistachio dubloon
rack sun correct ratchet
           Dumbo in   size

  sign or hone win
    gold when aft
      whom   whine
it, state

clip
        in the light hapless snow-apes
fodder off a pencil
        gate tops & tongs
liar in snail

the cleats
gone hurry made slow of fries
        bundle dwelling
hairy mine
        copse stop

climbing it's
        no pike or hole in stop
    capes draining lozenge-ward
        flush hands thru coal
loot was pop

no.
        file prayer tines   luke
    a ward was at end
fan of tires loosing the 2nd
    goal burn near hairs
brine nearing

slowness
            kite numbing poles
    grass blue fringed
    fridge smote a cone back
        bung coat & smoke
throat clear of sky

this.
        the lesser lesser any a

contact back
feldspar   arithmetic
          pond

prune acrylic whose
dives
marls pays loops watts
lock mix deem
white apart
sass

agape modal serene
                less
panther orlon
                idler
                        pass attain
        bowls

ounce code orange
a
   the
        ohm
trilobite trilobites

dial urn
        sub phase moor
fours clue

        downs
mice alp cup a drawn
port
        slim react

of   about

since   dot

listene
secting
erences

miliari
ontempt
opposit

compani
bilitie
pontane

nerousl
ercussi
ndition

aluable
rievable
fluence

berness
ionalis
deliber

```
                        ace
                    act ado
                add aft ago
            age aha aid aim
        ail air ale all alp
    amp and ant any ape arc
are arc arm art ash ask asp
ass ate awe awk awl axe aye any
bad bag bah bam ban bar bat bay bed
bee beg bet bib big bin bit boa bob bog
boo bop bow box boy bub bud bug bum bun bus
but bye cab cad cam can cap car cat caw cob cog
cod con coo cop cot cow coy cry cub cud cue cup cur
cut dab dad dam day deb den dew did die dig dim
din dip doe dog don dot dry dub due dug dun
duo dye ear eat ebb eek eel egg ego elf
elk elm emu eon era ere err eve ewe
eye fab fad fag fan far fat fax
fay fee fen few fib fig fin
fir fit fix flu fly fob
fog fop fry fun fur
gab gad gag gal
gam gap gar
gas gat
gay
```

```
                    gee
                  get gib
                gig gin gob
              god goo got gum
            gun gut gem gel gyp
          gym guy had hag hah ham
        hap has hat haw hay hee heh
      hem hen hep her hew hex hey hic
    hid hie him hip his hit hob hoc hop
  hot how hub hue hug huh hum hun hut ice
ill inn ire irk icy ivy jab jag jam jap jar
jaw jay jet jig job jog jot jew joy jug jut ken
kid kin kit lab lad lag lam lap law lax lay led leg
  let lid lie lip lit lob log lop lot low lox lug
    lye mad mag man map mar mat maw may men met
      mew mid mix mob mod moo mop mow mud mug
        mum nab nag nap naw nay net new nib
          nip nit nix nod nog noh not now
            nun nut oaf oak oar oat odd
              ode off old one ohm ore
                orb our out ova owe
                  pad pal pan pap
                    par pat paw
                      pay ply
                        pry
```

pro
pea pee
peg pen pep
per pet pew pie
pig pin pip pit pod
poo pop pot pow pox pub
pud pug pun pup pus put quo
rag ram rye ran rap rat raw ray
rib rid rig rim rip rob rod roe rot
row rub rye rug rum run rut she shy sly
sty spa spy ski sky sad sag sap sat saw sax
say see set sew sex sin sip sir sit sis six sob
sod son sop sot sow sox soy sub sue sum sun sup try
the tho thy tab tag tam tan tao tap tar tat taw
tax tea tee ten tic tie tin tip tit toe tog
ton too top tot tow toy tub tug tux ugh
uke use urn view van vat vet via vim
vow wry why who wad wag wan war
was wax way web wed wen wet
wig win wit woe won woo
wow yam yap yaw yen
yes yet yew yip
zag zap zen
zoo zig
zip

```
                         for
                       sap set
                    the was via
                   led the did far
                 the had did oil low
               was and the the was had
             won was and was are the for
           and all the and set for tin red
          the the can one one was top can was
         the the and the the was the and was and
       the two and won new and end the the one aim
     not was had was eat ice why our and and sit for
   the the and the and was our had the the two had the
   was one was the the and two one was the was was
       the was the the had not rat not the but bat
         six was and one the the and our the his
          one the the and the and the not all
           car the was the had the low our
            and the all and who win not
             can the was and who the
              the the who and the
               and the our and
                was the see
                 and the
                   was
```

```
                    mat
                  bow lip
                urn ken mat
              bow lip urn ken
            mat bow lip urn ken
          mat bow lip urn ken mat
        bow lip urn ken mat bow lip
      urn ken mat bow lip urn ken mat
    bow lip urn ken mat bow lip urn ken
  mat bow lip urn ken mat bow lip urn ken
mat bow lip urn ken mat bow lip urn ken mat
bow lip urn ken mat bow lip urn ken mat bow lip
urn ken mat bow lip urn ken mat bow lip urn ken mat
bow lip urn ken mat bow lip urn ken mat bow lip
  urn ken mat bow lip urn ken mat bow lip urn
    ken mat bow lip urn ken mat bow lip urn
      ken mat bow lip urn ken mat bow lip
        urn ken mat bow lip urn ken mat
          bow lip urn ken mat bow lip
            urn ken mat bow lip urn
              ken mat bow lip earn
                ken mat bow lip
                  urn ken mat
                    bow lip
                      urn
```

```
                        non
                     out non
                  out non non
               out non off non
            out non tin off non
         out non off tin off non
      out non off tin tin off non
   out non off tin out tin off non
  out non off tin non out tin off non
 out non off tin out non out tin off non
out non off tin out non non out tin off non
out non off tin out non off non out tin off non
out out off off out out non off off out out off off
 tin out non off tin out tin off non out tin off
  tin out non off tin tin off non out tin off
   tin out non off tin off non out tin off
      tin out non off tin non out tin off
         tin out non off non out tin off
            tin out non non out tin off
               tin out non out tin off
                  tin out non tin off
                     tin out tin off
                        tin tin off
                           tin off
                              tin
```

```
                        one
                      one bow
                    one bow who
                  one bow who old
                one bow who old ton
              one bow who old ton two
            one bow who old ton two owe
          one bow who old ton two owe nod
        one bow who old ton two owe nod pro
      one bow who old ton two owe nod pro odd
    one bow who old ton two owe nod pro odd dot
  one bow who old ton two owe nod pro odd dot too
one bow who old ton two owe nod pro odd dot too oar
  one bow who old ton two owe nod pro odd dot too
    one bow who old ton two owe nod pro odd dot
      one bow who old ton two owe nod pro odd
        one bow who old ton two owe nod pro
          one bow who old ton two owe nod
            one bow who old ton two owe
              one bow who old ton two
                one bow who old ton
                  one bow who old
                    one bow who
                      one bow
                        one
```

"HEY! YOU LOOK LIKE A GIRL!"

the "Erector Sets" were permanent they thought, & forgot & left
    the bridges up
wheel zimmer kids all over ("America's Famous Rivers") & the country
    might tilt, toward you, up dangerously
Look out! Fire Pa by the House Kite! & the Lemon o' the Lake freaks
    humid ventilators & mates quail-fish

O, let's snout & lunge, baste & hasten Popeye! (he came over
    in a brick faceted tractor glare)   the Three Kneeless
        Brothers!   O bejeweled terraced rims of Hoke & "morn"!
the limits of New Jersey have been legally equated with the
    limbs of tobacco   & Jimmy's wand
        wrecked his bridge-pool mother (a "family of 5 . . .")

a kind of Lockjaw discovered in snails only under
    cement & steel abutment bridges?   guess so.
what, a tropical fungal-film of green pin fish?   Geeks
    authored Biblical Humor at bloody stumps!   Yes!
& milk flange ups Vitamin C, & babies' mildew sold
    a solid gleam on carpets, & the mysterious black gland
(doctors hid it) found to provide 98% champion gliders of kites

the transparent mantids rest on highest knit girders for their nests, tho
    the belted cops have vacated Colorado forever
Chipmunk Berries kept the "war effort" hung in bulge
    & fire creeps to cement the mothers flee!   (Buy a Kit!)
        Bee grew a beard!   won a prize!

Cracker Jacks emit "a weird light"
N.Y. Times legends' flutters ooze crabs below Hudson's "Green" Level
Calcimine gives the air to ceilings & mush
 tone California "level housing," sounding like neon, crushed
   (road-like) into the landing sea

too loud! move that Grape, the beds too lavender, & lounge — "*is too!*"
 I couldn't believe either in the "car park" (at all)
  specially when you untied & left
   your raspberry ribbon that snaps
   & all & that too — "so true!"

toads in the mumble park "levels" humming by
ooooof! your lunch, I'd unlock my hand if I
 were wearing a glove. Love's definitely *round*!
& nothing has been recently found to be
  forever.

WEST

1.

agates roll and the bison flinch.
which way to the stormy layers?
lunch on which butte?

blown thru the bats, mesquite thumping.
Battle Iron, Canyon Pendulum Garden.
Golly Mine shelving.

Tin.

Eggs.

Thunder open.

lain out stone motor wrecks
the "help! help!" water mammal table.

2.

black fumes rising in the Sioux Bee tankard
watering growth, levels of sweat

gunk shaping azure louvres
granite in moonlit settlement

bronze boulder stick
calamite stew
beef breath
gulph
glyph

VEGETABLE INLET

massed disguise, pleats of calcimine train
of elevator, finely key boreal watch hits
wrist with slick thongs, red yellow
"watch that!" hate a long rim of dial rub

non-caloric feed mechanism, spine wheels
along gap, runway makes its move, packets
the beat widens, spread elbow larva run
in case of brown bags, the loose
picked to spur & chime silks flange

red, argot, sign under calomel sluices
in range of bracket trees (an eft!) soap
humming widening to wood road (a plant!) 3
spines hydrangea brusk, bruised graphs
ticking mash in tin bulks, the aged tin
imprinted "ACE" or none
the film the splash
rust bush left
a chrome set

A GLITTER SHOALS

the duster so back years embroiled
haddock, tuna fish, twin reefs, the sharp land sag
far smoke "tell you!" farms & after-carts, the wreckage cement
tarp glancing off at glow posts, sends rusts (Tow!) bends reefs
clacking glanker edge the hemmed bow chain, twisting chairs feel
Connecticut Hag & Clock & Barrel Co, many rends, chow sign
gall seating peanuts, muffs in tune, blade in excelsior gimp hill
treadle bucket, ear & lamps, extra tobacco laughs, spume & spit, it
glance echoed in lumbar diodes, jibber salt in tussle, the clay light map
ma, ripe talk in the sneeze, rough, jeans defeat, deflated glass, car tray
in sends: lucks, in sands: locks, deafening bead, can the held harps
aah? two-door bridge, decalcify lamp posts, more organ rift, warp rig
Amygdular Januaries in ovular insides cocoa dust, heck twigs most, gypsum
red, & slim berry cartography, smell ends in blades, sooner? taped wholer
the carp, a boiler, & the rest rags, the west coast of January

"pink hoax!" & the lamp snags & smogs hugs

MANGROVE IN CHROME

gas sigh invert balk
cabal ants too
    trunk
        if so, in case, sat soon

sump, pro
        down

   lump, lung, in toe, if is

saturday flirt
       sank echo chiming dreg, it
sank down dream so, concert your so self sue, if

———————————————

Benny's charts so pipe bark, kids cramp
back trudging allergic, stamp snapping
          fired
    shark 'lastic keeled in, ramp dun bird so?
  whiskered die & plectrum
        roll of ouvre   (Premium)
           clatter punt & echo

———————————————

shoot   shot   shout

        scup

THE SO

slender gel from cracking odes
"punch you," hot, "Hey!   Out!"
lime cool green eel key, echo, smite
"it at last," sag gum in
hang, "watching the wrist is . . ."
batter sea lode, lodged against, "much!"
silk is, argonaut match head
"Selby's crazy!", terrible hot tornado
ink licked in small rod, "Summer is . . ."
relic tricycle hit
smile, toad, rills, "Objection, please!"
mended seams, ripen that
remainder amphibian, "Xylophone right next"
simple, oh, "you!"

bunched zeppelins, remark, soda start
up in over & around, tones
back side slid farther, "monkeys!"
trim typecast, of love pimps . . .
barley satyr, in the back starling munching
cart & tell, "ugly!", females
larks, thermometers, batons, "her curl lip"
sunk past his, Carl's park
in head lead in smite summer, Tru-Ade Social
"Morley!", the rip
piles of sled, parts of shale, "burnished, what?"
marked slices you deck up
clatter, barns, suicide, slickensides
two faced, liquor, "hand me . . ."

tomatoes blow out, "face it!", delved
reaped, aphid, to land in
it fading & small, slowed great
ripped, sore & fall, to see
mire, song sign, is milk is breath
"monkeys!", kelp beer &
tirade, mulch sent, "harassed"
man mad bump, is scald
frame settling fear, so nape
in rod run, sun gad, "real!", savvies
is scads, family's frame
oh low, pirate shit, "my clean . . ."
organ site bean glade far
candle skate & burnish bar blacker said

THE AGATE ACE

grape pocket is seen, caught, & I repeat the radio's newness
sculptures of crabs & I wonder (itchy)
the plastic (white) may be porous, like ivory (weighty) 3
grey dims, bubbles in his plants, turned on & trapped sounding

(the gentle "Blat!" of fake jade)

(shreds of Our Love Tapes lost in the Sub Test)

(the window colors water in embarrassing shade)

Novocain before remnant "news" leaves
pour down hockey tracks, red & Xed, like turkey
tracks at 350 mph bank road with 'em
                    wide iridium Hokusai studs

Snow Mind blurs sentences out sheds I forget
the exact holiday count of high new england deaths

inside the thunderegg's a mallow, toast &
she shrieks ("ten!") & I'm straught in the plastic

the name of the game: Green Day
the number: You in the Street
short of breath & the exact pill

HIGH PITCHED WHALE

left from   gay behind private

      it is it   of hip it

 in have made   two one shifts

     drivel agony   also over

belief health over   remember

   him   riders of there   color whole is

    but is it in the are also awkward

 going of face   put kind on

    the out the   walls touch

 it out it in   does flowers

     get with a grain   the was the

    faintly color   out out clear   sense

image   as a in office   position prints

image

      beautiful as own

   last than   go dear

straps   screen her where here

    main chin this   overpapers

 the as car   flowers work

    sect to photo   soft whole sifts

      but

out go subtle   limp funny orange

   in been men   impulse to basis

 color thing out   star shown

to as   go is a two   to by in a the

  and are if is a   the this   the the is it

MOVIES

obsidian lasher, partly   pip oversmokes

                      in gym it

    pristine in boards setting and then cows

        very   the snout

     then there   very send howler call tunes

    squandering very squirrel limit

                   baby

                      bound

        blue-ing snakes

  grass it film

       guess   filter varies

 the, um, a snooze

Prentiss March : gulch, mist, "Gosh!", hyphen
ledge it glow harm, in variant, rye, rust
tumble hex an echo, last, landing sown stash on
burnt, barn & stools, caitiff, larceny, England, euglena
in trip, middle onion & stand, "Varmint!", pipe, thrush
arc opens & puddle, side cap, buck & wing-nut, sediment

    a looseness

SUM SUN ELBOW

trees blur, fizz, & peach
black, & snake, matter where tunes
the lack bulk finning sky, sack
luckies, & blend belt peaches
                   (toe linkers)
gullet parts edge & fidgets
                       (Reuben Nakian in Hollyhocks)
Breeze by, Honeymoon fit & blooms
musk of tilers, hits, lumps up, three bell zero
Haggard NAWSPS, Hawk, tree toad, & frilly
the Crandall's expert & husks marsh, can tweeter guns
the Ripe is Carlsbad, wrists in
sun-bar, the crisper, silts

mackerel blue-belt, echo, hitter
bunch crabs aerial hisser mix
Pastrami salve slides & hoo hoo
   (Gecko)   (Malaria)

Mistere, hollow bone, Grump ground lank hurries
the Bludgeon Hollywood fount's too
Siren of Murray's pelt, shad, the oregon gun
cloud eel humps, tree last
coat bloom bulge fuzz gulch, cat to the nines
the berry & mike, Crandall, factory

  "with such evolving of events as has happened"   (now here as)
Istanbul Connecticut HyFong Jamaica Texas Guadalupe New New Paris
pop hype marginal Hilton melange   (midtown hicky wrestle)
the block, block

the frame (block) in frame (frame)
toad mumble in wristlet zappy, leaf zot sun punch
stars hive myopia Hidalgo, jet syphon fan bug
shed remnant Nippon

magic crease elf's suction face, fence
gnarl go by echo leaver, the pow & mux
"how's the leavin' son," reed a giblet, creed oh
mix on

counter block ways turn marl cloud, Historo Monte
climbs brittle shout puff radio storm blacken static fur
slate grain clover murder non-rhyme
ago, a way

is hiss
down shaft darker spread   (eeler rug)
Beechcraft buglet marble yell
Matsumi & eggs fried   (trapeezer elbow reckon)
on cranberry bogs blue shutters down
arms on right mist the truncheon   (hick-up meson)

MOUNT NOTES

1.

grasps latching in rock bark of tree milk
the ledge of edge on leafy & more maneuvers
the clasp rickety in farm slants, too loose the rock monk
trail snarl in bristled peans, gonky moon shells
the grass shifts beneath sit it, miles of tramp void
the keys pearling in fathomless starling, broken pod seals
the gnash is too scab & light tint tip flicks
mount gossamer flea dungeon, it is too *raise*!
  — sifting quartz peas a butterfly misses . . .

2.

obsidian bunkers trailed marsh peat hit or missing
the grapes unwind unfound under scarp, the scree giggles
conception slab the mind tilts glancing, gloss on shafts
acid sharp front face riffing, vegetation knocked
undersoil lil' pika, drib milk the sod vest, echo
planked by side mirror azure resting block & snake
gone fright amber, tomb its husk, chant away so peak
  — vine stone fisty plain, the rattler void

3.

glance chamber muscular fans, its ribs, lips, tabs
soil suture plankton escapees ammonite stab at, risks
mighty church in lab the kinks, pines fir on thumb, traipsy
head grows pin in bark blend, the oval nose, sit, its sit
mumbly on pate tirade fire the glow slab, ointment rippt bunk
gone slant on last land, mike-ing the freeze hanger, 'gainst
sorry, piney, how's lee blend? the slab made fossil sad, band
mades tool & slabby gneissic chant, chart it in sawdust lab
bind at capsule robins the slab ash at dusk dust, tin of
— black lightning magnet bolt, its inner scab & lichen husk

THE BLUE POMADE : 22 European Painters & Sculptors

"I am not so sure that it was useful to invent that untamed volcano that lies concealed in all true art." — Jean Bazaine

"To help art regain its place, I should, I believe, dance & yell like a madman, & always be seen naked from all the creases of a professor's chair." — Jean Dubuffet

"I have abandoned the sculpture-object, & I have turned to bas-relief, so that I can more easily undulate with relief." — Etienne Hajdu

"I cannot speak of painting without a feeling of regret for a certain blue and a certain red, that's all." — Alfred Manessier

"I paint because my way of life is to need harbors, olive orchards, nudes or workers, everything that moves and lives passionately under the underside of an interior decorator." — Edouard Pignon

"I do not know if everything evokes, or depends upon, my portrait bust (which has its laws)." — Germaine Richier

"When I work I have no ideas about forms, materials, colors, words, painters, impulses, longings, models, pictures, points, worlds, spectators, canvases, spaces, metaphors, formulas, van Goghs, or experiences. I work, guided by an inner reptile." — Pierre Soulages

"I want to be jotted down, with great sculptural necessity, in a flying machine." — Hans Uhlmann

"Man seeks man. I am in danger of becoming a barren, empty & plastic, mass man." — Theodor Werner

"I consider it my artistic aim to seek, through a transparency of
vision, the *content* of the *inner structure* of window glass."
— Fritz Winter

"I like sculpture to look like overhanging, generous, & comfortable
singers, cooks, bullfighters, and storytellers." — Kenneth Armitage

"Real imagination is technical imagination, & I would like to perfect
in my consciousness the memory traces of a snail, leaving its
track of slime." — Francis Bacon

"Art which packs a punch is always near an owl & I think I may
have found *that owl*!" — Reg Butler

"If I look back on my work over a period of years, I can clearly
see beaten shapes. Sometimes I feel the need to weld in iron,
my limbs." — Lynn Chadwick

"I am horrified at the smart brush, or the brilliant canvas."
— William Scott

"I think my painting is beginning to break away from
investment." — Afro

"I can only say this: my painting is an irreducible presence, that
refuses to be both imminent & active, tho threadbare."
— Alberto Burri

"I must have been about ten years old when my mother took me
with her to visit an institution for the blind. Ever since that
day I have been absolutely blind." — Giuseppe Capogrossi

"I must feel in my hands and have before my eyes the assurance
of an absolutely intimate man." — Luciano Minguzzi

"Before speaking of the plastic idiom of today I should like to
draw a black & white hairnet." — Mirko

"In order to paint, I must capture enough tangible paint."
— Karel Appel

"I should like to be as amazed as a jar of jam, tinted with the
blue weight of stones. But alas, I am too agile."
— Vieira da Silva

to ea ut ue ir p es de he in ss
ob c te it l ly ou to ff al & a te es
pe hi & od ee ov tr t el al er b
as rd s f s th ri ra in er r l VE RU
ha er at r ha ve w s s ho he wh s
wh s do an o at al f d s r ck a
ba fu & in hi th ie ve c r se ca go
oi & de re pi & t t m ne ge in &
ev he m w le re c -l & f d r or on
yw .. an & gh o y & m 's pi lo
to me r. o em ? a d' om wn f r er d
l wa .t be es a re o la ' ke yo
r e t' ot UE MA S? ck ye el w h s -l rs
dr s c si l -b c sy a yo ig bu
cc nt y vi .. r' or hu rs ms an rp es
e ie eg ha un s e lo ha ng l l d te ng
gh t r t an ha ar n e h t an ru ..
yo hi he at o' be c lo & ck l e io ve
y is . ho gi g w g ts ug g es
th s s cu a in c r o dl ld he n
po in f el i ll ac a & e io on tc fi r
l r̄ e k in wh 's e m d al hi nc
l s lo ig et -S al hi ri o po ta
le cr li al he th w en an il t co e
ad or sn of is et t g rn t ut g-
o t er ho sk l a nn w I it y s?
oc ol an th a a cr i at at s th tr
be m ew oc w ow I ea m t oo pa y
s m n om ve av as o to sa ra o n
t fi r er ws me n b de an sh m in
ev bo s s n a we nn ed gh hi si wh
ut ? t el ll pp & le ot s l he no
b c go au o y la as ha o n n w ow de
ig pr rl tr ht e n u sl ve t
fo ve or e p n se ey y pu do th ay r
s s ze b ed ke e ck o ur en ly ou at
e- si ev da er re ty ke e am er w e
as y th s te is ee er e k ce ne w
's pp g? ea ro e th re la h e h ws er
ti ad fl ho rs d m ex or nc in rr e'
it s d th n ? OW ME wa un co su y
d b st la aw y sa mb 'l ri ra li s
on e p rs e y me ik co ng da d pl
en h ou un t st b k f fu ai s cr r
po 5 r en re no ie u r s rd mo g
b -w s tc i o me sc c cb t e ce on ou
I ke tu c st t ne & n' et s m ik
ne g to an ou he dv d ro .l r m s e

SUITE V

taps

.

buns

keys

ohms

cans

arms

lads

inks

hats

gars

pins

wens

webs

cups

tins

jets

zoos

bins

airs

ores

lids

ants

lips

eves

dots

mats

fans

cams

pads

nobs

mops

eels

peas

bars

hips

inns

DRUMMERS

for Larry Fagin

Jimmy Zitano
Ronnie Free
Jeff Morton
Nick Stabulas
Frank Isola
Art Mardigan
Gene Gammage
Lawrence Marable
Joe Dodge
Lloyd Davis
Herb Barman
Chuck Flores
Bill Bradley Jr.
Frank Butler
Joe Harris
Osie Johnson
Shadow Wilson
Al Harewood
Rudy Collins
Bert Dale (Dahlander)
Stan Levey
Chuck Thompson
Nick Fatool
Cliff Leeman
Jack Sperling
Grassella Oliphant
Pete Littman
Johnny Crawford
Roy Harte

Sam Ulano
Jimmy Campbell
Mousey Alexander
Alvin Stoller
Mickey Sheen
Ray Mosca
Charlie Perry
"Sticks" Evans
"Specs" Powell
Chauncey Morehouse
G. T. Hogan
Tony Spargo (Sbarbaro)
Donald Bailey
Dave Bailey
Ron Jefferson
Frankie Dunlop
Alan Dawson
J. C. Heard
Al "Tootie" Heath
Al Torre
Frankie Capp
Bobby White
Lex Humphries
Al Levitt
Jake Hanna
Denzil DeCosta Best
Tiny Kahn
Joe Hunt
Bill Clark
Billy Osborne
Steve Ellington
Rudy Nichols

Larry Bunker
Charlie Persip
Ben Riley
Dennis Charles

WHILE

broken bridge
hummingbird
the ladder

tranquilities

silver discs

trellis
breaking hue
longitudes

intrigue
lamed

chet

mem
tet
air desired

high

saraband
terranean

twined columns
twined columns

while
orange column

pi
moving in
nineteen

hot half
no end

THE MENTS

1.

the   but   ments
                  over
the   forms   Tions
ternal   of   monly
cance   Tions
      an   trate   ists
        aving
yond   vance   quent
        and
to   not   But
to   Mund

2.

did   one   ly
      thing   utes
      icance   ments
          bines
          tions
          istic
          ical
bines   been   stead
  tive   judges
          act
    as
        and   and
    in

3.

all   put   cal   to   cel
the   ness   for   Emp   Tone
          an   4
          ac   two
   as   aca   crea   num
Roll's   Erous
         bailiff   cassia
the   though

4.

mundane
      ture   and   cal
              surd
duced in
       is   ing   the   line
in   eral   ern
      rated   and   in   as   tic
vanced
vations
      be   the   sev   the   inno-mem
two   tic   erri   ous
the   lishes   of   an
      upon

5.

and   or   sence
much   gated
from   haps
tional   is   pass
  ist   for   from   onances
ogy   some   ing   forms
  to   such
                        as   the   ab
                            the   de
          and
on   the   close
of   ly   ner

6.

tive   troll   oughly
tempts
          a   the   to   tory
  the   dinariness
chon
        ous   art   nar   thor
    in   a
    and   ways
                        heatv
at   in   fan
  a   spicuous
          fan   two

7.

are   tinctly

       ges   ate

   that

   ate

          tions   ough

     en-thor

     greater   lating   lutions

     HONING

          dis

          ver

          in   recog

    BATIM

      an   one   tinctly

8.

monly   date   of   co-ous

one   should

not   of   ning

    art   the   art

    tween   tween

be   ness   of   Ly   ty-eight

ous   ness   of   sign

mo-best

in   For   Box

in   full   And

   two   pro

    that   then   own

ness   ty-eight

      tion   two

BY OF MUCH

by one of
of and a

by the   not

of the and
and for is

for the   and there

in
than it is
half or
but the
been

is of a   can are

same be and

has are some
a too a
as tends are

to the   to the

clear are as
if is the
is that it is a

in not   it as

    the to

    in those
    a in
    so of which

the of   there of

    in of
    of no

    be can
      main

  and   and

    the in the
    the all as and there

as until   or most

    they are they

    are the of
    most and time

  red   ors

    and are

    and new
      one

                    the   or   the   could
                        it of that
                              like
                        isn't an
                              and

    of the other   and the other

                        is that the

                        a it's not
                              a

        then since   of much

                        about
                        or of is one of

                        too of is
                        it to two

        the much   the main

                        just an both
                        it and with

                              either
                              their

AMONG THE NEWBEGINS

as   es

the   une

be   tain
to   ate
         on

ele
re
oth

er
lege
an
tor

as
an

gone
ie

the
you
you
you

so

a
to
that's
is

cer

could
is, of

got   the
niche   the
us   and
out

         to
to   which
can   le

it is   the
most ances
in   the

in
are
and
in

in two

not a

out

of

on

SIZE

tion
petts

dner

egories

tip

discuss
discus

guage

talline

secor

net

sur

ha

nating
veying

coordi
mir

sci
sur

lan

lin

lan

SIMMER

picture ethic pithic   head blanch O's   balade entrench hifty
dump the
        or coil ore   grabd sleek dents   match-matic
bubble you
clags mump if it limes   gork crab   stem beans   all or
rod house bee have
        smithic bents slab or gel rose   encleeps
smile-o-ray   swift shove pie curative
                enlapse   cong tripes
glab it   combs bent drave
  or club whole oleo-oreo   stymy   calendric
nines
    climb sleeve core bandit   blunt ade for snide
claps
    tree bounce   collects   hawl missive caw mistake
snives off
    trip it fend   glass or flower the
cave cable
    dynamic & frame long rips time signs   or glow
Metaconkanet brute bite
      whelm nail or love   pipe mosquito
break howl whites
      gong animate whites whites call
smelt
    song along allow whizz pin   or a gonk it   or
piano
    sent for sneak souse   noun of rub it   caser in
spine trim it
    at ache sent bat   pre-butter   ran neolithic
or come a trap
    cum perhap   allow all bitter ride
mount notes
    tree hand ash   kraut swim brisket   tarpaulin

amaze farm

        fount   fir   collapse add act   nick snout

pipe pill raise

        meds spills ack sound   tom   tom

spun   gull idler

       matic steams impress   sporadic hum at up add

spy heater

      Gorilla Gomes   is a is or is   elastic

  I or I or I

       salter humid   below bromine band

  sand cross cheese

  calmer or mer

      thaw tar

        or whizzes

moon silent mike breasts
paper sign gloaming contest
coal avenue mirror lump pea
Styrene damage arena

     gong

arette   simple TV   freights
mallow
     range pump
hashee in a bloat of flight

    gong

steam end

end

SCRIP ANT

just road choice fifty ditch   away above pipe peers noon
chance not hysterical laugh   it lap just car been
slowly & factory wearily   petrified call room   state him tion
walks stops aura dow   banks room arms   and not and face
sits up kiss moves   white water waves white   looks strikes
under away apart closes   away remain   out shouts out
cushion style same blonde cushion style   road pats late
kiss while comes slowly puts still   upstairs is comes
too him that stairs mad   heart roof better bends
that that tell that at it's   very there by starts sound
goes   squeezes   less looks flawless leafs   pulls two too
lakes   distilled didn't concert gives go   takes shaken
bottom when light thing   left looks loft pelts soft
things soled fringes   morphine morphine   must difference
under arm package   flowers   towards jokes   wig house
don't fifty   print house please please & steps   a can
seat   wind upon besides   climbs   is closed cold
goodbye final nearby shack   keep keep to quited large
a fin   pit caps copter quieted down come   soons
or runs   clapboard door   of liked   face clam drag still
brokes of and sacks   back sorry box goes   aren't?
sound mud storm dress   thick is short a haze   haze
under until depths oar   already breasts   usual rubberized
lust shark   sailor fit   away a few sand and then
bulk room   sea boat   gifts guitar   moves slight away
pitch after   landscape   were all throws piqued
encircle   by number abashed   number sleep to last
cod pounce   shot saccharine   yacht not the at book
grabbed   swim   lanks sleep at looks   isles a tred
pump part enter kiss   backwards the a nude turns third
pocket ing down   same around third   slanted nude
tight sand blonde   fifty held   masses   slant
bite glass   lame very time lawn   elderly by wings
walks she she   is angry form   at the I say
lump number   carry cold only   red glasses
cent day!   coes   ent there   cap thing
fleeting spare   eads   and sion pulls
erable   ment   onds   knees
po   sent   tion   aged
him is thing had a him is had a him a

tam moil
       peg sluice
sun big
       aft pound
sigh loot
       par sand
lock tweet
       steam parse
lag bead
       stump fan
fast slate
       am hold
fleece dock
       twitch plate
dun loss
       tam tam
ad lodge
       fume buzz
arc nod
       fill spot
ram blip
       dunk hedge
tie murk
       hog don't
die sail
       stain tight

DHARMA SNOW

dread snake Podiac
barrette duress, clung face boards born
new eave in leek-fats, silo crab
syndrome patter fat, leasting finds
dew rat

"Fon-*gu*!" mazed lap tureen buttress
zylocaine pontoon meat cement
rabies!   saw tooth scan beak puttees
pylon flair scarp in ruby cenotaph

elk scone keep plum
the major hover reason major
the
half & can pun gates & core aft
                              bond eat

lifter lace head mega-shovel
turpentine no key lag mist twelve
fan in dud
        coiler deans
    fin shack talc
    no talc pawn
    newel purr

PONTOON BONITA

window of a stone turned
hint bane   & a cap moody wait
repack oblongs & hedge grail dome
brass clap wick hum wheedle whole
duress him-bark time cold alum mace
   — dose —

parturience slab teas   a mackerel roil
boob-gum sub-linghum   caressed market
chaffy & cool red ink stem-lains
dew voter   disturbs on sewn water wish
scurvy   sand actual lab chats

mated sigher   carbons on bell weeks tarn
fame: sign goo   carrot: shovel-L cram stain
paste hello dryer   Scheissliche Camelot

but Elmo Lincoln silence bath-ink   (loster)
cam but lobster   raid man shelf a fail see-eth
door funicular pear stumps   diametrically silo
but half but grape   tureen piler bats
style lakes, everso litmus mast cancel, goalie own

electrical

          (middle eats)

permission douse a taint blunt
pelican

demise   a wrist   Toulouse   a march
plately

house
vein dent a ban slap
new vent dude

plause aid
phantom   a fame

node toot duel
ray hinge

may mole

       nerve

rice
once   car
           harp

from WHOLES

A
tian
dello
the

in yet
actual
but

flow
ic

flat
tion

ALL TALK

in many buildings of them five rows
pure to the those those move

the each course

       and the wait catch
       one dont passes
       to spot pool

one in past print the old other shells

is but over middle of the off appears
       like to do is sit
since ago to even years

on to them to it at all
and when the skim so much as anything
must soon in the widen fast while

notion

       it in an

            all well light

than true
       some tall

SONNETS: THE BLANKS

for Ted

now is the time that face should form another
a liquid prisoner pent in walls of glass
strikes each in each by mutual ordering
thou shouldst print more, not let that copy die

holds in perfection but a little moment
by adding one thing to my purpose nothing
and perspective it is best painter's art
to march in ranks of better equipage

anon permit the basest clouds to rise
I make my love engrafted to this store
eternal numbers to outlive long date
and, darkly bright, are bright in dark directed

a closet never pierced with crystal eyes
to cide this title is impanneled
against that time, if ever that time come
the which he ill not every hour survey

since, seldom coming, in the long year set
and you in Grecian tires are painted new
which parts the shore, where two contracted new
be where you list, your charter is so strong

if there be nothing new, but that which is
even of five hundred courses of the sun
in sequent toil all forwards do contend
increasing store with loss and loss with store

and the firm soil win of the watery main
when I have seen such interchange of state
to live a second life on second head
when yellow leaves, or none, or few, do hang

the worth of that is that which it contains
and that is this
now counting best to be with you alone
so far from variation or quick change

to new-found methods and to compounds strange
and keep invention in a noted weed
and therefore have I slept in your report
who is it that says most?   which can say more

which should example where your equal grew
and so my patent back again is swerving
to set a form upon desired change
and do not drop in for an after-loss

some in their hawks and hounds, some in their horse
that do not do the thing they most do show
and yet this time removed was summer's time
drawn after you, — you pattern of all those

but best is best, if never intermixt'
to one, of one, still such, and ever so
fair, kind, and true, varying to other words
now all is done, have what shall have no end

of others' voices, that my adder's sense
seems seeing, but effectually is out
as fast as objects to his beams assemble
bring me within the level of your frown

no, I am that I am; and they that level
our dates are brief, and therefore we admire
lose all, and more, by paying too much rent
which is not mixt with seconds, knows no art

had, having, and in quest to have, extreme
if hairs be wires, black wires grow on her head
and will to boot, and will in overplus
ay, fill it full with wills, and my will one

among a number one is reckon'd none
in a cold valley-fountain of that ground

THE ARP

here the rope or a doze
and less train
and well are as such
roll
ten to less
of or sum

an old nap hem
or hung
under mile
here light
lint and bind
oil in like oil

come whale on granites
row low wash
and slap long skin
like the shin
rain on a squint, lose one
to get one tea as a jam
and bigger than raw

seem to mass a luke calm
ask breath like the water while
here is one till ease will
so hug the eye
whole, seen, sure, low
on and old from old ones

in white rough
loll, as if in tin sings of arm
too ether here will not use hick
bulk of a blur uses
hot ring

DEEM

like a nail on
the way's froze
by shell
from a bowl
in a light

the red
stops here
a time roll rose
to boom eel

MADE THOUGHT

made thought which of it
all of which a kind yet
best it in and on should must
whatever it is often once to do

in a while once is there and in
as it like it but often ever that it is
in which in separate that
often only very not in which way

all of this but this which as are alike
or in an only not what made as for
it in its well as made open as in
that which it once all but made but
                  for all as it is

A TANGUY

and so I returned to us the so
I reset the so
miles of tree cones
land pressed it
there a map rolled it
a crow isn't ants
a pea is near our day
ma is like dawn in the oil can
a dazzling exit dishes out
legs in interminable solo
core revoked in essential ones
leaks (or both) a mile lolls
lapis seed forks
lateral iron veils

the Iliad is a tool on a relief surf road
pealess noise gelatins it
and Caesar came here once the floor was final
to tessellate a dummy floor member
a hum to outfile Tesla's red lamb spars

the main sun files lead
on to open dolmen mirrors
the trail of umbrellas came over less anemometer
in a dollar's worth of sun

down file the engine rinds
a Dutcher but delicate hissing
to dub out the monday

octopus culled wheat edged
ores run on the resistance message
the solo said

using angles the silence deplaned the glacier
lemon in a mocha cracker seems our fist
the land it creases in return
leads resolve to echos
as a horizon permits little ridge

a nose shows no ions
a deck is a deck
the north set the final rate
as Selkirk's geode is par for soap
then a surd commands apatite
under "B" rising

COLOR SLIDES

for Ted

dream profiles
black pines
iceberg projects
yellow bird
hung piece
packed coast
ocean park
floor piece
cloud slant
late summer
tilted wall
white passage
double negative
wild goose
two yellows
love sculpture
wall piece
green blue
flat rate
black bottle
velvet rope
blue square
feasible monuments
carnal clocks
horse blinders
black olympia
square spiral
orange juice
your own

HORIZON

it was
it which

        is even if

   by

evening itself

MOROCCAN VARIATIONS

this of that
    this of not
that here

•

this there
    that here
then

•

here then
    that

•

does this
    that doesn't
even

•

here even
    there
that this
    do

•

do this even
   does that
there as here

    •

here that
   this there

here
   that there
this

    •

at that
  there
is this

A SATIE

the article grownups honour
the rest past the lobster
the latter at a height of weather
like the rest of the animals
was instrumental in the consequences
of purchase on a thing
at morning a bone is
　　　　most like time
when pupil teacher and grownups
honour the freedom in a system

PIN ELEGANCE

for Bill Berkson

a halver
a sung in emits
a toll annealed
a silt dowel
a mild
a parse fitted
a lane cloth
a nine
a back site
a more still
a badge
a long
a so far
a rule aisle
a number of
a clack
a mute pint
a rail dome
a tuner
a pole noun
a flick
a dine
a mole

DUMB AGUE IN OURAY

blue treads last in time
tinnish not ovoid rests
blank as is soils of teem

    the bound.

a knock of which straightens films
in a band to group dimes
touring age and low length wrist
start-motor: a trim

    this vault.

out of globes lacks arcs
over newel tines in link blurts
out balms and out sodas bulk stint
a variable the

    tune of throttle stem
    a nine in the blank
    and stream.

THE BASAL STRINGS

for Dick Gallup

behind the around of many block
of down which way back in ten
lifts wide depths

    totals
    dowels
    tonals
    towels

        is since a knob plenty bulk

diurnal slid tuckers
some as the same as a rest

a mist lead blocks askew
parts air past a tile
pins the munch

        picking the maze in a blimp

    fresco

ten pastes as adhesive as a hinge

AS APT AS SQUARES AS POUNDS

one large day
cot to make jump the cut
more even to put in an elevator texture
rather free fall to row from little plots
letters keyed to folds often
by those still bear beside
   even whole a child
   name side down

•

a more simple number to even open
                      an even band
all of a whole unit flat water
the nob number
   a white been jump
   but it made

•

stair pounds at the door
there more not let wide
one less is apt to be side itself
needles as exact matches
the fewer the colors the larger the color
   pods paired anyhow stem

•

the smooth dates lateness of finish
duck brush letters have a nickel
as can the simple build is to pick sides
as to circle
of which so much
so idle well to date
the springs trace a cone pose
as a spring traces a cone poses
little as much as almost more
the speed of a numbering ovals by

•

side dimes using good inches
field the tall trail lights
the room's good right inch
   moves match whole locks

•

what time the place maps holds as still
wharf with trace of treble
as ground is as light it
the overthick place to date
on a cup, in letters, so well
set circles through
   sharp dates bore stands

•

lip leads blocked
an apt to pick sides the dialing thresher
whether it not well still
water top which still are wet
whether can it keeps and not tell a front
for meant zone much as close to it this
   pads

       bear

  pits pins

•

such an hold of age hold of it now
small shale shy away
can chose there
of ever in turn off
part in a round
or the narrow bit dates down a drain

a looming lunge over backward

•

well made post can only
   abstract crazy hat
   largely surface figures

a flat places
the bun hub

•

less kept on a best kept even more
some draw
off type still though some another
plan
turning to yellow moving white moved
the turn so as
there that are lots

•

they are
             colors are as
                        things are
                                upon
                a blond
mineral
             patterns where an edge
                                meets past
a like and that
                is made an other
they are what
             (colors)
                    it like this

•

large flush of pop exact match
matches along the bands to and from
smooth key image one
side down
the one whole starts
around a green devised
blue down

•

as keyhole paint never caught on
in a pack like a deck forms halls stiff lights
nails saw fit the square
paper one into the room comes back effects
can
    lights roll
      spring
    ties

•

to do it, hold off
of it now, it wasn't such

•

      figure
      pitch

      paper
      over

THE SKIPPERS

for Ron Padgett

The Edwards Three Records
Edwards Roadside Skipper
Samoset, Scudder
Records Samoset Skipper
Scudder, Dusted
Dion Edwards, Conspicuous
Black Dash, Metacomet Harris
Dun Skipper Mulberry, Massasoit
Wing Scudder, Hoboken
Harris Skipper, Aviator
Broad Airy Tones, Argos
Skipper Delaware
Edwards, Formerly A Delaware Skipper
Antediluvial Camps, Sachem
Pompei, Little, Glassy, Edwards
Wings Wallgreen's
Ortho Egremont Cement, Scudder
Broken Dashes
Polite Cornea, Cramer
Formerly Pea Peck, Peck's
Skipper, The Polite Themist
Tawny Edged Phenolphthalein
La Trill Skipper
Fabric Of Polite Origin
One Record, The Cross Liner
A Chautauqua, Light, Styptic, Long Dash
The Hesperian Uncas, Edwards
Records Uncas' Skipper Backwards

A Laurentide Lyman Skipper to Manitoba
Skips A Pawnee Dodge, Edwards
Skip Doubles As Otto
Edwards The Auto Skipper
Aesperidian Sack Spanner Of Dakota
Edwards, A Skinner
Fletcher, A Mantid Bodes Indian
Parker, Pow Sheik, Ankle Slipper
Fabrician As Least Skipper
Pallas, Pale Lemon, Least Of Arctic
Loaf Skipper, Pale
Borean Catullus, Fabricius
Common, Sooty, Wing Of Grote
Checkered, Communist, Purgist Slipper
Aerie Of Keel, Of Ice Lung, Scudder
Dreamy Burgess, Dusky Peals
Brizo, Residual Of Duck, Anis Stippler, Lucullus
Columbine, Martial Mottle
Wing Of Horace, Burgess, Horace's
Wing Of Thorax, Thorybean Batholith
Smith, A Cloud South, Pine Aorta, Rung Pylades
Scudder, Skipper, Northern
Ankylose, Pale Geyser Records
Asparagus, Clear Cramer, Silver
Spot Skipper, Hoary
Record Of Phrygian Edge

BASIL RATHBONE'S BATHROBE

1.

a dump an octave up
dip a large it
rose on did

single of that on that sort
cord knee to lots pends
fiddle such with pends balds

belongs a cuff tint whole
air of trim
neat's trick wax amati mud

number no nor no
an arm in arm all down room
peck mere band diorite

ping morman mere
white pulls post milk
oath cork corot quite a little all quite wrist

2.

rose on box did the term
copernican it large as octave
dip of that on dump did

such with lumber brains cord
pieces soils and sticks pend
bread pends to euclid lots

blue bungler light forefinger
air wax number trick lights
squared belongs

rink all down in cork ping mere
pages birds cigar
pearl boy nor no flakey

rink band mean forms
diorite no-necking potato
smart final quite cork corot

3.

dip a dump it to rose that boxes
an octave
of sharp large single

sitting thought with such that sort
sticks the lots blotted
to lumber knee pends

to mud links belongs by number
tint by arm by all light large across
snow of head

mere head clear upon down
bird of an arm rink mean band
up at pages forms some frock whole

final s pulls were a little haste
corot ping pages amati squared flakey
quite mere all were when smart

4.

airy single did muscle boxes it
on dip terms of that and blotted
large

copernican boot sort pieces
it
euclid to lots bread a sort

fiddle to history belongs
a number mud
across tint by balds airs

no nor no
light belongs large
all across by foot whole squared

peck ping when cork mean
ash a bird
post were a such had some s corot added

5.

sofa walls it dips sharp upon rose
sitting dip so did the it
copernican bull of a single

sort such soil that brains
bread balds pends and lots
of soils sort pieces fiddle

to a history foot of the tint
limb light link tint all blue
to number of neat's whole

no forms pages nor mere added
no-band down corks post room
box forms tattoo

a corot all quite s
pearl cuffs when mean ping
numbers when milk numbers

6.

copernican that sharp
and single and dip the terms rose
and sofa bull boxes

thought knee with sticks to lots pends
on lumber sort that brains
the private to euclid soils such

a blue trim whole wax of history cuffs
the book belongs by the all link
to heads a neat's whole belongs

an arm in such arm all
down the finger post haste wrist
smarts some peck oath pages diorite

room necking the band corot
wrist s corks an s
a cigar added of ping

SOUP TENDS

Hih!   Whose.   abdomen alatch
apex angular a century small or less
from a can to black or can species

apex bristles or other not, yet listed
to the rectangular or absent

rocker mites slightly canada at base
times less than tube

cybernetical the diptera morels claval
it has been which is fairly automobile
as used should be tips or isn't

profile anterior starts
believe less than discal at base paste
as wide as or hinder than less, was
smooth under-answering as greens common
moron a cylindrical parallel
numbers sometimes back
under occurrence a plant concentration

type reports palps long, un-beyond
parsley leaves on a number
of leaves together one just together
a bar mell of swayed tims
Bohemes

THE LEAD CHAMBER

no more spaces
  had and do
heard of said
  it and one
were of them
  have what you
ever know was
  been it that at it
a think of time

do you do you never was very was such
  were sit was such rust to it
had and tried that
        the got

  I both was other and then out with get away
and to and around
  to be hours to the what it got
turned out what was got like what it sudden
all of a this was all there

  got in metal and or one was to that
    finger across would
   and to fuse have a big been fine
     got only broke
      that that

it had to green that the like you
   but them it's when
pick you can put a certain
   you and they
         material sometimes
  that earlier that long that time
 it for a then I put I like that
  that up moved and nothing but done
    kept back and right chink
     threw into a handle
   chink it did just that chink
  it do it's things just work

whole had any end front with that
  had it and or it was of it
    that on it
   of what
    that was and
   how that did
other being able of very was again
  the how to the it works
that's where you have it to gets its where it works

    whatever
    like was
    there clear
a lot of which there were a lot of them
  would it little to would it
  take to less to hold it larger
  so the and it is you another

size is that would come that goes there with that
that size with what you would do

if at it
          was
with a catch
up the make
    trying to was with those to do with it
what could size it that way pieces that
                          make it that was
              that that was
could can't was ever it is
          has yes was
              out but had
          that side was
              you felt
          a lot to do it that
                      held
      around a lot in one like place became
      to do with on them
    a like out place
          for a put on sees it

a certain long and time was boxes did that
  the time and still good
    an other later it had
    into the so is another in so's pieces that are
      and how that there are feels that form and how
  it had other did that
    out in kind that and no other feel
      greater enough that on that

seems in it would do as that
   whether or whether
to use what much a lot of means that little to do
   of a lot of about it
and a lot will do of things that

     really anyway it
      sure is like it
     as up as which is its
      liking in it
       turns to more
      certain and it
     changes a little
    back to and some for
         other how
  some more and then than in and much been known
   heard and knows
    about it heard as though
     that's don't do what it
   be want to what it
    is it's about

a lot of sort of with those
I'm as do I can it
sort of with
a lot of some with kind of sort
    use upon it
yes and I and so was
so I comes to went out much it
number went and was

a fall by tying into it
   than thing but that's a make
  an ought that's like
if it have no other than that of it
if that's all part of what you look at
this is all doing to
and get that well by doing away by all
so just to do it in like with other
                        words to store
      the you you door
         that next other as it's what
      next were that
         long as what wants it

  ten
  little
  long
  whatever
  ago
      before whatever becomes usage in that there
   it now kind of move but it sort it light
   a lot put it sort of that matter too
  dealt for notes it can't first too
that it's out of a lot of the time that way
   a lot of then will have
with a hap and a take so a little in case together that is
    then the scale of how will have of it some in that so forth
    it had within what of more another this one of a thing of a sort
                       than made
    one of what it is to sort of want
no one that's that and this sort a lot in mind
these where looks take time but at that it was here now where it goes

there's another around show or keeps either by it somewhere or
about the like keeps it
 it readily would be kind of
  that's up to stack some thing and if you find that it's out
 about how can pull it had to be off
    keeps goes
        some and you
     that out like that

put it in the goes in on and out
what with that as goes and done
and takes goes in where done have everything
what got in there that were on there not about
none had first what was doing there
                        doing there
with what I made it had gone out this was
point and it felt that out
with what this is what to do it
every works to get then there
and a lot of couldn't to run things was one
which wasn't that just didn't
that was one thing to do to a lot of things and to that
        do out and sent about out
        this is it that really does at that
        that's it what it did so at
            that were what set
        that's what one of others were
                it's that it means what it
                 set it gone on like that
                and it's put that can that way
                    take with it is what you do with it

than it did
that they sure more there by being there
it was the very one that said that
this was over there then
thought about then here
all of a where

in doing what a very little then is and gave what to get that
if very little has gotten it then other never get it either
by it
on your
back to
own goes
whether one is the more your one
it doesn't have to occur to this is one of them
that
this of one is them whether
doesn't when or then's not
other
a few and you'd be
over with and who all here hasn't
neither is that
is what goes

more with and that's what forever seemed to me
either and harder even to more either the one
rather than were both
liked them as one may a lot
a both one

I felt that as it was just as I saw it first
it didn't as it wasn't felt trying to tell
it was just some as it was one

I thought it was there was of just something
it gave toward as it gave off itself something
              else it gets there
        that passes that that's part of
           how about else

I really deal with how that can do this
and this that made and this to be making that
things that can feel it to be can be that only
        that exist in those some things

when at that time that there was what to do
that went on as a while what it was did as
        to things like that what
found that found what was this does and who made it
found this whole out and why going
did it take so long out of to get to
do it

THE BEELINES

for Ron

white john, bell jungle, radish high
robin hull, velveteen, berry hill
rice obedience, chilly
ground view brig, counting goddess
step commerce, hydrant
lounge rounding star, overripe
hominy cucumber, junk's pliancy
kingfisher, implicit
childless hyphen
marshall tracy, typhoon
miami hearse, mammy horse
chronic riffraff, mounds
drown dine surname
no watt epistle
practical pawnee county, fiery, burrless
crag husk epitaph
cardin pitcher fidelity
grove patching pottawatamie parasol
roughshod roosevelt, warranty melon
thigh height sequoia pigsty, tormentor, cherry rider
sheer clay chevy, union grandeur
vintage suede heats initiate watts
whitehouse hilarious, amateur onside
in rag's air turbulence
star lion in airy porpoise
beryl tailor's barn-all erasure
broken arrow nectarine
hatching caney linear valley

cartless corduroy graves, ideal dale
equilibrium pretentious
belly ward polarizes delaware
gangrene hammock on pew scuba, severe
drumtight matrix
integral wand of huff
garners pious ammonia
linseed home of cactus anonymous
sparks deterred, roseland winter
omega taciturn, buck pacifist
low rate oolagah, exhilarate
everso rollicking guppy
pleasant pioneer vale, chancellor
graft city granular, malingerer brawn
larceny qua paw
sand springs carver, vouchsafe
gainsays king canasta, seminole
garcia skyhook, crotchety
amyl stickler, filibuster
borax still water, melee
manny cow ate a miscellany
round wooden sun grater, justice
delayed by a bee, afrique dent
word arrival joining, dawn on a spell
woods on a honda, just pallbearer
bum garner mercenary tulsa, veronica
cellar bartlett, valiant
eats of bixby, ragamuffin
blue jacket, skink
stone barger, corrugate
clay more forfeiture
deliberate tailor crushing homonym

candy bishop, dewy abbreviate
digital foil of car rue
guthrie, yokel
holland edifice, hall of boil point
conception immaculate, toaster villainous
ball of eight kelvins, nola renovator
barren darling grew creosote crinoline
seven kelvin heifer, gibberish
ear of self, kiowa scenario
ray of born pawnee congeals, panther
cherry crag, superstitious
prague pew, monotonous
salad saw, hereditary
conifer shepherd, pupa diocese
banana magnum, sparrow-jaw mayo
may count tuberculosis
braman ray bob, sacrilege
cherry hue, okay plaintiff
iron lewis, okay mulchy, peevish
miles of car key, bow ring windjammer
cherry parries lariat off paula's shin
ogles counting washing, raucous
palm talc, expeditious davenport
loud deck alice, kremlin gar counter, tabasco
don a ticket, chandu promissory
lenten hops, husk of myrtle
lend an ash, bury whole family
garner inclement locust, jettison
vociferate, jettison walls prior
lithium chap of bannister protocol
fluvial strobe lender, linda
offers maestro wagner

crescent watts, volition baker
cherry nullification, sousa
tulsa maquette, dawn of hierarchy
dun land of drain, mohole
gardener at beck of raillery
severed knee, monolith

from THE MAINTAINS

laurel ratio sharp or hard
instrumental triple to or fro
granule in award

one to whom is made

nave
bean
shin
spectacle
as the near wheel

of all subdue
a overhang
or bear over as a knot pass
the spread

that fair
the part
of the part plots
ending in for the most part bolts
as of wholes
golds
come to as risen divides

paper a half surface certain salts
such as full sit to the waist
turtle
dative object
flute or the like bonus

soup spindle
cloth ink
pit spring
bones to the axis of the bore to part
holding to do that draft
mar
a pluck comes close to
cones hence or ahead
issue
as or for one dents

humph
that wattled
place over hence
with urchin
which occur in the not true scales
slow green off with blue
more side
also and of those he was suffix

of the clock
note
terminates as an one leaflet
steps
or white person

bid protein
quill in full
lit square flower sulfate
or of another with each other

as a tremor with quoins
game
tape
red bill
also any of several serrate jars
the only place force genus
cause of roll
start from hat
state

or this natural or video
poplar forms meaning coke
envelopes
invert leaves
or more up from middle
blunts
leaves dash by the slip tick
as on

as at which props
a twin
and full agate pass
a jest or the like wad
waff
act in them
as a mote looks on or speeds
whole hence tablets
a double button

coat to send glass
see bill
called a swingle

is so hung as to beat
hence of woolen
lacking and also having
quarts

of flam of extol bean
of using chem
the pea suture inducing insectile
furniture of pole divisions
sending forth with the fold at the top
lens shape back phase
as some one of the nodules
woody and rind
preposition of either
the arboreal mild

a width of the like
most used rapid paste
a small
away or small
between without the mob forms
icing disc-lobed blend
cue tailed
the fried acute

acid
non-czech
also any hours as a chaplain base
after the one to take to not appear against
the painted but having no dim
not one nor one better than none
a state of being the like

intervenes
talc
often noting no milk of the suit lead
to render for sorts as hence
no sort yet left
a disc on the head or the like
one's for a term
repeats cast off spring
sound state in materials
shuns

bleater
the dry hub
to loose or draw
has been like also to be
back or aside
wear or blink
dims and acts

past of blow
blimp one home
blister copper as sap but one
due from ice at tennis
around a cent wind
cynosure
any of a central able carp

dropped
edge of other like
contents that will run out
of several blent
minerals eyelid

to raise in a canon
less flex or more canned hemp
and is much as masses liquidic
canopic
sonorous same kind uranium
dipping which by recipients

row or summons
of being commencement
with a coo or coos
not classed as silk is wound
the coupon
courts in reply to another
habitant
the face of a type

steps also this
as in the mast of a running suit
now only in some set tip running
see court
wholly from the main dormant
broadcast rodent
one shoulders
an amount of the day of the dope
used for does not
fend and right reason
dulls or to the doodle plants
fish

a dime
as the one or that which hums
limb in reports of the tube

kept hulldown
gathers in huddles huffs
cards near the resthouse khan
such as cathode meters a cow
cognate realm
or gradual hollow tuft

stances cover
number and neck
as a part in what one is not
subject
matchlock to a masterpiece
or the like things of immaterial scope
lower journal
mongrel moth or mastic solo

called pole
called made or right booms
a mono or diurnal linen
during life
more name
used of a mountain range

•   •   •

such like such as
of a whist
a bound
dull
the mid eft

lulu
the mode
own of own off
partly of such tin of such
the moo
which which
lably laugh
meter it's too
too maybe
lately too
same the marge
noun
by down which say
such way
ken ablative
sand's off
the lend the so
can which of
townly
the one the last the none
so so
which so such as
how lately
more stem
the go the stowed more
through

the such the pour as as
ton the hum
tire you
such tire
loyally views

the dodder one of the other
the love too
time as to way also
worn the such
such that shines which
when
said of small case
friction of about
the may which
that next over which
said so which
as to look to flow
such as about
in striking about to
grain in such as are which
the laws pose
such as about which one poses
ton
the mile hence fuse
more and
that this as to
to but as form this
such that frames this frowns
last or is
such's steep about
which ton too maybe
term as in
is lately bound of a same like such
like such which things croach
nail
by for to
as as

which
mean implies ing as often
period
means by which
made for also
by ever
a picture or picture
light on and then in as which
then such
amorphic not either
as even the like from
the loan the gram the duck
so so by such
as is
is which the stop
then that is first this
deals with parts
since at that
with into made such
it's too noun
off such
and has one is
the having own
having nut it's such
units of the number nut
it is
no
low where the no all time
cell
this with the wherewithall
such's which stirs
which one is though
no since no

mother order
for general past part the feet
each upon which its tone
often a like even
the stump stock from the pole like
such's tonic
than stop off or the like
a may a close
a one that some close
likely in grayish type
by fill hold back
having as means the such
has used for which even so
so that's
so through such
so what's even that
as such said so as much
which this seats
as stope works

stone hence period
as if such would come
that's one for fish
check adjective piece
one due to move off
which fill out this
much much
hence such which as much
as few point the touch
brace
zinc were then since
off as is

these which spice
down sands the lend one go
so which say moo maybe
arcs at such even names
it so
so's this
that say
says circle
round the even
might yet state
pound the may
din

maybe such yeast say
such says the last same off
means as
or if evens
any of
acting on
down to some
last at the same the done
much as such
the last go more through same
as it's that is
more as one that this hence was
done that this so it's moo
circle yet say which so
such even more hence do
lead henry

a pounder that's
certain as same what's
which though such
for lengths for enter sinks
that often as singly
bound to left to
its light as such
even off the part thumb more through
nine
tin
due
to put all in hence to dash as
in or to every lastly part all the way from one
the covers one
such small thing of which
is this with term though
such as stirs likes its such not
none as there

that's what often meant
among meant which said about which so about such
tars the one
ends the other
nines the done
say so
even's well
may as

timers
such as
which's said to
part to

done done done as what can was is
point
lynch
a par for such which's even now in
as on is on
the much a might the so
the bend's through
which though even noun
about such even lately yet
so as to said so maybe
that next over which one lasts
even or as
as yet
part the like such's close type
grain one
even so having as means
which what such's this means are about
the left more the left sinks the so

pun glean apter much sunk
more than through
can which it might one is
yet shines the so about said so
maybe though might
so off the can part even over
about with this that such
a yet a too
might that which's even now
about
this which is so
such and even
done and that

means and maybes
so to say as so's said the one more more even than as to such so
since such's close to since
since such a such is close to
it might yet pose such since this's such about which one poses
through's
so and such an ever

a nouner
that then again
a mile or such
a maybe moo which say sand's off the so
maybe town down
which as to look about as poses its fuse
a main shines about which ton frowns
this maybe yet even a then hence
its so even pieces
that other such even as one closes
on or in the next over which one's even like
and has one this is
deals much down that say means
say yet again this though
a stowed more since as the tonic seats this tense
through this hence more moo
it is
no
such
as no one
has one
says so as so such's through
as rose a more and then this look to flow done
through over which clear as move

such as whole about
such as it came
left like to that cross that side as like side
such that said so what's even that
is through in it
such loss most likelihood used
as if piece much
off as if out in
one such which thing of tin due
leans that such as one stirs likes
sinks hence the done said of a roof
that's what often meant among meant said part done

might that this which is so mean so to say as even since this's
though's so and might such since the more the more
from stop either also done and that even about such
to current plants it might one is yet
very much small
the very so
such a such
lasts even or as means are about the so
said so to say mingles means and maybes
the such's part close type part the as yet grain one
yet is more close to such's since a means a like having
a sure so and such an even ever through
a yet even too over part of an even said so through
so's just about then one more once this

from QUARTZ HEARTS

The mud of the bulk of the back yard.
Itch of wash. The sun through a board
crack a splinter up it. Noise or
rail yards behind white sheets. A nose
turned in window. Lock it up and smell
off the brass shine. Two steps by
a cat. Air and hewn lots. The view
across and the walk back home. Blocks . . .

•

Soda pounce. Three blocks of tonal
disbelief. A sail. The cigarette
slips through a basement stairs.
An air of cut papers near a fog.
A pocket mailed through the slot.
Crowds beneath ceiling.

•

The car had an open top that he never
looked out of as he drove straight
ahead. An iron mushroom.

•

Doubtless blame on a machine on sunday.
It was planted in the feldspar section.
A pan of white circuit matter. A last
strew of the peas.

•

Black shoes and brown shoes. The cat snaps
her orange tail. Aqua water in the toilet
bowl flushed away. If the disc was certain
one could put it to the man. Lime kiln
avenue in a shower going away.

•

Standing in back of a building with the
frost on. Large circles painted to the edge.
This is the last week before the books
are returned to the library. The museum
on fire, just a frame house. How could
one push a stick into rock. Too many
papers not enough rock.

•

In back of the painting was a stocking.
Pulling the plastic off bolts and the
mind on coffee. Near the edge there
was the room. Enough to stretch to the
far end of the canvas. Where? A clock
tolls. I wonder what's inside a telephone.
A click behind. Lock up that book and
recall the papers. A dream of three match
heads and later stalling. He threw off
the cap and began to plug. There were
three degrees of cold, lengths in the lake.
Altamira. A brush for fingernails

into the ashtray. Books will not last
long enough. The house is too full but not
enough things. To think is to sap one's
dreams? I stumbled on the root. They iron
them flat. The leak from no visible source.
That's left, this's right. No, yeah. What's
it got to do with my arm that I can't see
where it should go? Teeth. Poles on lime.
He said death is mica. Heave the books
up into the room to stop a leak. This is
morning, this point here in the black
which will come around. I stood up the
stretcher and backed away. Flat. Coins
in an image that won't amount up. Dumb head.

•

Before the wall the war stands up.
Touting as a list would I don't fall
for it could at all. Plentiful nevers.
A dot on a ball of salad in. Yes that's
as less than it could. Awaiting the break
of initial waxes. Piling lie stopped.
About can it be as near to as it. Left
at all behind. Brought out as black
as no red. Penny sitteds. Mar scales.
Brought forward it's not as total.
There's a vague main toad belongs to
a boil.

•

I caught a bird which made a ball. Open
toed. A house inside a house. To have
to demark repeat. Lightlier. Cone ledge.
So far as darks part. Settling drinks.
As flat as let his tongue came out.
Staves. Pounces.

•

Back on lime kiln avenue stopped a lattice
truck. Rods or milkbottles and a sky full
of glint. I go back stopping at them all.
Bimbos having sandwiches. "I'll have no
truck . . ." Coming to a plug a style like
a fleet. Missed. Copper weighted down in
pants material shearing. No moon could be
thought as mild.

•

We came to the zoo. We locked the upkeep.
A bird knows. So. And so was so so. I'm Mike.
Your land is mine land. Well below it'll
make you water. I linked the fence to.
Pencil in viaduct. Wheel ones over there.
Phone seen too. Come back when seventeen
strikes and film against my firm. Car
keys under woodpecker. Come to mind I'm out.
Lip in place.

•

Isostasy water sounds itself. You take a
quartz cold I see. Rose shale to
inflect audience openings. Verbs halted all
north of topaz. Taut morning chip wrinkles
vibes. Take quartz verb to calm feldspar
stress. Water that's beer. Chalk that dense.
Time that bedrock. It's a syntax
that stains sounds.

•

What is seen, not known. Billerica highways.
The beach in Nevada. Putting back the rusty disc
to cover any strata that might be loose.
Maps. Straights. Caves. I'll go out on a
temperature mountain. Cent calls by the way.
Vista cardboard. Subgum forks. The Seven Caves.
The tribute to the aluminum cylinder. Packed
to line up the sights. They buried the openings
among the blocks to be carted away. Ball
courts. Dogs should have license plates. Front
and back. A plastic thermometer. Stalactite
plunged in cement. Fossil tubes. Animate gossamer
rides on amber beer. Gothic Avenue is dusty.
Selected AM radio stations. Cod portions. Vermilion.

•

The seven woods or the open range. The
bulk of ideas. The coffee change dry
gales. He was willing to do that so long
as it mightn't prevent his seeing at

least where *he* was. The letter flounder.
The pin at the heels in place of
Newman's art. The series of meaning (continued).
Put on a dressing gown and house shoes.
See fit to the toaster, the pinnacles
abutment. Even to work he cannot
abide, thought could be possible. Sham
muffler pyramid music by Henry Miller.
A boy in glasses lives on mulberry trees.
It like comes and goes. Some. There was
a large iron ring tacked to the news.
In it yachts the size of Stella Polaris.
Nowadays more than ever. Will. Oil.
Snake Butte as a youth in Los Angeles.
Cans of our times. Doing one's best
as a cutter drummer. Dots on enameled-
steel plates, singly or in groups, by the
former. Nourishment at all hours.
White snake. Alexander Caverns is
now under what?

•

Nippers. The cave is a hole in itself.
The goes for miles. Rock a claw. A cane chair
placed in a water closet. Sun going down
and on. Pepper sliced eaten. Longness
within plain box. Black and gold sign, green shine
of papers, magenta corduroy album cover, black
spackle covers notebook. Copper rings of steel wire
in a red cylinder. The paper lining it has
got. I see black lines on the white opening.

Goes in, repeats, endings varied as poke holes.
Rock's time is stopped in measurement. I've got
a place a turning out to be. Looking out
for what's beyond the ground. Biotite letters.

•

House at L'Estaque. Pieces of belts.

Houses that look like cubes. Houses that
look like tubes. Nothing looks like
anything. Nothing looks like homes.

Chet Baker and liquid in glasses are
vertical.
Jay Cameron of baritone sax unknown.

Is a house side sent from here. A glance
of the eye is not there.

I walked on the street and closed
the door. I passed trees (my height
and other). I passed another. Thinking
on changing one's mind. The glass of a
store side comes up. A fish on wooden board.
I don't go in the door's shut. Small rings
and catches are they brass. The grey feeling,
the air glasses, the walking down. I
don't sense I state.

A pebble next to a pencil.

from POLAROID

stand point lap still think close near may seem
may you seem stand point it laps still thinks of close nears seem
standing points lap it stills thinking to close nearing
may stand for pointing a still laps seeming as thinks it close
you may close it for points then stand close then nears last
one you stand it points you thinks even since still may
per act a still stands as point for some it's back near
you as point of act standing close by seem back it nears
one by part to you point it stands may still seeming a lap
just nears may get to one still as you think close it's standing
from how to stand as still why a think as by close points to seem
from long thinking of close to a point a let stand by all leave
it point to up stand close near may it seem you all do by
one still point at same as once a hence since both may near
even yet and as still too pointed as thinking close may seem to stand
one just part about you close laps may seem thinks it may
or go say tend to match points move cause turn let it may be
why over whole closing stand off points as near than about you
all points whole both and close the lap so still to thinking
of up of yet by act here point all to another thinking close on seems
to be standing just points only all apart much to once by nearing
you than one as a still it though then along one thinks close
on seeing it points apart near to kind of a stand one point
that's about one it you are then may seem a point on thinking
of its near to point close seem a match pass tending so to say
it just to you pointed stands out close as near thinking stands
still points stands just down from means you near forth from
a stand point the way points thinking of close stands point the way
a thinking match passing still thinking by still close seems
a not thinking as point of acts just near a pointing to close

by standing to a point stills one laps close to thinking may close by seeming
that points stand

amid then along apart while as seldom matters which as past you
here then just a tending may opening apart is ever is some other
amid then and just a some where along one goes during fewer
you and ever still matches it will then along then near into either yet kind
you have fewer matters least along the point of then you
then what some amid stands to tends to because of a point think
lasts then along a seem to bolt tend bend as its thing as it opens some
the that that this could some ever along amid then
you and stand and just and single point of who past as seldom bolts
the might as its the during matter along had lost and you
the still stand its got thing at its amid then how have you
a match to least initial you as then along may send a let have think least
the much of it being the you a then as an along it could as
soon an aside then amid at it bolt turning its you to
stand just maybe then along amid open more aside of yet such how come you
matter to leave it then and of a then amid bringing yet to lots do
you then while it stands just amid the bolt could be around then along opens
                                                            to leave
a somewhat amid but then still tend to you near down back past
its some due to acts here then you how come by but few
appear to got apart may then will you as some ever a very between is
nor with much will it points along then it turning you lets see
back past seeming to say think of it then you still along tap during
its miss to let aside clad or place you in amid the then turning points
to a then along with the light nothing missing matters
not then at all then you be it along with and still to be
one lest could it be left you to think out along to by
singling amid then along by everything turning out with and by you stills
the point to just stand the then of the along amid lines

up into match it in itself by your amid then along being
its still matter of one and the then along as it stands you pass it
nothing amid then along nothing to be back past what then stands you
                                        think you

few part once and then one as around leaves close stays then some
of you few head so forth by whom why leave either to go
part and it leaves once you then some do you within stays besides
either few or just some once of either leaving miss it to close to it beside
the either one or it you part per whom via either one or
few do stay once it's close to you missing the whole either one
still few part once and then either it's around you or some close beyond
once and then one as few as ever or either it's you or one close to did
it part of one's staying why turn to some one other about to close
better once a single than few parts wholly to thinking it's seeming as at least
close to once a part of being either whom leave or why stay
you part once from thence a few ones could stay but leave besides
it's only a part either way one close to leaving you misses either heading
the part once and few then ever leave it around one might
say a few parts once stay then what of there being then one
around to leave only then one its leaves close then some stay
either forth or within still around say you do it by
parting once and then for all some as around staying it seems to leave close
its few once it's apart then around soon near ever another seldom gone
to once apart leave it as you why you if and when to stay leave it to part
leave it to close as few leave only to part once come to
stood around as it you miss seems apart as few may be seen to only the once
the part the few the then the one as close to you as once a part may
stay to you when besides leaves one to you doing it still staying it
beyond a once better single few parts the once whole few within
the one stays forth so close by a head nears part closes few stay
once one then leaves around the being one may still once and then some

will part once you few close around it leaves fewer open than one might
either part once or then stay forth and some few leaving you either say it say
or leave the why to some whom once it parted to better close a still whole few

out past thing without nor with much both there still is
a you to seem a thing during but yet a whole turn of both a thing is it's you
past the point of what this or that thing least does lest it still stand
but you may most make the thing out by past turning ones tend to wholes as
                                                                    they could
but nothing missing send for to let by seldom turning from in past openings
                                                              toward let out
you last all thinking aside matters without often a thing around to
turn during out as a whole it may seem open past nor near yet a means
a single thing how tended to beyond let it's really a one you think to closely
by more than seem a one such a thing yet a one you nothing may allow to
more than think in a light not aside from any at all matters it close or other
a past thought thing out not seemed to turn in a lot still one acts here
out past the thing of an act said whole passing you yet but a still just maybe
                                                                          thing
still past though out there as a thing turned whole beyond point or you still
mean matters as a past thing without but with both much will whole
it our why not may it get aside much by you thinking matters any as a past
it within matters in itself you hold it by as up a one
could it but match past both at all and single wholly itself with or you by
nothing on past it a thing one very besides to you a nothing so let thinking
be out of a thing it both has as past and turns you closely toward
out of a thing itself the past the one an it one you why least if both close and a
                                                                    thing means
you as wholly as a twin it might both the past and this leave off to
leave up thinking of one thing missing nothing you could as well leave past
a whole during one point to as some might one does
think out past the thing is a least close point it out to close near

the past its turn as any since during or past one it as say you does
what does think or meaning to close on leave a thing to
be its other wholly twin a thing and meaning you it have both matters
as any so a past may mean to matter as such one thing to you
nothing missing matter timing one means as still hence as any some allow to
you out past thinking a thing as a matter of what one closes as near to it as this

same via some point some just stand
as of just you still about it via a same because a turn matters
some of you stay just seem a one down on letting cause same to place
one some it then's the same to you a one seeming matched to same
as might one lest get via some same either one or you does
it some to the same thing that's your still matching along toward that
does some means to have it matter to one the same you means
via same said thing passes to stay via the point of still during the one
means some via the same point of still you having let lots place toward cause
one to a means of letting some in via points to it thus one's it
a not turning least to a match the twin you meaning one single the same
will other kind of beyond a same all a really part for another via
you stand same via once some to point to everything least during stand it
still some points still to a matter of time least one
you may come seem the same close the everything points to part to
the lot of via part placing you what same to point or stand some
around as same as even more singles than via points which
part at the same very past still ones open to time the same
via what of you how the same a matter of some the another means
to often everything because of stands some matter of you mean
a same as via some of just you do that means a what of it standing
for same it tends to still you instead of a lot a whole means
the same of it pointing you to just some of it then letting
a said thing pass by some or more same just still
one of you the same via what then of you the last one it

turns hence this or that the same the via some the you yet
will to often anything the same to it all the some one yet is
it all the same to you might for a time matter of these means to
still the same at some points to which you could it let lots come
of same via points to some you are the one close to parts the point to
everything

whole often match the least cause due to initial let
it often whole same itself place lots of the still last matter of
match it last to once part out of its the ones to matter seldom matter
those think and the whole turn often it's of this single one nothing is
matched is it nor least of matching any whole often same now acts on
often it is
match it is let to initial the whole light leaves the place the least
matching may open initially whom much tends due to the one the whole
the match and often the whole and turning match it point by just let time
open below those its whole my turn the point being matter closing
its whole often fewer than the let match least light on it stands on lots
still of the one matches the whole its often its since it's the cause
one to last matched other than rather some to least matter nothing to back
one its up matters a place a think to match as time some of near it does
often and whole match turns and place still on the lots each a let point
still missing and opening clad or not matching come
nothing it still would matter to and not lest a point come to whole often
this is around such let a turning the closing place a lot a whole matters
by how it's still often one closes aside a bent aside tending to match one
everything still single or not staying twin opens to a close it
matching the matter with the light turn the least of what its being around got
turned to the lot due to it lest it matter often still whole
a single everything an often mattering a match for the closing near
still a match is apart to the lighting on it of lots often due to the placing of it
nearer than a few acts forth may turn out to matter it

does often the whole time one by its one last matched
nearest and to the least it let point the closest matches
nothing misses in case a quite during time closes it
matching it turns one often whole and close to
it's one to miss turning back initially to match the whole can often match
out all seldom whole and often still let the light match
it is let closely it is pointed to a standing one wholly often is at least once
close the match

dial around forth enough means that there since
it's still lest closely light dial an around times as yet lots
dial by seen apart than by lots as forth a there that this leave
in case let lest dial really single a matter of one tending may
a lot of match twin seat case will dial leaving places gottento turn around
aside what's due this to least it's that still may turn lots to tap
head per think dial forth past still going a one some turn let
apart it's and light via but such still and the back but tends times
and is so dial nor even lots around it's come nothing let seem post bend
nothing
the may during and the come stir by how dialer single around its one
to point to the tend it's then sending open the dials it to part to once then
as get stir as got dials the bend lap of time let be still around
the by now such will onto around say brought tap say bring point
it's everything go because last nothing amid twin along still around
letting least turning cause it and open bend and but for lie stay
which at of yet dial around everything forth to places apart via
the where the one other dial the its one to due closing forth as
a non a single apart lot seldom because very will beneath
upward of all of it on lot dial head matter think lest time case
it dial it stand it just point enough of during forth to around go to see lie
really match what some every singles on all dials most lot of which
it can if it's sending got may to go send to lot last

still dial and just around say forth then often on itself bend
head light turn come upward into near kind stand just
matter let lots past timing casing the dial dials a dial
to or on as in turn in case due around the forth
come may the matter got still its say past why brought to stir
tends loom dial still around on it staying from turn means down forth
the fewer this miss its thing back in a matter due a dial
an it per pass upward forth see from post at bend on
a miss dial a long but close light means those below will like twins
around those then just back away still dial forth
as like tends

twin may what single everything
loom nothing lap lost seat to lap to may twin may what
stand just pointing seldom to matters may act open here a twin
all brought leave and why place it to one past the think bolt
have fewer this what its twin may pass per light per least by all onto tap place
                                                                upward
initial it lest it let its due to have that means from a whom forth a those by
nothing miss may it loom twin a match it and seldom let it seem may turn
twins it do time its open clad about one everything by point in standing
tending to initial back by pointing past its least it's light a twin is
act here seat there loom lap by amid such before as a tap may since onto
think see in case due let matter closely least its dip
matching the single twins just kind of near to may around
nothing let missing as acting here under so often of
due to single the twin heads nothing one or and closely
kind into either in a way to cause the why brought clad nothing
pins dip in lots and place much whole under and other yet both
it's a twin and it's since along or a time a senting reach
place open and miss apart its matter its never a reach may aside
lots and nothing brought one along since bolt thing closed left missed
                                                                around one

there hence since or may twin let one time upward a stir come to reach this
last the gotten matched tapping a really pin some dip that this
pass one its twin dial along as twin as tending may send
just and still or may and got it's a due lest closely least
it open to tending a never between during a standing
its seem to say twin think on one as seeing things as all itself onto doing it
tho pin cause way place since must over it's a twin one
via heading twin to send close the nothing single to the point truck
seldom lighting has to have to draw everything one match to its loom
twin
may what

clad aside no while light least as it not doing point
because last clad nothing pointing then do leave pin placing truck brought
everything seeming to say clad aside clad
the right deign tap by the pin lots reached appear as appear and
or just or pin go tend as one's clad lapping a time in its case of a matter of
due lapping at act clad here clad in asides the one pointing of everything it's
seat to lap which to what will during a think time a case of
will down a beneath is under an aside by thought never seemed here
a head a clad single everything point out the tho still the stay bend
missing may it clad be gotten a seldom still matter gotten to
matching a post bending a capper to the line appear the clad in its still
ever which some as a dialer any of which twins by the clad aside
bend it's a miss post a timing case via seat lap in its stay seems
the matches really the least seldom loom clad in point in dialing in
of this of aside what's to matter in a light clad each seat
miss having due going because a clad
amid such a clad around the one twins its thus during last gottens
what miss via very besides apart its send and reach causing inch
tap it at back tho all due to still at a same when boths gotten
clads about and matters timing single a cause to why go tending back

in its flinch twin right apart let close a besider the another
come pass pointing the dialing act here a may clad aside upward truck
none and seated back past to its lap open to the stir coming near kind of other
a back it's nothing a cladding light think casing matter
of dip lying will among its case among till due time light
clad standing the place get the truck down means
a clad and seeming light a bent a downing come aside
all singles of everything point till time still open all
its tho its ever on the light things place tending in a clad
this veer lines reaching matter lots on its
go by during nothing
clad least

point seem thing or never one may turn it one to matching
all whole point all seem to a thing a may turning up this it can during
the light of the everything single point to its seem thing
its lap seat head inch truck still least due to close capper light
acting here sending missing matter to a point the thing veryonce yet may seem
the open of a match send it this bolt to think just standing point
a thing there till within hence all over means to
single till the reach point of everything a heading tend go say
before match around some tho still its emitter seldom the one tho cause about
matter
during the let matter the think a point may sending seem can thing
a single match by how long before everything as point to of middle inch
still backing tho all parts may apart by those kind must aside
twinning musts and lighting keep to these say a point to nothing
a whelm keep lap such as the amid on an only often
leaving such place a still tho flap a bolt each thing
of miss nothing looming the lot in match of place the till yet
matching the whom passes the dialing into out of becausing last stay some lost
matters it that the time

trucks turning in stays of lighting a must seeming light
this thus having to may such least a thinking lost the match to a veering twin
one enter tho still a massed line emitter to the stay the since points
to which upward turning gotten aside past the lot it keeps taking
whiles of ago letting the light one may nothing near
see bolt think past the head the lap post a still twinning a bulk along then one
then capper that's what
a capped in that deign twin what's that stilling
to say by seems to staying miss comes its nothing seeing
being or let the point miss one just standing
for or by and of along since the beneath never between very amidst
this nothing one misses tho time and still or light of think loom

place pin bulk dip tap inch

AS IS

A metaphor is a sort of retina
that comes at the end of a stick.

*

Judd

things
that

exist
exist

*

Johns

one says this
thing is this
thing

*

shape
        much
    of the about
form
        as is

                    *

Stein

I
dreamed

of
pieces of

electric
lights

                    *

Webster's

Mere: absolute; undiminished; apart
        from everything else; bare;
        having no admixture; pure

*

as
words

as
well

*

The Fifties

for
one
brief
moment

maybe
say
six
weeks

nobody
understood
art

*

that's
true

and
of
course

so
was
I

we
all
were

OF TANGUY

1.

Underlying nonetheless.
The edge of the door is a pumpkin tray.
And the lights let down. And the dry
of a pin a witness. May this plunge
and take the edge aligned.
A mote in the cellar, of the soup
I say collect. Time your down.
Ramps to the list, say, apricot. Glimpse
of common field can . . .

2.

Miniatures

the portion of
ever in motion
palimpsest
a drink of talk
pine
and dip
a great grey
tonal saturnine
height fracture
dome latching
escape top
part
catch as is said

a noun
plate
done in a setting
waltz
rocks
jot

3.

But there is no sight. The eyes open up
to nothing more. A slant to the paper east.
The lug. And the pile tuning when, where
in its haste. These are linings, these
lemon pipes. Standings on the rail to
tuesdays. The notion of north to the jay
on the alabaster. Whip cups. Stay capes.
The whole all going broken sky attempts
and lies its silence. The film buckets
and the hair tin gnashings. A shard of
marbles on a paper on which is written.
Coming back to the same lack of going.
And is not heard, but is black as a
word. And the shelf left its spread deeming,
filing for the flats an agate takes on.
My left dreams. Pins in wheels their
settling. A clock is a rock. Cinnamon,
an onus on the tundra. The pages
are whistling through the stain. On
uprights, on legible pea husks. The
dominant, the clogged as it's palpable.
The wrist in short, the malleable teas

to mix. Motion is a complex, still or
no. And the line of nights has grouped
a day. Nothing beyond, seen, of weight.
Except, left, nearly twinned. Stand down
the night, a floor submerge. To see
beyond the hammer, the first latch of
substance feared, forgot.

THERE IS A CATERPILLAR THAT MAKES A VERY COMPLICATED HAMMOCK

A hole, then the strike, on a pin buzz
the bugs are particles-of-life, pass
the clouds, the print-out on nothing,
far-away roar of the sound-whole, birds drawing
deergrass in sea swirl moundings,
I have occasion to see sky through hole in leaf,
creak. I move, I'm a relative.
Where are the snakes? the rocks?
Grey or silver, yellow or paper
birch arms and trunks, nothing but a
jet cracking air, down here among the cubist
beelike makes a stroking call
in the jello of pesters, sun through
leaf patches on rope netting
cackle, plane, divider, toad stomp along.
I've got feet slippers. I go in, sun out,
lightbulb on, phone doesn't ring,
silence while I'm out the room registers,
somewhere I'm not wood shifted an inch.
As green points the sun through an oxygen,
edges of leaves near fall, a shadow
drawing of a toe. Where's the cat.
What is a cat. Greener in his sleep than
I not in mind. Sunburn derm cooks bones
inside. I can't see my houseroof. Glass
does not exist till the birds don't, birds
don't watch. A Cessna 150 with easy carb.
I've got no idea about but write it. That
gimpy great sentence to the lawn. If

so-called green's a certain wavelength from . . .
If he called me would I hear it,
would I hear it if he called me.
A pile of logs starts up and pulls off.
A glass needle plasms through a cloud.
He had to go to great lattices to get them.
He had to stay beyond the saturday of no light.
A dome is the intermediate stage between a
needle and a liquid. "Also I've been a little
envious of you being a cloud," says Irwin
seriously. Time the skunk left us
with no yellow-jackets under kitchen window.
A flake falls at the end of the gaff afternoon.
Hairs blow on the rosin my arm is. If
I could see myself I'd be
along in the afternoon, put down in a day,
feet up in a tree, somebody about to be
calling me. A dented old plastic wading pool
upside down. Birds practicing
what is up-ended. The glass is still
what is the grass. The trunk array
behind each other. The "front of the house" is up.
Green shoot starts up and stays, blows
points, marbles elsewhere under the woods.
My lowers, my uppers, a mushroom with
an emerald green translucent cap he saw
fit to tell me, to wave away a fly pattern.
This is the writing creature under the sun
even with nothing on the mind so shouldn't
but, but do. The sky is nothing, doing nothing
and everything sounds over this line.
Imagining stringing illimitable twine

up in the sky, tree to tree, wholes,
afternoons taken, Bob Raymond and I kids
Brenton Avenue . . .

Lately I'm just going to lie here and not take pictures.

RHYMES WITH MONK

Dimly seen but off-center. Wood irons in the box.
Reflection in terms of rapture's granitic. Clench
plant an air. The picture is of, overhead chimneys,
slant, then from above. Ring till extents are sound.
No time in the practice of rooms. Stairs that not
repeat. Any window, that's dust. Park car by means
of meter. History coined as bridges that abut.
And there be more holes than. Equipage rhymes.
A vest of interest. And a member close to any closet
darkens. Rings that oppose what one's wall might.
Beeps on the button. Fend might to its original.
Duckings that rhyme. Fingering a plenty article.
Traps that settle and are bridges. And to the side
it said, and in time. The paper on the window
scrape of speakage. That tugs are ever down.
This won't change it winters. A cap that place
it so, it stays. Wood, so untoward, metals. An egg
to a city. The rafters, whistled by. A book's center.
Says one, to someone, find me zero. Sun, and the flat
keeps pace. He would laugh at the dock. Stroll by
means the having words. Gleams mean the brittle
instrument. And he goes, green the rest. Space
to light lets to equal. Mishquamaquoddy. The pin to
all weights. Not forgetting it won't and then but
does come. All, but counter. Have to move to move it.
Shifts by no lonesome. Music a matter of walls.
Breathing in the place of record. And a make that
ring. All beside sound are views. Goes in the channel
of retraces. Just here just there. And it's handed
down that bridges be barred. Chimneys, says the eyer.

A staircase at any event. Place by help of, say,
that ton. Helps to make to have made, and being sound,
helps to see to the seeing it through. A brick,
and it sides with its corner. A family solo farther on.
Procession to the nailings. A cap to pop and he seats.
How work is lodged. Rhyme the chimneys with what plays.
A tip of dawn, no books are on. Clips the parade
in time to stripes of coat. The holding world, my
pocket top. And woke clear of the bop. Went work in
slants. Shades, to spot the sun on hand. Or tunnel,
to hail from. Right as rain, the rights of coincidence.
Lightbulb as hat, piano as light. A thread of wood
styles the thoroughfare. As an hour is only a face.
Face it, room enough for the doing thing. Fly takes air,
and has weight. Come look to the sides of which are his,
the broughtens.

As the room is quiet for the one who listens.

ALBUM — A RUNTHRU

I look in that one kind of dwindled. And in this,
look up, a truncheon in my fist, tin pot
on my head, the war. My father, I'm looking at, is my
age then and thin, his pants streak to the ground,
shadows of rosevines . . . His father sits beneath
a cat. Here the shadow has more flavor than my
trains, elbow on livingroom floor, bangs that
curl, opera broadcast, The Surreptitious Adventures of
Nightstick. I lie in the wind of the sun and hear
toots and smell aluminium smoke. The tiny oval
of my mother's youth in back and the rest is dark.
Sundays, the floor was black. At the beach, here
I'm a nest of seaweed, an earlier portrait of
surrealists I saw later, a stem of grey what
rises from my scalp. My hair is peaked in brine.
And this here hat, dark green fedora over same green
corduroy suit for a trip to the nation's capitol,
how far askance I've been since and never another
hat. Chromium rods, the hand in the guide's pocket
seems far removed. Blurry shoes on sandstone steps,
double and over exposed. Then in this one the SECRET
points to my head, shaved, and emblem, OPEN, striped
in "pirate" T-shirt and HERE IT IS. My elbow bent,
upright this time, behind a pole. I had yet to
enter at this snap the cavern beneath my sneakers.
To the right my soles protrude from beneath a boulder,
for I had trapped my mother and she asked Why.
Taken. Given. Flashlight brighter than my face,
another grotto, where the ball of twine, indirection,
gave out but we never got very far in, Connecticut.

I swim out of another cave in a further frame, cramped
gaze of sunlit days, apparel forgot. Later I reel
in a yell as my cousin takes a bite from my shank
beneath ranchhouse breezy curtains of Marion. On a trudge up
from the gasoline rockpit in the gaze of Judy Lamb,
she carries my pack, my jeans rolled as I step on
a pipe, Estwing in hand and svelte as only youthful can.
Most of these rocks remain and she married a so-so
clarinetist. My greygreen zipper jacket leans against
a concrete teepeee, my father looking bullchested stands
before. Perhaps we had just argued. Central Park cement
steps of pigcons, the snow removed. Overexposed
whiteshirt at the drums, stick fingers ride cymbal
at the camera raised, livingroom Brenton with orange
& black "sea" wallpaper and orange&black tubs. I wore
a wristwatch then and never again, drumtime hitching
me past it. I graduate from highschool in white dinner
jacket and diploma and frown, too many hot shadows
back of the garage. Must roll up the bedroll with
skinny arms and lam for the caves. Dave & A. Bell by
the Ford Country Squire first time allowed alone to tool
Bleak grass scapes of Knox farm. Rope down a crack,
mosquitoes and Koolade, sun dapple leaf moss sandwiches, ache.
Then in this group more drums on the roof, the gravel
and the flat, a cover attempt for no album even thought.
I tap and step in the dim known street. Lean on a
chimney to inhabit the sky, deep with drops. Here
I'm pressed on a wall of Tennessee limes, stones-throw
from mouth of the underground we camped in. Too many
thoughts, elide. Then lie on a beach in a doughnut
pattern shirt with a stick, a pipe?, in my mouth as my
cousin grins shiny beyond. Truro, also waiting for the

caves. With the poets then I'm fat and the driveway is
dark, the clapboards all white in a day of all talk.
This then all ends in color, my red bandana and shirt out
on Devil's Pulpit, open hand addressed to the grey
where Hawthorne and Melville now view of a highschool.
While the water still spills, and the cat squints at leaves
blown, my father wears Brahms, families lean in on one
for a group shot, and the rock remains shattered in a star.

A NOTE

I think then I live in a world of silence.
The language has become lodged in itself a background,
wall of rock, black and resistant as basalt, then sometimes
as viscous as heavy grease, poetry must be reached into
and rested from in a cry. Meaning is now a mixture, it
recedes to itself a solid fix of knowledge. The words
of poems, once rested from the mass, cry shrilly and singly,
then spring back to that magnetic ore body of silence.
The longest poem has become a brief crack into light and sound.
The candle flame through the sliver hums but must be tricked,
wrested out for a mere tick in the radium dark.
The rest is all a walk in stillness, on the parade of
the tombs of meaning. Or is this all still the highest ledge?

BY THE ISLAND

A tree-lined street, or sides of grey shingle.
White-washed whaler church tube columns thin
but don't ring (wood). And the largest elm
on an island. Peacefulness with persons.
Walk along the edgy brick as autos
whiz you. On summer grounds. Thoughts,
or beach (hot) particles. Shades grey
the sky the sea. Air the blue and pink
the skin. Blacks own motor launches.
We'll move the sand nearer the sea with
our bare feet. Ocean lacking raft.
Out there breezy with no movies. Or
inside the Bourgeoisie in thunderclaps.
Night bikes and car lights. Water close
beyond everything. I see Otto. I see vanilla.
I see the back of a menu behind the
flat of my hand. Bandages in drugstores.
And a walk after cones after dark.
We talk over Wagner and the lobster's
brought in. Sense of rings, sea levels.
The time it takes a boat to dock. The
room it consumes to talk. Meals.
Regular hours and starfish turning. To hand,
a daily paper, waited in lines. Today it's
lemon, tomorrow a balloon. A hedge
darkening line of rain. Over the sea,
weather mass and steels. A chair on a beach
is funny, set up. Talk takes hold. I live
there, I did it, tell you. The island launched
from the bottom one night. Autobiography
jetty light.

THE CAVE REMAIN

The past has opened its doors, the tube
in the backyard lifted from its hoists.
I have gone that I am here. The word "again"
perfect as a hole in its closure.

From all the roads around we enter the landscape of the past.
We will find its door. Among weeds, some grown to arms-breadth,
in a mound. Turning in past the collapsed foundation of fossil
slabs, once house of the tall old man who hoisted them, a dirt
track filled with potholes from the winter brimmed with water.
How deep, each one, will it break the car? The Roller Rink,
once noisy with marbles rolled on polished wood and all night
long we camped in the near field, now filled with young trees.
The past is a hole in which the present grows. We don't stop
till we park by the sink. A fragment of stairway stands like
pulpit-hanger on sticks above the damp hole. Hell and slide
down the dirt. A two-seater refrigerator on its back lies
in muck. The rockhole entrance in, rusted gate lattice hanging
into dark within, swing on its bars as if a ladder and step down.
The passage dipping into glooms appears as a mine adit littered
in broken stair wood and particle mess in the dank. Is this a cave?
The memory is of Grand Entrance, stepping under drips from
ceiling point a flashlight at brachiopod in Manlius ledge,
head up and gay with entry. Now it's darker, and ends in a
drop twenty feet to the floor of first dome room, a red and silver
steel ladder bolted to the edge. Climb down in darkness, arm
over the rung, feet stretching dropped to the floor. It's a dream
of darkness you can touch. And filter through on clay feet,
tromp through wilderness of ghost tourist. The cave failed.

No one is here. All we do is lock up the past with such
appearances. I stumble over myself hunched over sick stomach
fingering a chocolate bar as it's noon outside. Where is there
a cave that turns back?

Passages through lungs, ribs of keyhole and vacancy of a frog.
Drip and peak, the long fog passage out of my breath. A long
layout of avenues on my nerves. Words to a friend between
foot steps. So long ago we've come to still be there. Our words
are the cave, each going out like a light, into the telling
black. The tube called "Gunbarrel" closes its optic end.
There's no way out but in. Grunt and compare the stretched body
to rock in its literal sluice. Enclosed in the stone panic of
forward then back then again, again. Clothing wrong on rock, it
sticks motion, clutters passage. An arm ahead, another arm back,
the head somewhere in between. Friend's boot bottoms disappearing
out the far hole, into boom of standable room. He's through, I'm
here. But I'm getting. Is the right word "out"? Through.
A flat space, then a rising roof, we once found prunes in here.
I look at the smell of the word. Memory is a tangle, unlaced
it goes flat. Room rises. A slab seat bench erected to stand
since we came. "Bloomfield, N.J." painted on wall above this
bench. Sitting on it one can't read that, but "Berne Streakers
Team" high on the wall across. Were they naked? Roger deJoly
negotiated Schoolhouse in a jockstrap. I don't remember the
temperature.

Friend is yelling through clatter of breakdown slabs. I go through
the cake pages. The transitions are longer than I remember.
Time has extended the spaces between events. Will we meet
someone? Going in coming out? Going out coming in? No one.
Names burnt into the wall. A single broken white wax candle

we may have brought in, we'll carry it out, this time. A chimney
of chocks looks too high, though we once scaled it. We had a rope
we don't have now. Turn the other way, down Canyon Passage
thinner and higher than memory has (had?) it. Tenses are mixed
in the cave. We get all wrong high forced up in a dome and have
to turn tail lunge slip back down and reach under to slide
through a lower slot to go on. The same direction. In is out,
of this position. We have seen human time in a broken stalactite,
its helictite adjacents still present, twisted. To the end (do
caves ever end?) of this hall and the high up adit we thought
might go on, but too dangerous (then) filled with big loose
stream cobble. Surprised someone has carried away the cobbles
and we climb to see the sought end, might have been continuation
but ends. Clay. And a Milk Snake that can't blink at our lights.
Interstitial beast twisting in cracks, clastic homings, he's new
from the surface?

We can't snap the link to outside but must unwind the cave to
emerge. The cave is our-size to a point, then it's snake mouse
worm gnat size thereon. The walls rise in friable sheers, feet
slipping and sifting soils from roof shingles, no patch of daylight
up the well. We don't and turn back. Quicker out. The whole cave
quicker "because we had a purpose"? The walls return us. The cave
is a clock running out. We have taken the cave and move it. The
labyrinth of joints we shuffle, remains in perfect lattice, off
step and balance. Stuck in the barrel again, denim bunching up.
The history of rock and cloth binds. Then pop. Elbows save the head,
bang on hollow metal clay on rock, heavy densities sound empty.
The air bubbles in a bruise. There are no chairs in a cave, even
the word is wrongly placed, but "bench" . . . of slablike extent.
I have wandered to this twenty-year block in my past. To see new
trees growing up through limerock, dark shells to be stepped through.
We can't step on, to make touch, but edge amongst, pieces of a past?

The mind the tip of a long body shifting along stone tube, as daylit hours go by the boards. The passage to outside plays through bigger and bigger spaces, upwards putting feet and armlocks to ladders, spokes of the great rock wheel turning us out. I encounter daylight and suddenly loaf, back against a warm dirt edge. Ice blocks melt by refrigerator dirt and no beer or pop.

We, out, take snaps of each other, hovering at entrance. Will these bodies do? Scraps of chemical paper guttering in a sink to be passed on. Placed next the earlier pictures of the same spaces, the younger objects in newer-older time. Caught-time aging at its own aging speed. We can touch our bodies, we can touch the rock, the warm refrigerator, the words on the rock. We leave the pit, and the trees grown into the rink. Retrace the car through potholes and park by the house by the road by the well the water we used to use. Robinson's gone dead. His foundation smaller than the house memory had. I'm covered with mud and pick up heavy fossils to place in another yard. My house will look smaller than memory had it? The cop that pulled in doesn't remember the things I speak of, meaning he's younger than I am? And should have snapped a picture of him too. Speak some of the same words and go home.

CAVEMEN

The cavemen walk far beneath the sun.
There are miles on their walls so
no distance is far. They feel the sun
is only just beyond reach. They stomp
through signs of trees and enter their
caves in full.

A caveman opens his mouth and feels
the sun enter him. He never moves,
but stands there all day. A tree
grows. A rock ages. Cavemen
never bar their entrances.

A rock is the inside of a space.
A caveman thinks if a rock were
moved his life would be ended.
He wears the cave and decorates it.
Its stillness is a sign of life.

BETWEEN YOU AND ME AND THE LAMP POST

she wobbled a bit in speech of memory
but wait a spell and ever the day came clear

the time Bump Clark drunk froze his tongue
fast to the gate post of crystalline iron

or the night I age six spilled a whole prize
bag of ancient pill bottles at a lightless corner

she was exact, though of an age
a husband interprets the news in shut-up frontroom

puts a smile on the face of rue
an iceball broke the glasses of, the priest ignored

she cheered plumb from a heart of fear
rolled boulders before her bedroom door her sleep

to secure and lastly blind and deaf as a
door nail made up mind and shook this life

my grandmother then, older than
her home long gone

and now a post office

OUR NATURE'S FUTURE

1.

small smells, plenty of bounding
and the kind of placement elapse
we are used to get left or, subject to
fleecing load, tremendous scan of pouts

in the loan division aching flairs
to sponge out the buckets, an eye
where none before worries wobbling
a whole bead spun from the short end

and indicative one reaches less
to apples than to shovels, the sun's
ascension less prominent, the rails of any
fence magnetic to nearest city

intestines contract and the bolts
of a muzzle-loader lock to ground
there will seem toads but no one
will reach to touch them out, assert
the exact purchase of what we don't notice we know

2.

in America abandoned vehicles gild the land
and pace spools off the hems of neighborhood fronts
glass sides stand in for back boards and
I listen to what burns get tuned, I listen to the holes
but the blame comes out quicker to greet the sirens of jazz

just as mere or rude a mention of Zoot on the Paul Harvey News
the pinch of sex will gather, heightening powders to the lips
of combustion suits spanning years

the glassine pinshot arcades missing, but the ring of brass horses
                                                    still around
the hot meal for chain gangs just a bowl of steam
but worry none, on top of the world is a streamer
our cordillera a little rope or string

the newspaper clipping accordions out
like the magazines of a radiator
cascade safety to China
then you turn around the world
when you sit and brush a drum

CONNIE'S SCARED

The wind came up, the radishes died and
the peelings continued. No one could be
more hostile than a species enclosed in
a chimney for a century or so they told me.
The lighter fluid on the other hand might warm
your nails. We deserve overtime
for dealing daily with these mistreated burdens.
The milkweed pods for no reason in the world
we could see ignited and the frog is loose.
The mail at last arrived but you had better
proceed to lick your envelopes more heartily
as they all came empty. No one exactly states
but everybody thinks the whole world level
has been lowered and continues. If the flame
goes out the food will spoil, remember?

Then there is the problem of the stray moose
to be seen from the road or better not, bring
apples, take pictures, but the village idiot
had his son throw rocks. The later thunder
around the sleeping household was a mere
five minute herd of cows. And Rip Rowan thought that
thunder was produced by two crickets banging
garbage cans together. Tomorrow the snow will
be higher and the school fail to attract. I pay
for entrance to this life by my exit, can't wait
each morning to treat of impossible questions and
have never been depressed. Makes you wonder,
all these seacows spitting on their tails,

flashing lights on the spaceride and even in my dreams.
Claimed I awoke from the fight I couldn't win.
Chained my warts to a snowcone.

Across the street are many stray dogs but whose
fault are the cats. Something terrible's going on
in the woods the rabbit is screaming, the cat
distinctly calling your name, nothing that can't
be solved with gold club and pistol empty. Lock
your house when you leave for the auto. The company
that brought you pasteboard frowns on too many
fallen trees. Check your son's teeth when he eats
or he'll end a blimp. A crib death when a baby's
network lapses mid-breath. The television not collapse
but slowly burn out. And that cooking by radar might cost
you a few meals. There goes another roast beast.

The adult book a human gunned down as he left. Seems
the nature of crime to go unsolved, covered up,
never caught. Sal Mineo, for one. If so, wouldn't
you want your kids to stop it. A gay couple hated
for their foul language not their sex. But the fat weather
woman terminated as a lesbian. Stamp out discomfort
and lift a heel for bliss. Heaven more attractive
now that harps are out of style. At the loss of life and
limb remain cool. Their son last seen chewed by
croc in pool of steam.

There is no longer any Florida and Christmas nowhere.
The men removed our home sometime lastnite while
we shook. Asked me how I felt and what he could do
with his mike. All my girlfriends have been raped,

some in basements, some by families. Even in the movies they don't know they can complain. Reels mixed, eyesight tearing. Heard they've even left the lights on in space. The dawning hastes and subsequent vagueries.
Never a morning wake but I congeal.

AT THE POEM

You must have missed the signpost, took
the wrong turning, ended up for the sore moment
in that mud without holes. You must gaze
into the sun here to take your rest, suspend
motion and speech on a point of
zircon sand. The only articulate surfaces, they
are also somehow sounds, are buildings which
as you approach pour their facades at your feet
in a rush of the purest substances.
There are no faces to be seen since all
that is human here is you.
Numbers are become animal forms: the pounce,
the adder and the lynx. The things you loved
are all shades of moss.
Your only index the very grains of sand.
And somehow the set of things has you again,
a fascination in love of self.

from A BOOK BEGINNING WHAT AND ENDING AWAY

I don't have an instrument. I went back in. I'm still to the use and dig the actual doing. At the time that he was also dug I don't remember his name. That made for what I don't think. I must have been playing something like the Transition record. I did admire Horace at the time, I still thought of Tristano, but I was really involved with Miles's playing and Milt's playing very much, and Sonny's playing and Monk, of course, and Stravinsky was not as much in my mind but he was still there. I had all those sources I was still drawing from, and of course, Ellington. I never would have thought of playing the piano without thinking it out along Ellington's lines, and that's the base.

He used to say, Cats don't know this bass! On my sock, on the beat, on my sock. Monk's said it, do that again, never forget that, and don't know what I did. Up and going to tell him to play something he knows that you don't know anything about. He said I'm glad he doesn't know anything about like I thought to play. Does it. Cats used to say used that. And I did something and the other and the next thing I still don't know it was how he said it. That knew how to like you do. Been in music and came out he knows. I was something like used to there in the corner so over. Picked and played on. So I still don't know who said that he did not know and split. He said he was glad how he was said to play. And you know like you said it. Said that he did not know he knew how to do that. So I said you really know, and they said no, not you, and I said who then it is said at this time. So I said, does he know anything about the bass. And he said I don't know anything about the bass. And I was doing like we know him, how to play, and I was glad and used to say, but you don't know this and I don't know that. And he would say I know and I would play it. Been kept, whole tunes, all.

I must have been playing something. Like the transition. Record
I did admire. Horace at the time I still thought of. Tristano but
I was really involved with. Miles's playing and Milt's playing very
much. And Sonny's playing and Monk. Of course and Stravinsky
was not as much. In my mind but he was, still there. I had all these
sources. I was still drawing. From and of course Ellington. I never
would have thought, of playing the piano, without thinking it out
along. Ellington's lines and that's the base. April in Paris.

I should care. Everything happens to me. Remember.
You took the words right out of my heart. There's danger in your
eyes, *cherie*. Memories of you. Smoke gets in your eyes. Just a gig-
olo. These foolish things. Sweet and lovely. Body and soul. I'm
getting sentimental over you. Liza. Tea for two. You are too beau-
tiful. Just you, just me. The man I love. Nice work if you can get it.
Dinah. I'm confessin'. Darn that dream. I surrender dear. I hadn't
anyone till you. I don't stand a ghost of a chance with you. All
alone.
Standards.

                    Music.
                    Let's face it.
                    Face? Is there a face in music?
Block.
Block.
Block.
Block.
        Worth it?
        All of them are worth it.

                    We see.

That's what I want to find out from the best way to know, like to
find out.

Let's call this. Think of one.

Cool it a while.
Fast, isn't it?
                    Well you needn't.
                    I didn't.
                    Worry later.
It's good to sound good to a thing of sound.
Like something feels as if it's something's been through.

                    Let's cool one. Think of one. I mean you.
You ask a question, that's the answer.
One time I talk that figure, and sometimes I feel like talking.
                    Worry later. Played twice.
Every place can be big. A small place can become the biggest place.
                    We see. Who knows. Ask me now.
It's so far back. Time flies. Let's see.
And fingering on the piano jumped from that to reading further than
that.
                    Let's call this. We see. Think of one.
I started the keys to move to play on the piano.
I saw how the rolls are made.
That's all you hear about on the radio.
                              Worry later. Work
Black radio, black book.
I played the same kind of music in the moth.
                                    Think of one. We see.
We're looking at different horizons.
                              I mean you. I mean you.

          Cool a whole.
          Hold it fast.

Monk's mood. That's what. Monk's dream. Anvils in Petrograd. Trinkle tinkle. Coltrane, Coltrane! Ruby, my dear. It's so far back. Round midnight. I feel like talking. Coming on the Hudson. Ate in cafeteria. Light blue. Heard it all ringing. Ba-lue bolivar ba-lues-are. the same streets as outside the theater. Bemsha swing. The best of it. Brilliant corners. The smallest place can become the biggest place. Well you needn't. I didn't. Straight no chaser. Gathering range of whole snow covers. Criss cross. A tug bulk. Hackensack. Faults beyond. Let's call this. Billy's buoy. Ask me now. Peewee's white. Reflections. Bright channels. Worry later. Frisco dreams. Crepuscule with Nellie. Light coming on the plains. Off minor. Red bridge abutment. Let's cool one. From the top off. Nutty. Engine back room. In walked Bud. A collapse dome. Misterioso. Questions as Parallels. Shuffle boil. Diesel trees. Pannonica. Keeper of the flame. Little Rootie Tootie. Junior. Thelonious. Baking soda chimney. Manganese. His ear hole. Eronel. Face of the bass. Work. Counters. Evidence. Of what just. Monk's point. Of the mica plain. North of the sunset. Spinning in place. Functional. Sounds like. Rhythm-a-ning. Dictionary remake. Skippy. Long to learn it. Played twice. When the red light's on. Blue Monk. Came late. Bye-ya. Ah'ma see ya. Think of one. Count two. We see. Brands forgotten. Locomotive. Ferry theme. Friday the thirteenth. Stand on the same corner. Jackie-ing. Frame askew. Four in one. Zero is even. Epistrophy. Set brake. Blues Five Spot. Jam hours later. Round lights. Fugazi Hall, a round pillow. Bluehawk. A capper that's the answer. Who knows. The alternate take. Humph. A lot of sidecar Bacardi. I mean you. Slats gerry-guilt. Gallop's gallop. His own mind's essence. Bright Mississippi. Brown version. Hornin' in. On tap. Introspection. Ring knock. Brake's sake. Call it whole.

Bright bands of those very same dark whiskeys. Applications of the going. Wanted to see me out. Were going to see I ever hear in my life. Wanted to see together again and continue. Were going to see while someone else was playing. Wanted to see cold — bang! Were going to see softly and develop it. Wanted to see. Were going to see that was a long time for a while then as now. Wanted to see a storm up on it have really done it. Were going to see the big fat part that was left and started using plungers. Wanted to see that's one thing I'd like to know. Yes. Were going to see minutes of just the other kind he played in a sign. Wanted to see octagonal shirt and fancy pants. Were going to see just as some people find the plains. Wanted to see like either one ever distortion in the world. Were going to see that a guy has first to play or writes. Wanted to see those lines it isn't that at all means. Were going to see it come back on where somebody else has left off. Wanted to see with time I'm sure it could be done. Were going to see. Wanted to see way back to that first hour on one night. Were going to see room there one of the first things I wrote. Wanted to see a curve in the future and come right back to where it was a kind of plastic board. Were going to see night. Wanted to see from the inside, or more, all wood, a sound. Were going to see rats piss on cotton.

•   •   •

Light on Lime or the Hill's Makeup

A book on the sun is out on the books are out on the sun. The hill's tops are exhibited into rocks. Flats that come back magnified and as bordered damage. Cones, we don't know do we. An apparatus as light as the manifestation, its traps. This loose membership, a marry of tone and topping. Wire on marbles tosses their surface, corrugates mumbles and pronounces. The time the slope. An entrance of much room. The case elapses, framed skywards. The match and, in a flash, place of join. Tributes to back portions rock, cellars of closet. The mumps, had in a crystal stem. The hill, come back, this time enclosed, trim in paper. Plain sky part of sewn perimeters. Gurries and wobblances. The handtorch shows the tune its rock to turn. Accompanies in marbles its stringer, pulper in double stave. Cord roads in striae missing its night. Apartment in tenor, the appointment on tenor. Semblance of tone on bicycle of river hill. Turn around in fake novel. Much the part rock slight sandwich. The whole of a globe of ice paunch. Delimit the fill and ice the bunkers. Yellow magazines on typewriters. Metal hill on low. Bethlehem in fumes. Live by a bubble ever alofted. Tantamount to neighborhood slackhood, lath and plaster crogenies. Prize down the rock stair. Mention of half a quarry. Times the tunes the road casts match. A whole case of axes, sun on and rotating next. The dinosaur came through the carburetor, temperature in the dimities. Slickensided, false novel. The foot times the rock seem plain. Reads the word rock. Stands for dust spot specimens. Diurnal and finger-popping. The double marble turns up sounding lost in matrix. Put down that hill and go housing. Ghost geode in the sun and web closure. Fist in the museum. Scree slip to a stop and this case is closed. Light in the hand against weighty of map. Particles that magnetizing say you.

Hill aside, slots from the inside. Violet shine of the instrument and the block breaks, all trap men awork. The foot was found of tree and entered paint. The train abutted cliff to a stop, the photo toned in sepias. Hand to rock holster, toned granite or songing timber. Grotto flaming own phreatics. Wall of cones, site of overhead blues. First day covers the ink in mines. You go home to whole rock. Black as noise and full in trimmings. He thought his twin would need the stones. The man put by a paper in case. Knowledgeable but buttressed. And part of the path word language goes to the mouth. Lasts till the sun day, its amounts of particle palimpsest. Could be a band of chalcedony, drops to the hill fretted in lime light. Drink the book down past the box canyon. We live to the trees beyond the aerial cubist. As the hill suits its vegetage. Stick to your punctual geomorphs, lodged in brinks. And wouldn't you know the entrance to it breeds its stalks. Turned over the hill and door engaged. A drum within which to center its axes. Typing up the rock to its one day gone. Once heard all its doors ate cones. Lime sheets of domestic furnace. Hill to hear the all roar. Drove on slate all day, tendered the phonemes from the mine. And all the hill was loose, the shelves. A doppler of soda and fixative of purpose. Sand it all came down to wallpaper. Rock slip and night is drawing nigh. Shadows of the evening ton above the mine. Eyeglass of fossiliferous slate, nobody's adding now. Sharp the case into the sun, pyramid a kind of volume on axes. Place the star mole back in the test hole. The cats will match your azurite. A penny for your openings. Class place for standup bariums. Beneath the ledge the auto came to gas. Dim but audible in readable layering, the lowering sun. I read the book on the wall. That rock is above being a hill. And beyond that any possible stone being blue. Lop a chorus and stone the keyboard. The sea is drawing boat. Keep the axes in mind. Latch the housing to all polishing specimens. Arrive at the mount in full speech. As wholly terminates wholly. Watermelon tourmaline next to the hill stores in a box. Cave me the picture in the light. The cat stops pebbles from attending. A base of dendrite for all flowering tourniquets. Muscle the sun from this cleavage. The housing of hills, a make of buildings, crust of cakes to fall dude, to strata a mere uppage. Line this book in slates to chalk. Bend erase.

The hill arrives blue and in cap of Mozart.
Films of monads in a sun. Fingering an any instrument lets see. A prime pink ledge lagging, set the car to its score. The outcrops must pass the house, housing leave room for light and gone. And veins and leaving. In my solitude I parse the geologies from their leavings. The cold paste from its cap. Tip the mine from its tubes, a montage. The cat leaves its crotch, flowering above and bending then break. Eyes are stipulated.

237

The hill caught its back on a hooked ruglike roof of shallows. The spine proved stiff enough adit of the mine. The cave, well. I encountered this enough writing in a day. Of housing, the hill, its minerals of particles. Collapse dome and make an airshot. The sambo had come to, a millennium. Growth of stone is of metal on wood. Miles to flow before it cap. The mongrel mineral in hill terms. Summary of all the films to a mockup. Whole newspaper on a mountain. Solos on the terminator. Let the hill's health have a lever. Corks to the pole. Sheer trouser. A gumby let loose to the hole on the tube. Got to onions like a mere hill. Cylinder for apples rolled to a slope. The hill tenses the rains. As black is as warm. Lock froze and stars out. Merge mine with rock.

• • •

I turned Beethoven up to graze the ceiling. Progressively heavier objects seem black against sudden light. Light tends to crowd one wetly in the mornings. I want to pull myself into a run from any interruption of rest. Moments one must prolong correspond to the metallic spaces between storm clouds. Wait a moment, then move on the condition. You will never have another present, a rainbow that will soon be dark. Imagine the origin of a straight line, or the birth of body hairs. They rose while the mind rang elsewhere. I used to introduce a daily language through the use of hairs, proceeding from a single stem. The Marx Brothers separate their sensational discoveries into several marvelous piles under the usual conditions. What idiots! They were only safety pins, to the consternation of everyone.

A sweetness, as of lettuce outlasting bread, turned me toward the violin. It was tall, much bigger than I, but so thin, and had come undone. Startled, I concealed my head, and knocked it over, twisted it, crushing it into a hundred pieces. It had become more compact than literature, when it sheds some light on painting. Each syllable a hammer, one for each finger, to stifle the silence. Only thus could my opinion become lightning and the incident closed. I turned to the professor that had mounted a skeleton.

It was locked so he forced it open, the top of a lung, a rather circular picture. I wished to compose a masterpiece with my head, to shave with a pencil under infrared waves, to look unusual. But how could one do it, whereof did it consist. Does one ask how one goes about doing it. It might be discovered that I did not know it, that I never could have done it at all. Everything turned for days on my meditation of what it might well be. That I might fail in the light of it would dash me.

But the rocks, whose tips accumulate suns setting in mineral impassiveness. Only these have enabled me to trace my life in the tension of shadows. A stone beak in purple light, an ephemeral height. Or a dried olive slowly swallowed in a setting sun, the very flagrant proof of force. All phenomenal things are subject to geological mold. Take a potato on the moon. Or an olive, greying to practically nothing, on slate. Tiers of insects tend to descend as the granite blooms. Attached to the face I prepared to fling myself from the hot pink edge. But the earth is as grandiose a phantom as any absent wine.

Seawater crushed the grasshopper. In the midst of class I found my book was made of glass. And those horseheads, composed of bread or gum, or gravel, or a greyish paper. Those who find pellets where there are none take up all the space it strikes me. Everywhere carrots are considered flowers by traveling salesmen. Several other men were seen pouring pails of hot glue into an animal. They were considered golden by their country right down to the bone. But only I can only blurt out the letters of my own handwriting in public. This is called slight speech in the outskirts. No, no fun below zero in a landscape of numbers on rumpled papers.

I did so. My hair is elastic. Silence. The one in the middle sucks back in as I stand up and you bear with me. Glue becomes blurred in a glass of water. Paints in great numbers, parts of my speech. I could not hear the flag, turned out to be laundry down the street. Used the scissors on a brush which caught fire leaving a blackened hole at which I contracted sunstroke. Billboards seem unsuccessful holes, sheer mechanical obstacles to sleep. I found a marine in a pail of water, became critical and waited for death. This occurred on my roof during rhumba. It was at night some claimed to see a connection between neck and foot. I listened close to the submarine and began to count the hairs.

My tie-pin features a meerschaum cheek, and silver sideburns. I was growing, and so was my hand, and so were my teeth, and so my grin. It followed. I could never struggle more than a day and night against anything. Handkerchief. I was learning to draw myself up in wait for a better technique of intervals to stop welcoming vertigos and agonies. I kept repeating all the faith I needed in my tools for book purchase. A calcium deficiency and a taste for plaster. A spring to the eyes of tears over a certain definition of the moon. A few blocks in the outskirts of Descartes.

Where is Zoroaster? Never an uttering word. A few fragments of Ice Cream Konitz. Complete calm, a slight hollow in such a calculating coldness. A few burnt coffee beans. I lowered my nose and blew it. The course of all play is in creating a suitable quarry. The technique of lipping, between the bridge and the turnaround. The only fit subjects are these seed balls from life. Some skulls only answer to wax. Jackets soaked to their pockets. I only take a walk in the rain with my letters, and end up rolling them in a ball on the waves.

Rock could be mechanical, and produced in a sheaf, like paste. That we would. And, remaining seated, sea salt seems an extreme point, symmetrical and without twinge. The lightning seems to be getting fatter.

Two white balls to touch the cypress tree. Blackness requires the heaviest pencils. Pebbles to boot, a lasting slant on realism. My ponder gets lighter, my shoulder comes to light. An apple is nothing but a child's sky painted red. And the setting sun keeps the stones from noise. Conversation, a smudge, an hour, or else a cutting thing, all through its stairways and columns, a drawing of some science. I'm afraid the point of my scissors is a boil.

· · ·

Let's have another tune, perhaps you will grace us with another one? The berries turned out to be bugs and attacked. A cathode full of hay vanishes down the dirtroad. Turns on the tube full of methyl blue dye. Sits on an adjacent rock and her shadow on the sand flat. No one parks here but they sit and eat. The fencing in of municipal garbage containers raises eyebrows here and there cool in town. A corner in New York across from a corner of Pittsfield. Change of image fast as a waitress might be moved to bring you. Back around to the neon entrance an occupied cab below bales of rag ends. He found himself synonymous with the myth of tractors. Blank got loose in fields. Damage to trees, mustard dispensers, barn doors. Had his shoes resoled by a lawyer, then entered the church through a fishmarket. Moby Dick's birthday again, celebrated by only a few in schools.

A record of Lee Bontecou's attempts to construct an industrial washing machine. Many people injured, others in flight across sandpit outskirts. Bought these marble beachballs at the Artaud Jewelers. I'm satisfied with the way these stones are piled, let them remain understood this way. Then the unreadable sign was shoved over. And the city receded. Between buildings out of a closing door. She finally captured the orange Mexican by means of telegraph. Then returned the TV the size of a kneecap and started an oak farm. Found out earphones reproduce best if your back is bare. And the doors opened on a whole world of ice. See you next time past. This year they're celebrating Halloween on the moon.

Well what haven't the trees reached. Once in love everything went blurry, even the fire under the coffee. She took a seat just behind the pilot and tied her breasts in front. Heavy objects hung down from necks producing breast relief. But once we're home no more lip. I want all the leaves kept from reflecting in my windows. The sky to stay just like that. Only vegetables unaffected by gravity. I was raised on sheer boats out in the sticks. Let me have a perfect map of the front on that building. The grain of that road. Once out of sight and it's nobody's sweatshirt now. Raindrop the size of a kneecap.

All together they haven't the strength of a nickel stanza. Portrait of the garbage attendant at Saint Mark's Church, stands at attention above his own can. Walked from the reading and focused on sand grains building columns. Sky in everybody's wake. One possible position: embrace. Another: itchy. New Yorkers get a lot of color into their lines. Stand outside and watch them wave. Note the cars go down the river. Collect leaves inside your window. The sky goes over, collecting and dispersing. The passing scene, in the embrace of hair and eyes. Reaches for his pocket and finds a window. The opening out of my country in reverse wadingpool. Left-hand-drive: cloud seeder. Indigo snake escaping symphony hall.

Saw the Battle of Midway six ways while in the service. Then turned to other pursuits, such as the design of diamond windows. As the owl ignores the plane land. Points of distraction in a dense fog. Wore a tie-dyed sky on his back and vanished into the dark glasses works. It's no breeze living in a waxworks. And such as that the cat does not think. So lit all the burners and played all his albums at once. Slipstream in a boat, ankle deep in sails. His childhood backyard features the lowest possible branch. And he bought a cap that also served to hide his notebook. Turned twenty-one the day the berries bloomed and the fog finally lifted. Turned off the light on the toiletbowl and drifted into serious cirrus studies. Always wanted to say he lived near water, even if only sometimes a puddle.

His poem was replaced by a photograph of pieces of board and broken glass. Bottles of pop used for port and starboard running lights. Thought of the dishes while watching them wash. The machine tended to leave out all his h's. In the mirror the statue of a famous officer. And the store went on trial for unclassified candies. Unidentified man wiped by blue plasm. But up here all the weeds grow sideways. And all the pavement leads to ruined firemen's muster towers. Anything at all you could wish beneath our cylindrical light fixtures. Then recall the derrick you left out all night. Cars follow the curve of the lamp poles home. Going on in the sequence of sundown. Of a single substance could be chocolates then postcards then parked cars. Everything suddenly held up by the pop bottles he had extended.

But the cat looked frightened underwater, he said pushing the light out the door. This is all a matter of country time licensing and reflective of commerce. Letters against itself and whatever lowers to replace what had been of our day. Out the door, a toy. He photographs the hay bale field in all its seasons, held up on the way to the wires. Plants line up, mowers lined up, it's sensible but you wouldn't want any, going away. As people make triangles of their walks. It glows inside the stone. Makes of wall. The retinas grow large at the bookcase. The Case of the Headless Nude on the Sheet. Pall Mall on the dash weather, little time for reflection. Slows to a walk at the Jersey wall and speaks of that thick taste of Pepsi and subsequent guns of the trees. Snowballs turn left here.

Tiger lilies screen what's new about the house. And how is the world treating you. Styrofoam doughballs in no line up at the ready. Food-stuffs in an aluminum lighting. Cage reads his Lecture on the Weather over the phone. Is a marquee proclaiming WEDNESDAY today. So hunch on a sack and appear to be sobbing when only trying to change the film without allowing leakage. Garbage cans in a cleaning light, change of pillows, yellow ball all the way to the wall. Robert Creeley appears to be applying for a license but is only paying his check. Shell over every car that halts. Everything near some kind of weeds. The top floor will always appear newer than the lower. A printing plant on fire. A carbon mine in the rain. Scraps in parturience.

He's got no friends but a script he has written. Deals with a murder caused by overexposure of clouds on a meadow, solved by the time a girl read the correct passage in the right book at a certain part of the neighboring marble pit. Puts his hands on her breasts and starts the tape. Aerial hums in wind and flapping glass doors all night long. Cars as offshoots. A truly encyclopedic house. That certain red is to keep you in mind of Mao. And sit you down, find your cup, redress you. Poppyseed lights in a diamond. Skull fragments that form chords in an icebox. Turns out he was there twice but at the same time slipped off the roof. Engage your clutch and hold your water.

When I see myself I never laugh. But think of driving through all-out sunlight to take your place in the woods. Nobody's toothbowl an in-kling of difference. Stir your bare feet in the reflective depths. Sitting this complex game out with hobby figures on tiny squares. The object being to occupy your own space as subject. Brought the floor up to shine speed at window level. Found cellophaned larvae in supermar-ket coldcase. Left the light on under the pot and went home burning. Served up as so much self-image at sundown. Then repeated the chain-saw problem to three different age-groups. The log remained notwith-standing. Getting the city from a distance as a mere congeries of light points. She remembered her barn as sides of that fixed mass the ages are.

Notwithstanding night. Quick glance at a horse made of hemp. He views what over coffee at sundown. It will come but meantime things made of wood. Going down increasingly fused in the mirror. Same as learning to type without looking. The things not focused on later take up your time, the sight warps at precise angles, the instant his hand touched her knee just once and lightly. Hung the used-up lantern from a maple frond. Her friends would only see her soiled dishware in the mirror, so nobody care. And the car turned away. That he did. Melons on sale at the smiler's. Clams to speak from signs to the contents of moving vehicles. A movie nobody saw was made in this building nobody knew of. Drop your sights on fabrics. Come to in a glass bed with tractor problems.

He never knew what building would do. Drive around the block till I get my fill. Intrinsic interest of rubble, forensic tacks hung out with the day's wash. A film on black&white tractors missed because somebody threw up down the aisle in a juniorhigh. The potatoes were enclosed in red, the tomatoes in yellow. Somebody hired the room for a steambath where a party eventually took place. Cars spinning in empty rooms. The man in the skyline T-shirt. But where will I find the feather in such impacted city. Lie the buildings on their sides one by one. Then take in Come To Your Senses with cloud and dog.

An impaction of hulks that hold machinery so it can be brought to bear. Rass, A Place To Relax. Fine wines should always be stored upside down. Devises a TV to correct his windows. His constant drawing criticizes the sky. He smoked so much the day grew grey. Later she had to call someone and inform them so that they came and ate the cookies. Sign advertises cows by the road. Sign pointing out wires by the highway. The ceiling catches light and the footprint reveal an envelope in the ground. A bullethole in the sidemirror if there's any lack of clues. The house extended straight to the ground. Thought of anything's unusual of you say so. Brubeck formed the first national camera quartet. Cat transformed into triceratops by a log. Kept note of all the circles in one life. The plastic bag load somewhere in these woods. Burned nitrates and played a Bach Partita to increase cabbage growth. Nothing works as an office.

She needed three hands to study the Indian. And a parasol above the new aboveground pool. That light just makes your sink. Collects Kandinskys in a notebook. It takes two men to shear a haybale. While the trees shine like Tiffany glass. I'm going home to my quilted towels. I'm holding a barbecue for double exposures. I'll have to ask you to hold your trees. Face this way not your idea. The coming weather noticed through a filter. Only then will the socks be sufficiently soaked. That you can stand by the pumps. And light up with old saws.
Space only for light enough backs. Coupled his own brand of lighter to the pack and suffered notebook on bareboards all the livelong day. Sing a song of webbing. Leave space for a chorus by the spider. This room has never been left alone. Never even her friends come to my pool but they call first. I always try and look at the sky when I phone. A few drops of leaf and some sky on the planks. The dog turns to marble before your gaze. Knocked over the tablelamp during the fight so the first thousand feet were cut off dark at the top. The shopping center was shivering as it petrified and the newest houses all coming in upside down. I never knew whether the barn with its holes belonged to me. I never used to take shots at the sky.

Found a wooden cup afire on the wooden portion of a Chelsea sidestreet. Wouldn't move her head so I never did get to see that storm. The towel getting left out because I thought it was a rectangle of sun on the porch. Then at once the sky rears up. Car lights turned on the sky touched with pink. Settle down, the wires are where they must be.

A conceptual mistake, you're talking about wires and wines. The frame continued to show nothing but blank sky and the voice was mine. In a word, your face, your forearm. A catalog of muttering in New York. Listing neons down a sidestreet, you'll lose your finger that way. Back on the bus to a clean metallic sink.

What of it continue to the who are you. Rainforest stratatubes. He swings from the luggage rack scattering cheapest sheets. All up on the floor. The where we erected the dictionary drama. Wire New York. The frame's the same as the sky in the glass. People come down here just to walk by these books. Easy in the seat, scattered letters on his shirt. Begins to dawn on me the sun's going down. Lettering all over as the earth turns. As eyes come toward you in the night out on the tapes. Nobody knows it but time has already started to run backward. Pages of the big So What. Carbon-dated the film, stepped in the pool and began to write it all down in reverse. Enclosing in a small-sky daydream the proof.

· · ·

But I can't write this. Next, I'm never to know what happened next now it's gone. In the nature of words to lead away from what they lead back to. Words of the never recollective stays. Impossibility of the thing at all has caught me. New Jersey, with its harking newts retentive of nights to the open train set rain cellar morning of lawns. Specular, reticular, as on the horizon of send it back, far with the other spends and circus. So long I have not delayed to type the mind.

Then he walked. Then he rolled. Then he standard. Platforms of puff white in the causeway blues. Where the liners of cabbages were roses, and heat stumped the darners by harm screen. It was too plain in engineering the darkness, the skim stars and the stolen cars of their cement. Fisted bunches in fly rooms too, but he was street sent in the city. Papered out in laming screeches and noting weed spinning in car wheel. Seeing the strip maps in glass of market street. The beers when got down to desk in stove in beats. The cog lengths of confetti hum in cowls of store, you know he made a laugh in lair. He made a laugh on a line with crinkled blinkers stopping.

But this will all be a head of match-up stalks and moo guy flaring. The cow plated out of the thrust tunnel and uttered my veins. I don't think I know any but pure about this avenue in solitude. it bats by. Living on sorry if not stony roentgens. The heights go up in strong and the sheets in bury roll down. Surely and bituminous I've had many colds. I kicked in the lockers, the reefers where they fish the chicken. That avenue is bronze. This vent is sugary. And nothing is known to straighten all out but tombs around the poles.

What lies, but the ameliorative shocking? One vast sweater tube adhere my skiddy body. Yes is sticky but no is gold. Harking back to early standard blame time and the lemons on the ball yard radio. Zoot suits first hung back there behind the grit on tubes. And I guttered with them, gleaning their righteous tremens. Hank Shot, the brief flaw man, arriving with onions tarred radish-red on diamond gurry wheel. Rang a triangle on his three tire sand. Bartended in my biology kitchen, behind the signboard bread shards. Leaked berry sulfur to my witnessing ma. Shot up a guest roof over neighborhood avenue.

I came back grey shot with flesh, looming in bated lair mind, scouted to the foldest corners, mildew fresh in the tuckings and sun up over the mainlawn flood escapes. I wandered in merriment avenue, green and blimp light, listing the sticks I leveled past, a grunt turned to a faucet, a grinding like flutes as I watch. Till sit in winter sticks shooting tender, when cats look at eyes and never wonder. But that was, hefting, later. Oh yeah, I've had my pie histories too, to rattle berries in rotten battles, appleside dusts form boulders at my snail. And the sitting fascinate at a tiny silver disc flush with kneecap, was a thumbtack I hadn't realized I'd kneeled on. The chowder oak passage I didn't know was room of school.

Of rose fabric smartment broadcasts, as the boards lined up, skulls grew shrill and the sillies all pitched. We iced our inks and closeted our parents out of cardboard. Our minds on wicks. The buzzing cat to research us in or with a barrel of ointment gingerale. I'd dreamed my mind was kept loose in a certain ceiling, hovering on blue drizzle of jeweled shuteye circuses nap-nights. These were the dime flash years, spun from muckle and clingish roam. The rinds were open, nothing to stop a scar. Now that only sunset can be iodine, that tangish burn. Adjectives more adverbial then, hung on the lash of an eyewick tip. And all the caravan cabins of minder children and their tooting duties, that rhyme with fudge whatever they'd put their noses to. Must have lived for yards in sugary shock, barn owl pent. Passing shelf-sill shortage luck-poems, scribed sun-up in room alone. These were my milling storage years.

AT SPHYNX EDGE

I.

sunshine turnstone of various shade makes
acid blues out to the papered edge it leafs
through work through glass of elms encapped as
later as is, it was said, they fell first through it's
blown away under fishing vents a type mole plates out
undertow of the bunched plane a big light hat and
I've seen this all out beans to be true to tree slowage
lying biscuits that allow on vitreous tuftedness
the pattern of low beef to the siding with its pawn
of its later maw lane hefted and lift shedding
dolling in lake bent rise the pith comic fields one
so as if of them were to do stand for it back a way
the list of selves houses decks ounce a spate of
how could of it don't sat a film of labeling tsks
twins of men and ands the screen business threshes
a count stack habitation rugged in lieu poled of gum set
upon as are nature bolts drub and seals many
too length than in waves apart cushions in a hold down
a pin listen as of concourse a mulch due to the deigns
kite like disposable match lock to an ester cease
the selved down cities give for lacker a belted
score a sense ticking all lightly points it lips to
prolongs of certainty equal press of ones I must do today for
it's all but streaked among the cold a like to fend how to
plaster of paris levittown behind the him molts and urges
the plug-gull trenchant why not as much a rinse on domes
so alike as to face similar seals of continent signature

2.

the cardinal cops the leaves which semaphored bounce
the masters scienced my eyes have not the ledge to facing spill
acetone in present free will to the chord balk lime house
this is not cape presence to what sign the dormer have you
I'm a member behind the britannicas you dawn on cusp of brill
the cable sends you use it over position a dim sound as brim tents
                                                     could stem
a count an egg a standing wave to what such as you use it
all of you pawning new yorkers unknowingly it raises pinks that
guile as a house soon's come the block to the seine out back hinged to
a vaunt or a glance divide leaf in hull too plastered hinting remnant
arranged to silt a tin prompting marks of benzene after a storm
lad in its white skate landed pocket blow as ever ride bottled to
porch stained in from tone plant circles its palm fend more than
leaf one to cover it tines prado sands as coin as it marks off
tondo beyond plane elm at match hitch told at half
standing to tree belt snore cask down to name a
count to a man's will pin sigher to a plaquing north
been turns in before the sign brights up marsh fleck a tap
the upon it tooth upons unstop beneath a dip a have had
mainly a spin pun a self if to pile at a clip a tone map
dough or rather hoists or bar climbed sum its crease as its
point is to district fill pounce chink or halt brims
for use or to reseat stratum foil darning hollow escapee
the needing vend to relax it whiting back films you do
I assume a catch letting what to the frame the bolt lams
to whiles comes go the light chair does view climbs which
file down and go it lets aback a main stack a room boom
in spinach rest in dark in eyelet ribs wrist sit
aloud this fell and green and ouncing places abatement

acid of the whole stein thanking points under the blue
scarp that fumes tub the many off a floor card its tinning out of
I'd must tune out lots as he frets the sepal counts of a march monk
hen about lit to faint from in front doubt latch mount
clip close off the match ring houses a main door as dining as or add a one

3.

the inside all these are a dime a dime
or cancel it is not can as raised on a bunk you sham cups
akin to a lot of tent yet a prompt of miler steam
horn bees let the sky type pass the chance to house a beef
how kept the sum of it is which voids the jam of a loaf
could sawn there free a copse rack the veer off a bending
its either leaves fall or some of ones tend it to leave
scope and the will to toast out of film light endings
stirs and veins a cap aloud more coil to the heel base on which I
turns out could stay the rejoin rooves to the cave parts
from a nearness to you sign one up as pointed as leave out
the pike the self housed lodging in a turn farther down
make out light of it in disposable matrices throttled to the spread
rib cages the ticked off the roofs marble up the strands agreed
things on things on the heart stands in thumps for my due
bevel to plate out thumps in entire for plat presumables
coiling disposable biological as the moon is down the one's in the
                                                          shower the lake
houses wood perempts up parts deplete the coffee tan out back
for how the occasional I am ribbed less the numbers up bend over to
                                                          stout out
this choppy whelm glazed to and or backed to but yet
on a switched to flash by color able deep from the up back to in back
sign as buttered skeleton key how color amounts to add nouns of

greens slight angle one what is part line parts to martian irish novel points
as giving it pay lieu means sand hewing stable matrix as sun sets
hoving leavings and to the fore letter slots in kempt of elephant
dial ace permanence as eaves shoot means stick to table
pipe signatures of return verticals to a mouth it an out of house
some of I'll be slant draw'll be type the
door into be back by chalk reverse it'll humph I'll moby dick
night stove breakers above wind each fainter fact to be go do so
raking odds but be in so leaves its type back venting newel
the stopes from trees lime crayon hair line an ankle
stopping gasket reaching fills lopping a switch out of stays threshing still
                                                        until and

                        4.

the whale then to bed been it so as
snows on a morrow meters points off earth island it
commas getting about the be him is strange to
wake to bark cars and easy fielding the green edge blue is clench
twig of some make pans arm place with the will use totals phase
then apart boom exercised the ever take socks be short
within it's about all somehow landed rights of remain shore form
the bird end its wind of course be wall its first iron lighting
some tip as make cleared and slided yet past of
dials flat an ammonite cleaned off to its core levels formed
blue dots helicopter and pool goat sonance get let and range the
fish I escape from bowl that not to enpin refries
water rows in a stunt understood it's been geodes as all thinking rolls
whose floors a silent too well to not have did been the may pause
stains on cairns of the will pose a slight roses could it had
one tin will heal the march counts out of bounds in echoplex
tom gyres will stem what hurt off among out the duly mesh

whale though that manned spectrums a dowel coining summer matched

coco-veg

was type what spoke in the same even its paint glimpses such afterward

grammercy

done bairns hokku was meant to I see you beside went
supposing short off aloft to do the tank lent punt the wabe
and undo lead puff seeming vestibule sky to contrast fictive
what's been rend tops a very a might sound encapsulent mislead
and might done be left in tray a noun of but pawning screening
viable as the tween that might be easily cut sign of amounts twinning
stay flash and bound to still the sift capper told meeter
lean fall of gets stormed I run through ticks barking
stern rollins map turning in on to palm a malibu stripelet
rat on the year as folds the kiln pigeon
stemming returns in dice a close can't a laugh topped
then clone its ad maybe points to a screen yet hitches
spectra to advance no paper yet wetted the glass rose
a nothing noted wired to take again a blent "should I?" means no nears now

5.

what it would be of the bottom of the polar surmises
last took the canvas cake downwind divers proceeds
and what there may be still of a narrative in this subject to entire
it takes yielding up exert latitudes in marbles explain
a bit brings back the sides with little into a day
why then the all done does here step one forms a rolling forth
not by the strict charge of watch it off to some one
not half it rather with all of us or for other thing yet differing extra me
while now upon us but so wide that so much gathered what is more
into portable oblongs much like blocks the name imports with us
and within the short and long of it is

the body uses the following as elegant a language: the external by
    its circular rings joined
the thing waves as a house stands for a while of each is this
certain story as the frame of great odds took
in the picture capping three chapters of wood
seeming bounds or bone with no small name to recognize
but it is so far faster than the rock of some other ground
provided with each other much the same the hand in hand would
                be made

as not the smallest atom stirs or lives on matter but has its cunning
    duplicate in mind

MIDDLE BORDERS

I.

Cristo's range of Eccles Cakes. Tobias Johnnie on
Mount Sterling. Lee Majors winters near said canyon.
Texaco in warm sulphur. Shoshone Caverns long closed.
September Blackberries up under the furnace. The
creek closed down. Under Indian springs. Near coral
spurs. Antelope and onions in clutches. Negley's
Passage disinterred. Sandy cigarette. Clark's
sheep near Corn Park. Mountains sprung over the
Alamo. Alonzo Quinn's Gypsum Cave. The mahogany
stove pipe at the Wells Hotel. Panuche emmigrant
in a store front. Nivla Narruc. Pinion jays circle
the piper cub. Fish pancakes in punch bowl. Preston
Foster, John Lund, Richard Egan & Chuck Connors pass.
Ruth has one of the largest holes in the world.
Dixie quartz like salt on the table. Strawberry
diamonds from Tonkin Gulf. Harry Callahan's gold
shutter. Babbitt and Hawthorne were termed Lucky
Boys. Jimi Hendrix, the Tungsten Midas. Red House
Golconda. Stu Sutcliffe's Seven Troughs. The mineral
with pass powers of Otto Luening. Ragged toes from
rabbit holes. Jean Shepherd proves dry. King Lear,
a duffer. Fender Rhodes Cocoa Marsh. Send for a
cone as pilot. Indian airforce base. Basalt Queen,
Dyer-Bennett. Petrified endives bare daylight. A
mine groom or burning-gat papoose. Beaver cathedral
in view of jackrabbit. A charcoal oven full of
duck water on the ward. John Galt in the Valley of
Boats. System Auto Parks come green. Who plays
drums on Far Wells Mill Valley. The game of Five

Miles. Grapevine shells. Fibber McGee & Simenon
pick out rubies and Beowulf alternately. The hole
in the mountain. Young Leander leaves Cortez.
Verdi Midas, a sort of Buffalo Orpheus. A sugarloaf
ryepatch of obsidian. H.D. drains fish from punch bowl
in Metropolis. Benjamin Franklin sails the Pequod to
see Shaft in an oasis. Pitch range of a triangle. Teals
are right hicks. A sandwich of cedar brakes. Harlan
Ellison's balmy battle for galena. Robin's got the
silver. Warren Beatty the bloody runs. Glen Baxter's
ichthyosaur on Bunker Hill. Black sportsmen reach
new weed heights. Cris Columbus, Henry Miller and
Thomas Hart Benton nearly meet. I sit in seven troughs
with the rabbits, elevating troglodytes into the
Trinity. Calgonite blushes like copper in a sink.
Clark pelts a duck flat with Bay Rum at Mahogany
Crystal Pass.

4.

Ronald Reagan will touch only a Baldwin. Richard Tuttle
opens a Robinson Crusoe Arena over Pettibone Falls Cave.
Melville spiels to Edmund Gwenn the grace of a city.
Mose Allison stumps for Merle Oberon. Cannonball Adderley
has little heart for huffing coal. Joe Dodge zaps Doc
Holliday. Bluegrass in an eagle's nest. Jeanne Moreau
fires steel from timbers. Fairfield Porter bills Teddy
Roosevelt. Gorham Silver turns to dolls. Grackle on a
street guide. Tom Lehrer on the edge of Freedonia.
Marion Adrian turns Irving Berlin. Strontium oaks act
as cogs in a strobe. A minor Havana as a kidder. Whole
hill in head after marshmallow. In polo there be re-hits.

A bullhead less than an eagle. A red scaffold on green grass by Cézanne. A rattlesnake's laundry an act of faith. Miles butts Jim Bridger in Howe Caverns. "I'm working like the cat in the grind dome!", says Roger. A white clay composes Stanford. Ray Draper and LeRoi Jones sight on Vivian Merchant. Pressed Holes Are Ideal, by Pete Hammill. A white carbonate carburetor. Pen by Carter on white wood in Murdo Sound. Porcupine winded in chimney. Jack Collom undoes Tom Paxton's carlock. Keith Andes and Barbara Bel Gedes in Bones Of Steel. An olive minnow takes Turkey Center. The unity epiphany of Judy Canova. Art Farmer and John Mitchell watch the river flow. A yet lower Indian does a big knee bend. The Corsican auroras of George Harrison. The looming twin sockets of The Corn Palace. Dim hocks of violin meaning. Midway between tea and waking. Banked knees of Alice Playton. Bad blunt canning meter of Pierre. Bird-medicine's high holy days. Frank Capra's Bad Toe of Gabby Hayes. Buffalo wicks of the hay igloo. The lead owl at a deer's ears. New England pretty and rainy. A new town catches the Charleston. The Mohole near Minot's ledge. Philip Roth scours a garden bottle. Signs of derrick sprocket in Munich. The crystal ham of Valhalla. Grafton's steel door opens on the Gates of Eden. Bob Cummings' Clyfford Still climax. Mama Cass risks Pillsbury Camp. The cotton crooks hit Hartford. Viewfinder of box elder. The Cartwrights trail Arnold Stang to Trenton. Hamlet's Alamo, the Crosby Open. The Opening of the Vulva Plaza by Albert Pinkham Ryder. Johnny Mercer picking prophets among the pelicans and turtles. Ferlin Huskey's got a good Goodrich hurdle. Roberta Sherwood's antlered bass. George Stanley at Belsen. Ross Bagdasarian has a lignite daymare. Walt

Whitman parking with Nick Adams and Major Hoople by the River Handel. Lou Donaldson live at Carlsbad Caverns. Browns learn grace at Wheaton. Troy bolts to Stockholm. Jasper Johns ignites a Coleman lantern on Mt. Sinai. The Rolling Stones clear Vincent Canby. A log of mantid caramel. Ward Bond enters Brookings Institute. A Hudson worth its salt. Philip Morris finds Rosebud. A Mission: Impossible by Charles Olson. Aynsley Dunbar's creosote valentine. Glad to see you used to be Isabel. The Keystone Cops dam up Mt. Rushmore. Provos fill the viewer's field. Red earth and green glass. Jeanne Moreau considers rabbits "deep." John Lennon, glad of the thunder, wolfs down a boom. Sulphur is opal to Marines. That's a pretty square pearl coffin there. Bill Russo has an invisible shield. Mott, maker of teepees. Veblen took baths on whole hills in his head. Michael Fried seeks more air on the page. Don Judd says "I'm Napoleon" seeking grackles on streetcars. Emerson's noisy plumbing. Snowflakes through windy gates. Pilot kneels on bald swan. Edward Everett Horton prefers mint to carnelian. Kennedys read the Marienbad Tribune. R.D. Laing hankers to write on rock. The Certs Twins table their caving plans. Wagner trips on an Armour-Star at Avon. Bird's tea farm near Lenox. None but James Dickey turned numb. The felt twin Adas of Georgetown. Geof Muldaur, for Brandon House, signing off.

CHONDRULES

Fictitious and dotted chocolate object
red fellows, the pink to redden
revolver chewer, a world in yellow
pigment, piano or marble
a radiator and a piece of paper
inkpot house, captive balloon

If I am good to you will you cut me out of your
life? This was also a disc.

He was also a passionate etcher.

·

Fictions and dotted houses that have no
backs that let in captives. Red
chocolates I object to and piece out a
radiator in yellow. The fellow goes around
and is fictitious as he chews. Books are
that pink to redden. A corner on salt
does them then.

Bartenders in leaf. Agreed and that I
cut out of a book the disc. So the pink
and the red follows. Revolver of spines,
the dotted seller. Will you also
piece this ever. The object of a
fellow even.

Nines in a barrel. The fictitious pink
over the reddening radiator. An
inkpot in yellow. The chocolate one
was also cut out of a disc. Will you a
piece of paper. If I am good to
your life. A cap on the red, like
the yellow captive. Also as one
salt objects to it.

●

Some one itself to obtain rice.
Hanging or else sleeved corners the envelope.
His least perhaps file awaits my piling.
For how long an etching have we needed eaters.
The same appearance of round buttons snuffing
holes of comfort. The others have limited
their get cold many realm. Holder of
given comb left no mean rice.
Obliged to cage large clocks the furriers.
The best talking turning back the like to milk.
Some staves in the hose its own carpet.
So at present out of linen bells what?
After hanging was in front unders of
worst corners. Marble lurks then corkscrew.
Itching our small animals before five less
missing elections. Same time intimacy
a precaution, poles in desserts. Strong
ions or else file envelope the sleeves.
I'll have put batteries through the draft
pricking bottles in a hundred liquid.

Consequent balanced parenthesis on side of
enough rather confusion. Choice tomorrow flies!

•

The halt goes over the stunt, to piece
the bait to a staple.
Its have ridden. Colors of thin flat
covered surfaces. In a list the blacks
background after all. I'm over that
marble marbles. Cut also of a disc to it.
Pigment, piano or marble. It's as it
has willed you one a number of them
according. The hill of the ridden awaits
my objection to chocolate the rcst.
A lap the others realm. In peat of a
capsule chewer the ingot house. Flat
colors are thin covers. At last some
one piece has even dotted the seller.
A world in yellow salts a hidden
radiator.

•

The plight and coming back the
light burnt ochre. A bit of more.
The lights pink to obtain a redden.
And also gold, a bit perspective.
Obtained by light the silver in this light.
The pink burnt ochre burnt deep by umber.
A bit lighter of the more obtain.
All the more the bit of, pink.

And light by the white the more
burnt obtains. The Cyprus of also Sienna.

The black and deep the reds obtain.
Of gold to silver a bit. And also
black the pinks.

MOON DOWN

Impact is all they'll allow you in the spite sweats
knocker of cabbage at the vocal bulkhead
sit bent out straight as sticks awash
at sound not a bulge but cracks
a cranium for openers
whatever powers but you fist

There is a man in the sky, you string to,
clocks you gorger of edges
mimic concatenator of the hiss that strikes

Impact of the crow in whistle castle
you grudge the board that lowers
ladder back and have at it

Forget the sun rules
light a shock at the rim
coil in the cringe of boast and score damage again
stiff the merrier

You're gone, but the tracks of your blockage sing
clog the brightening core fist out
deep and crisp and even

HEAD BROKEN OPEN IT SEEMED LIKE
AN EGG WITH A CAN OPENER

The ladder tells me how to think
on all the questions in the doors that I've passed
but never having raced I now expunge them
send the moon a caption

Do you deliver meal, through what brand of grate?
Lock me an elbow and I'll stand you a tendency
rules the world from a sloganeering home
that finishes a bubble

No one's glad at this place I've gone slack
on a bender all of them cabled
to wish the race be run on clifftops overclad
slated for and booked into Stonehenge

Thus and so but yet I come
starving over shellfish also lighting up my inkwell
the liver gone dark and the lateness come to stay
whenever whatever strains come due
gone in an inkling

AT THE POINT LETS HAVE US A TUNE

The moon has lain on a short apple
to strike us mouth, now lying is
as slow as twilight is said
to be late to last

A shorn pig shivering out
under the ounce your fine words
amount to a boulder of a landing
gain a notch on the blown heavens a boil
stills such hands from the guttering stone

That candle owl in plaid pants
has he wrists of a tightening lets see
and airless all over now forth will he walk
crisp at the hems and wax up the duchess

NEW OLD CITY CHIMES

Jet-throne vacuum cleaner
    chimes over Allen and the bubble
and the oil stopped with stones of all of us

We read the histories of all in
    our magazines of city today
so, where is Peter's "cave up there"?

The day the fuel lopped off
    the valve on top of the bubble
nobody wishes to cease to turn

Saving the revolted urn
    we look at art but its hooks
only hold itself to the walls

And wonder why a painter would so
    rebore a musician friend's ear
lozenges of Jimson at twilight

Here spread the avenues
    but not their source for me
and shift seats hovering downtown

Not a place but a radium
    under no one's control
multiple radical

NYC buckles
    Madison's lights need trimming
where is that exact bronze doorway

Allowed me up to the pad
    of the girl in the Chanel ad
nowhere near Wittenborn?

De Kooning's couch has flown
    on pastrami across from Stone's
let's hope from peanuts

My breast inside don't rattle
    I'm sitting in Larry's cabin in the sky
fishing for words in refrigerator heat

The register gone
    better stick a feather in an amethyst
than shiver at a pistol in the morning

So loop the phone jack off
    imagine a bracelet of jet Bakelite
the Sex Pistols' Substitute's a razor

And Pandora my jailor
    not even Bluto had as beady eye
cold bones (casements or moldings)

Roasted over Chinese movies
    in wings of the audio backyard
as a capper (mute)

New York's sky must boil
    to the hue of exact silence
send me something to steer clear by

A set of metrical tables
    on sky shelf seat
Plaid is the name of a book of knowing

We must seed help to each other
    if nothing other than nothing more
than Creeley's eye

2.

In this city Venus smiles
and the only thing happens
all the windows roll down

The courts break
to allow the bread escape

The sources of voices are rusted
nobody's control of their gates

The ball slips from its cord
the world dangles down

A prism made from corner
triangles of broken panes
Imagine?

The books the fronts
of moving vehicles
that harm instead of
horn move your eye

This curling breeze arrives
from citrus cans
thrown away on rooftops

For so vertical
a city so much
flat

The sky a skin
of deep dim blood
you dip toward sleep

But why are these rattled
drawers full of silverware
flung at my window?

"Cooper Union Blues
the Moozac is too sod"

skirt to the side

                    BRASH

What is needed is
Eliminator Rooftops

Puddles that animate
at string tugs

Aluminum propellers that inauthentic ring
drill above the Church

A sneeze in the night the color
of a lion's eye lampshade

My love's the valence
even as heaven

OVER TIME

Tristano dies, rattles in kitchens
jams a tune out of lox and hair
you'd have to grow female
there wax rocks and dice

The aborigine is an elephant
the lower register waffles
the speakers pass on as a carbon
brilliant of axes in the rain

As with music there is no saying
no bridge made fit the yawn of a day
the dogs pure faucets turned off their chains
of pros and cons Tristano dies

LEADS FROM SOMEBODY ELSE'S NOTEBOOK

I used to have a copy of that
but something happened to it in the copying.

Me is not a word.

His route was marked with delusions
all over the page.

Stamp out phone books.

I have always wanted aisles in the margins.

The dubeity of a marble house.

The clock ticked so much it began to ring.

He finally had to settle for a window on the rest of it.

TimeSetters: people without wishes.

All drills should be of diamond once.

The night the cats take out their rubber plugs.

Growth as an adage.

Asleep one more time than awake.

Space as a reminder that gravity is egotism.

Why wasn't Wallace Stevens a pianist?

A MONOLOGUE

What did I say? What did I say?
I could tell you what's going on. What it
means but not all of it. Just a lot.
A lot doesn't mean much. It's whatever
I can stand or not. I can't remember.
What's the good of it. Nobody . . . The last time I . . .
There's nobody here of course. Not a bit of it.
Lots of it went away, by, came loose, went past,
gone away, not bad. Necessarily. They tell you
things but you don't remember them.
There's something they could tell you if they would
but it wouldn't stand. Lingering. To linger
is not to stay exactly. Stay what? I can't
think exactly. I could try to remember
to think of what to tell you and then it wouldn't
be so hard to stay here. Without.

There's the evidence. It was passed off by
somebody as a black maul. Passed. A passing
fancy that in time may. But open
the question with a deterrent. Like me.
I'd never pass judgment on the here today done
again tomorrow. You like it and it has you.
Smile. Talk about. See to it that the cables
all appropriate. Joining in takes a lot of solace.
You see them about it and they tell you to wait too.
They're a margin, marginal, tangent to the main
ounce. I'd like to put something by me.
Something for a late month. The time the sun
turned out a ton all broadcast. They couldn't

all find out to take in. Not even the wheat.
Rows and rows. Sandwiched between and now
and again a sort of strain. The moon will
not train. We're not solved to entertain.
We're to keep to ourselves and I'd say so surely too.

Night. It's always open in this place.
Closed in spaces all up in a shovel scatter.
Books, the andirons left a space for, or moths.
Let's have a notion and build from there.
You'd carry anything with little strain, less decision,
if you had the memory. The likeness.
Duckpins blow over in yellow pools of torch.
And I told him then, I said the man without
assignment must stand in the rain. Without
spoil. Now the tar gets to leak from the
battery last beam up to the left. The notion
that's not worth its shoe leaves its slots for
departures. Nice to pretend in this last
light out the walking hour. Demand of the
little import it be stated.

Got to bend in the basement most dictionary place.
Possible to have it be aporia near Peoria?
A quiver. Night raisin the dogs bring me and stop
signs. Get rid of these words and not hoping see
them thin into place without plan. A voice
does not terrace its ends. Stop theater,
ceasing volume, raging stun. The mother, the mother
of the child rhyme, sunset sign not enter into it.
Pedal out of breath. I live near this moon
by the house.

A broad dry thudding winter with the clouds
cladding down. I haven't been able to see it.
I've had to make away. To settle up the bill.
To stand in a hill until the sands remake.
I don't know. I do what's nearly already made.
No expectations on a corner lot. They've all
come down, sated among. Then the light's fluid
flashes in the frame. Words like brads lined up.
You take them down, settle them. Apparent, this.
No mug would parry. I half way enjoy it,
take a scad or two. Before the horizon.
Before the sun. In a lamp's nick. I could
have made it all up before but I had the
miles on dwindling.

It leads me into a world of strangeness,
every time I open a lick, a statutory lick.
Beyond intent, more than I thought, beyond
what I had to say, but never what I meant
to have. The world came around on me again.
This chair squeaks, when I move only slightly.
I hadn't thought it to be in need of a touch.
I thought to wait. I thought to myself.
I thought to pass but I never thought it.
When you think to say it you better mean it, none of
this turning out the same. Passing all right.
Passing failure.

A world all out of steamers, you say you
think? None of it. A stegosaurus on a
windowsill, brass, morning sun, collected. I walk
down the hall and turn back, my thought won't

hold me. I'd have to measure myself back
from the first one. I'd have to erect
great sand corridors in imagination and
turn them down. Half-light, storms in
the evening, expectable stiff interruptions.
I'll show you what it's like, half-hoping I
won't have to. I have my pride, I have
my eyes, the first thing you notice, the last
one to go. There it stands, the monument
to daylight, heading straight along the horizon in
the window frame. And at night savages,
fitting appointments, ruby running lights.

Actually it's not a matter of the cup's being on top
of the other cup. Actually it's a matter of
the putting away. An awful horn went off.
My chair. The putting away is a matter of
knowing without thinking where things go.
The things fly from your hands into their slots.
It's so right. You don't have to think of
anyone deciding, though it's your wife did once.
no doubt. Stillness of things entering their
places. You, an agent. And then you stretch
out your arms to as far as they go and nothing
more needs a touch. It's right.
What's that on the stove? And so still
you miss the pleasure.

There are diamonds under the ground. I
think about them. Then I go flying.
I reach out my hands and there's nothing there.
Wonder. To be the agent of absence.

You're solid, of absolutely no standing at all.
Mistless. Thoughtless. Where is the mistress?
The mattress? The longings and more or less
the short of it? All gone done and out over.
Diminishless widening thrall without the plummet.
But without the plummet where are we?
Nice today. Tourniquet. Shelf. Amalgam.

I could live better if you would move over.
We could share. The ointment is on the ledge.
These are my chairs. The ones with the seat back.
And the elms, no caring for them, the windows
enough. You sit by one. Put your hand where
I wish. Do the same to you. Thoughts of
a vintage, a quietness same. I am as
able as you'd give me leave. I am as stable.
There are oranges under the table. We never
ate in those days. We shared a common fear.
Muttering. Rather the screams. What about
the Arab tribes? The marshmallow bill?
The weighted planks? What if I wrote
this all out? What would it take me?
How would you take me? The olives
that rolled down the tube and plunged into the fire.
The oxcart wreck you wanted a picture of.
I remember too much. And you too.
We start out along the walls, the stuff, the beds.
We are consumed.

A man needs. I hate that stuff,
it screws your mind four ways from winter.
I don't want the people here, the persons,

the friends. Let them make their fly-bys
out on their limbs. I mean to be
incarcerated. This writing sealed in limedwell.
There is a mystery that must be preserved.
I must live to hear the words. I will not speak.

MONK, A HEAD

What could be seen in the back of a panel truck
allowed to be seen, Monk allows
that isn't thought, not so
much quickness as not thought
never to go over it
all in the head

a small bright round hard object
felt for by hand if not accompanying
eye

three silver sailors
watching the edge or ridge
picture on the back
packing of a harrowing marriage
men at large
in a lento or largo
argentina

Monk reported
hard eyes and riskier fingers
the laugh as interstitial haste
or click lid of grace
no brighter than the violet of Ruby
My Dear

Needn't
be you
takes a laugh at the sun
they could bring

back your bicycle bent
from the atmosphere tamer
black as those skips hard to track

the entrance to the phone was left blanker
white noise in a television toy
or eclipsing of plan, a sealed key
on the orangutanian piano

anyway, he beveled round streetsigns
lamps needing touch, felt answers
and brightness in the wall of friar's cell
he knew it possible to sheboygan encaustic
Monk weighed in at earhole possible

and the largest of suits on the sun
the barrier moon, the trim trees, the saddle
of lacy scandal, the impossible
to trace valuable variable
though it's all visible

Mind cogged best when laid up on the hip
then the gentian gesture dries, then suspended
month of sundays, the icy single plan
that it sound backward, but intentionally
surmise, he held the piano
at length as a sort of Spain

then children rung in the kilter twilight
needn't but, they do, we see
he do, and the liars set out their
empties for him to

Monk held cold hope
pressed that momentum never even
still the kernel waits his marvel

                    jazz
his adventure
                    bell
his bubble
                    dark
his friction
                    list
his tension
                    hoof
his pendulum
                        out
his function
                    down
his arm
down his arm

from SMITHSONIAN DEPOSITIONS

Suspended over space, we hung one above another, like laundry between tenement flats. The corners, dihedrals, jam-cracks, bulges, are all indistinguishable parts of the great, overhanging wall. The pitches never end, and one day merges into another. I recall only bits and pieces. A horrible flaring chimney sticks in my mind, and the most difficult pendulum in my life. Always the overhangs and bulges keep us from knowing exactly where to go. And I remember a wonderful Peregrine falcon eyrie deep back in a chimney; soft white pieces of down stuck on to the crystals of grey granite. Banks of suspended slate hung over a greenish-blue pond at the bottom of a deep quarry. All boundaries and distinctions lost their meaning in this ocean of slate. It was as though one was at the bottom of a petrified sea and gazing on countless stratigraphic horizons that had fallen into endless directions of steepness. Syncline (downward) and anticline (upward) outcroppings and the asymmetrical cave-ins caused minor swoons and vertigos. The brittleness of the site seemed to swarm around one, causing a sense of displacement. Each individual crystal in the granite stood out in bold relief. The varied shapes of the clouds never ceased to attract our attention. For the first time we noticed tiny bugs that were all over the walls, so tiny they were barely noticeable. While belaying, I stared at one for 15 minutes, watching him move and admiring his brilliant red color. In the direction of the sun, a new bar now rose up behind the previous one, which had hardened into a uniform, confused cement block. The sky no longer held anything but pink and yellow colors: shrimp, salmon, flax, straw; and then this discreet richness could be felt fading away too. The photographic plate of night slowly revealed a seascape above the sea, an immense screen of clouds, in front of an oceanic sky, tapering off into parallel peninsulas, as a flat, sandy coast might be seen from a swerving, low-flying plane, stretching its arrows into the sea. The light-rays, which were now almost horizontal, illumined only the sides of the waves that were turned towards them and left the rest in shadow. The water therefore stood out in relief, with clear, emphatic shadows, which seemed to have been hollowed out of metal. All transparency was gone.

A great many crystals of the same material start growing at about the same time in many different places. They grow until something gets in their way, or until they get in one another's way, and then they stop. Since they start with no knowledge of one another, they all have different orientations, and when they meet they cannot join to form a single big crystal. The result is a polycrystalline mass. Its component crystals all have the same kind of orderliness, but they all have different directions of that orderliness. Polaroid contains crystals that behave like tourmaline. The process by which Polaroid is manufactured turns all the crystals the same way, so that the film is much like a broad, thin, single crystal plate of tourmaline. But if one identifies and examines the words one finds them beginning to separate and act independently. The dictionary seems a vastly supersaturated solution of languages, roots entangled along sunken axes, originations buried in the dawn of man. Dangling amalgams of image and speech gradually propel themselves through all quadrants of the mind. A language must be carefully guarded and closed in common usage for its clastic energies to be held in check. Words and rocks contain a language that follows a syntax of splits and ruptures. Look at any word long enough and you will see it open up into a series of faults, into a terrain of particles each containing its own void. This discomfiting language of fragmentation offers no easy gestalt solution; the certainties of didactic discourse are hurled into the erosion of the poetic principle. Poetry being forever lost must submit to its own vacuity; it is somehow a product of exhaustion rather than creation. Poetry is always a dying language but never a dead language.

As for Apatite, fraud is a matter of bones. Biotite peels from Biot's sheets. In a pinch, Feldspar may be used as a field chalk. Garnet eats a granular pome. Mica becomes a lamina of the crumb. Oligoclase takes a little breaking. Olivine shapes an olive suffix. Orpiment, a gold's pigment. Pectolite is solid. Prase holds mastery of the Greek leek. Psilomelane reveals a bare black. Quartz, the German unknown. Take a cave powder and you've Realgar. A french red may be got from Rutile. Sphalerite's a slippery blend. Sphene, a Greek wedge. And then there's Spodumene or wood ashes as gems. Stilbite? Shine it. Tourmaline's, to the Sinhalese, both Carnelian and a suffix. Zeolites are boilers. And Zircon, a silicate of jargon.

Just as a supersaturated solution will discharge itself into a crystalline mass, so the super-saturation of matter in our continuum leads to its appearance in a parallel spatial matrix. As more and more time "leaks" away, the process of super-saturation continues, the original atoms and molecules producing spatial replicas of themselves, substance without mass, in an attempt to increase their foot-hold upon existence. The process is theoretically without end, and it may be possible eventually for a single atom to produce an infinite number of duplicates of itself and so fill the entire universe, from which simultaneously all time has expired, an ultimate macrocosmic zero beyond the wildest dreams of Plato and Democritus. And I am convinced, Paul, that the sun itself has begun to effloresce. At sunset, when its disc is veiled by the crimson dust, it seems to be crossed by a distinctive latticework, a vast portcullis that will one day spread outwards to the planets and stars, halting them in their courses. Pete'll hold 'em with one leg in th'air if they happen to be taking a step when he sees 'em, he laughed.

> Sets hard titter against soft snickers.
> Puts hard guffaws onto soft giggles.

From one side of
the dome around the edge curve to absent listeners on the oth-
er. Swelling brass and strings over fading pinks that have held
the acoustics to auditorium. From the flat diameter of chairs the
hemisphere begins to lift to deepening black and star points come
out of it. As if an upper magnesia peeled leaving bare limes. Spac-
es between distances between intensities from origins of lit time
could keep the eyes up all night. Buildings go away in a manner of
music fading. Then the double-ended rattle insect dumbbell shape
starts to turn, list in 3-dimensions disorients tilting seats, speeding
rotation overexposes retina lines. A whirling silence, locked emp-
ty, automatically no one to see within black globe . . . About Face.
Above Us The Waves. Alaska Seas. Allotment Wives. And Now
Tomorrow. The Argyle Secrets. Arrow In The Dust. As You Were.
Back Trail. Bail Out at 43,000. Bamboo Blonde. Barbed Wire. The
Basketball Fix. The Beast Of Hollow Mountain. The Beginning
Or The End. Behind Green Lights. Below The Deadline. The Big
Clock. The Big Night. The Big Noise. The Black Parachute. The
Black Sleep. Blind Spot. Blonde Dynamite. Blonde Ice. Blood On
The Moon. Blood On The Sun. Bop Girl. Border Saddlemates.
Botany Bay. The Boy With Green Hair. The Brain Machine. Bright
Leaf. The Broken Star. The Brute Man. Bugles In The Afternoon. A
Bullet Is Waiting. Check Your Guns. Cigarette Girl. The Clouded
Yellow. Code Of The Silver Sage. Colonel Blimp. Congress Dances.
Copper Canyon. Corridor Of Mirrors. Count The Hours. Crashing
Las Vegas. Crime Against Joe. The Crooked Circle. Cyclone Prai-
rie Rangers. The Dam Busters. Dangerous When Wet. Daredevils
Of The Clouds. The Deadly Mantis. Death In Small Doses. Desk
Set. Destination Big House. The Devil's Hairpin. Dial Red O. Docks
Of New Orleans. Duclimer Street. Eighteen And Anxious. Elephant
Stampede. Eve Knew Her Apples. Ever Since Venus. Experiment
Alcatraz. Face Of Marble. Fangs Of The Arctic. Fence Riders.

Feudin' Rhythm. Fighting Guns. Finger Man. Fire Over Africa. The 5,000 Fingers Of Doctor T. Flaming Bullets. Follow Me Quietly. Four Guns To The Border. From Hell It Came. The Frozen Ghost. The Fuzzy Pink Nightgown. The Gal Who Took The West. The Gamma People. The Garment Jungle. The Gentleman From Nowhere. The Giant Claw. Girl Rush. The Glass Alibi. God Needs Men. The Great Mike. Green Grass Of Wyoming. Guest Wife. Guns Don't Argue. Hat Check Honey. He Ran All The Way. Hear Me Good. High Hell. The Hitler Gang. The Hoaxters. Hold That Hypnotist. How Do You Do? I Ring Door Bells. Idea Girl. I'm From Arkansas. Incendiary Blonde. The Iron Sheriff. It Grows On Trees. It Happened Tomorrow. Jet Job. Johnny Doesn't Live Here Anymore. Jump Into Hell. Jungle Of Chang. Juvenile Jungle. Keep Your Powder Dry. The Kid From Broken Gun. King Dinosaur. Kiss The Blood Off My Hands. Last Days Of Boot Hill. The Law Comes To Gunsight. Lawless Cowboys. Leadville Gunslinger. Letters From My Windmill. Lost Boundaries. Love On The Dole. Lure Of The Swamp. The Magnetic Monster. Man Or Gun. The Man With My Face. Mark Of The Whistler. A Medal For Benny. Men Are Children Twice. Merton Of The Movies. Mr. Walkie Talkie. The Mozart Story. Murder Without Tears. Mystery Of The Black Jungle. The Next Voice You Hear. The Night The World Exploded. Night Time In Nevada. No Minor Vices. Objective Burma. One Body Too Many. Our Hearts Were Growing Up. Our Vines Have Tender Grapes. Outcast Of Black Mesa. The Pace That Thrills. Partners In Time. Pillow Of Death. Pistol Harvest. Pool Of London. Prehistoric Women. Problem Girls. Public Pigeon No. One. Race Street. Radar Secret Service. Radio Stars On Parade. Range Beyond The Blue. Rationing. The Red Danube. Red, Hot And Blue. Red Snow. Remains To Be Seen. Renegades Of The Sage. Retreat Hell! The Return Of October. Return Of The Ape Man. Rhubarb. The Ride Back. Ride The Pink Horse. The Rising Of The Moon. The

River Changes. The Road To The Big House. Roaring Westward. Rock Around The World. Roll On, Texas Moon. Roggie's Bump. Rope Of Sand. Rough Tough West. Run For The Sun. Rustlers On Horseback. Saddle Leather Law. San Diego, I Love You. Sand. Satan's Satellites. Screaming Eagles. Sea Hornet. The Second Face. Secret People. Sensation Hunters. Shack Out On 101. Shaggy. Shake Hands With Murder. She Wrote The Book. The Ship That Died Of Shame. Shoot First. Short Grass. Show Business. Silent Dust. Sing A Jingle. The Singing Sheriff. Sky Full Of Moon. Slightly Terrific. The Smallest Show On Earth. Smart Girls Don't Talk. The Snow Creature. The Snow Was Black. Song Of The Sarong. The Space Children. Spook Busters. The Square Jungle. Stage To Blue River. Stakeout On Dope Street. Star In The Dust. Stolen Face. Stop That Cab. Strange Triangle. The Sun Comes Up. Sunday Dinner For A Soldier. Superman And The Mole Man. Sweethearts Of The U.S.A. Swell Guy. Swing In The Saddle. Sword In The Desert. Take It Big. The Tanks Are Coming. Target Unknown. Tawny Pipit. Taxi. Tears From Simon. Teenage Bad Girl. Tension At Table Rock. Ten Thousand Bedrooms. Texas Dynamo. That Way With Women. The Thin Man Goes Home. This Is Korea. Three In The Saddle. Three Stripes In The Sun. Throw A Saddle On A Star. Thundering Gunslingers. The Titfield Thunderbolt. Toast Of New Orleans. Tony Draws A Horse. Trigger Fingers. Trooper Hook. Twist Of Faith. Two Fisted Stranger. Two-Man Submarine. Two O'Clock Courage. Two Smart People. U-Boat Prisoner. Under The Tonto Rim. Underground Guerillas. Until They Sail. The Upturned Glass. Uranium Boom. Utah Blaine. Vacation Days. Violence. Voice Of The Whistler. Wake Up And Dream. The Walking Hills. We Want A Child. Weird Woman. Wetbacks. When Gangland Strikes. When The Lights Go On Again. Where Are Your Children? Whip Hand. Whistling Hills. The White Tower. The Wild Oat. Wiretapper. Without Reservations. Woman From Headquarters. Women In

Bondage. World In My Corner. X The Unknown. A Yank In Korea. The Yellow Cab Man. You Can't Ration Love. The Young Guns. Zombies On Broadway.

The Pine Barrens Are Not Much To Look At. If a fire starts, it is like someone put a new chair in my living room. Wagons loaded down with salt pork, bedding, goods of every kind, rolled down flood-gullied roads from Ebensberg and Loretto, splashing up showers of mud the color of a new baseball glove. And just above the hideous pileup at the Stone Bridge, on a billboard at the depot, there was a large poster, undamaged by the flood, which several reporters made a point of mentioning. Put there a few days before the flood to announce the arrival of Augustin Daly's A Night Off, its very large headline read, "Intensely Funny."

guitar, with his quartet
cornet and guitar, respectively, in a quartet
piano
singing, with a trio
bass and flute, respectively, in a quartet
guitar, leading a trio
drums, leading a trio
tenor saxophone, leading a quartet
piano, with his group
band, with vocalist
saxophones, stritch, manzello, flute, black mystery pipes, etc.,
        leading a sextet
piano, with bassist
piano, with a trio
cornet, with a quartet
piano, with bassist
singing and playing piano
piano, leading a trio
guitar duo

The action is frozen into an array of plastic and neon, and enhanced by the sound of Muzak faintly playing in the background. At a certain time of day you may also see a movie called The Petrified River. Some artists see an infinite number of movies. The slippery bubbling ooze from the movie The Blob creeps into one's mind. Even more of a mental conditioner than the movies, is the actual movie house. To spend time in a movie house is to make a "hole" in one's life.

from SUBJECT TO A FILM

I.

They went off to make a movie of the land and on the sea. One if by land and two if by sea? The proportions of the job. To cover the land, and later the sea. The sea proved longer. It covered them, it turned them over, it washed their prints (which were however recovered). They waited on the sea. They looked through lenses at it, but mostly without them. They managed to alter the land, which after a year had managed to erase the marks completely. They didn't manage the sea. The sea remained.

Boats were upset, and the men on them. They wanted to return but they didn't leave. They couldn't until the work was complete. And its time, overdrawn. They waited while working. They grew ill. They stayed. They returned to the same spot on the sea many days. They urged themselves to mark it. The spot grew indistinct. It has always merely been a spot on the sea. Where they had to be, every day, through lenses and waited. They began not to know where they were. The islanders began not to know what island they were on. But there was always more money, and it overcame the weather and indistinctness of geography. The island went on film. A film drew over the island. Signs were changed, faces unfamiliar became familiar for a summer. Amity. We believe in reparations.

After the fact, opponents of this film found their arguments indistinct. They asked for reality (sharks don't do that). But they found themselves admitting the opposite. Philippe Cousteau after shaking his head at the film was heard to admit that "one shark in a million might be mad, might do anything unexpected." Another critical voice, heard in a record shop at random (also a writer), finally brought out a story of a fisherman chumming off a small boat off Hawaii, he turned around shocked at huge open jaws of a Great White bearing down and tearing away his fantail. Where is the argument? What has become of original intentions? Jaws seems more than an image, it is a language, a total interference with thought.

The sharks did not work. They don't. They eat, on their own time, on no thought or money. Their time may be only space. And money is not spatial. Weather, like money, only affects those above the surface. Men wait. Sharks move. Men found it difficult to sleep. Sleep, not as easy a change of state as diving under the surface. Sharks have found no need to change. Men spend their lives discussing it. Money as a counter of argument. Weather as changes of mind.

Could the film be brought off. The island. Movies never seem to have a separate existence. They are inexorably mixed up. With everything remembered. And what is forgotten may have been in fact filmed or not filmed. The remains are shown again and again, and always everyone misses something different every time. Alger Hiss is returned to the bar. Many do not recall even why he was deprived of this right. In the meantime he underwent analysis privately. After Arthur Penn's career had been thought collapsed, Night Moves occurred and he now works at The Missouri Breaks with Nicholson and Brando in Montana. He could not be reached. The Japanese refused unconditional surrender.

Many approved Eastcoast offshore drilling, with proper environmental considerations. Tax breaks applying. Steven Spielberg took off his vented coat and put on a wetsuit, then lay down on the beach and a picture was taken of him, that way. He was seen at rest at high tide. At sea the weather grew heavy, the camera barge filled and began to list and sink. It was towed and he was informed. Day for Night was used, as the sky was usefully grey. It would rain on the high-voltage cables. Feet and tripods in the rising tide.

I went to see the movie in one of the buildings that one of its scenes was filmed in. The preposition must be left dangling to point the direction of the thought with proper emphasis. The windows had to be left open at one side to allow the lights in, to point up the details of the selectman's chamber, a scene of argument central to the film's argument. The film was shown to the following summer's audience in a room directly above. The screen seemed to hover over the room now empty at night. Ghosts as matters of fictionalized memory. Rooms as a matter of boards nailed at particular angles. Image and sound are separate, in strictly two-dimensional terms. The mind is not a plane. Neither is it a room.

The moviemakers moved back and forth across land and water as if there were no change of state. Therefore the difficulty, and the money. And time and the weather. The artificial sharks waited. Their fixity must be held to. A preposition must have somewhere to go. A mind without memory could not make a movie. But it would be the greatest movie.

The alterations remain on film. The chemicals are all changed by particulars inexorably external to them which remain unaltered. The film is taken away, then brought back, almost exactly a year later it is shown in the very place of those particulars. One cannot say "its" particulars. They remain unaltered in the precise sequence of their own change. I have walked on them and among them, a year before and a year after, and I have seen that film in one of them. My thoughts have been removed. A Delay in Film.

People are starting to call sharks "jaws". They slip. One of the alteration products in language. The film has been brought to bear on. People have been changed their minds about the island, about swimming, and about ocean inhabitants. This is not thought. Films are not thinking. Neither is thinking about films. Films either abut or actually encroach upon language. Among other things language produces images. Films produce language. Language produces films and argument and certain fixities that sometimes fade sometimes change minds. The projectionists change reels in proper sequence. The narrative is maintained. Things go on remained.

I have no thoughts about this film. The writing is an alteration product. It goes on after and further and another language. The sequence goes: Yes, I saw the movie. What did you think of it. Another story. Without thinking my mind was changed.

The film was taken away and edited. Some scenes were cut. Some prepositions were remaindered back into interior phrases. Others were left hanging, pointing out. Some were faded on. A scene that gradually dims to darkness has a period at the end of it. We are intended to remain spinning there a moment, as in the interior of a pun or rhyme. Did you see that? Wonder about it. A certain word placed adjacent.

Actors live nowhere. In other words, some Hollywood. On the island they were housed. They sat at night and drank as particular configurations of nailed boards enclosed them. They may or may not have been recorded. We tend to think of them as living outside of such considerations. Books written from the outside. This is another one. Some books have made claims from the inside. We tend to disbelieve them, at least in part. No one was everywhere.

A way of seeing the film: you enter through a door and sit down in a seat provided for facing the screen. A way of seeing the film: you run off certain scenes on your mental equipment. A way of seeing the film: you walk through the locations and overlay certain scenes on your eyes. A way of seeing the film: talk over with someone who also has seen it. A way of seeing the film: reading language that interpenetrates with the film (shark texts, The Jaws Log, etc.). A way of seeing the film: something that suddenly reminds you that you have seen it, fragments. A way of seeing the film: sleep on it.

Let me get this straight. One shark could only be shot from the left side. One shark could only be shot from the right side. One shark could only be shot from above or in front. All of these finally worked in some way, that could be used, added to the language. A tracking shot could sometimes involve all three. That sentence is false, in strict movie terms. It would require editing. Tricks. Delays in film. Better: a continuous sequence of a few seconds duration could well involve all three. And often did. There will be many in any audience who will not see this, this way. They lack a language. They like stories. They see a movie as a story without language. Therefore they do not like language. They miss their own connections. They laugh and scream and are late.

Steven Spielberg sits in a small room with the door closed, one window giving on what he thinks of as nothing in particular. He hears vague typewriters and low voices from other rooms, and looks at a typed list of figures. In the back of his mind is something that will catch him later. At the moment his color range runs to black and white. His memory is set on low. A cup of coffee cools on a pile of books. The antique Edgartown fire horn goes off, a code, a language he lacks as a temporary inhabitant. This is a way of making movies. Of seeing movies before they are made, while they are being made. Someone puts out the fire. Or it is a false alarm.

The sharks live on a dock under heavy tarpaulin. Visitors are not supposed to see them. There is an armed guard, faulty. Instamatics are used one day and typical sights leak out. One of them is in fact published in a Boston newspaper. The movie businessmen were afraid untimely images would excite and throw off their interests. But no one is particularly interested. And most don't even hear of it. Publicity is an organ of timing. A matter of careful filtering. A fragment must sound interesting. Enough. It must be fitted, to abut or encroach on the language. The fragment is a filament of tiny content. Did you hear about Jaws? Not What did you hear. The businessmen do not even live here.

Films are best conceived in silence. But the moviemakers make a lot of noise. And it is finally at the height of the tourist season. Everyone pokes everyone and everything increases the din. The film is made in a context of shouting. Of high tide and uncertain seas and faulty machinery and labor problems and the polish of sea captains. Only the stars may use the waterclosets and mind the varnish. Beercans disappear for a time and wash back into view. Pleasureboats encroach on location and often enter the frames. Men must be employed to shoo them. As the cameras take their roll a single tiny cloud obscures the sun. Everyone waits till the wind whisks it away. A teenage girl from the summerstock has missed her mark (a clump of seaweed held down with a spike) and the scene must be reshot. Seagulls must be attracted to the beach with special food. Tables set up noons for extras. Dressingroom and cook and equipment vans appear in the background of a tense shot. but are finally left in the final print. Despair as an image of the final language.

It occurs to me that I could be sitting here gluing together a Japanese plastic Dimetrodon with wind-up motor (a present from the same island), abilities totally involved. The rain comes down, a jay is wet, and Jaws far from my mind.

A man named E. L. Doctorow has written a book titled Ragtime in which famous dead people are made to do things no one is any longer sure they might not have done. He becomes famous, and Houdini Ford Freud and Morgan again enter the language. A movie is shown. Many of the people in Jaws are still alive, perhaps all of them, and may be seen to do things they never thought of doing. I saw you in the movie. You looked good. You might have looked bad, looked better. I saw the boy who was eaten riding by in a car. I read about him in the local paper. He was said to be criticized by his friends.

We sat on the beach one afternoon and watched clouds move in over the sea. No one is shooting this summer. I thought of Charles Olson and the Grey Flannel Whale, and how Huston's mechanical also sank to the bottom of the tank. I ate biscuits titled Teekos, honey and sesame but they grew sodden. I imagined writing a novel that would be here today. My father read the New York Times. We had all seen the movie. We talked about everything else we could think of as if we had forgotten it.

AMERICAN ONES

III.

> "I am not a swan."
> —*Leon Bix Beiderbecke*

But why do I have to want to have more. Dichotomy, with com-
fort. The grist caught him looking. All the heads too close for a
mile, and repeat in their clogs. Why is the muscle raised in january,
a prune for discussion, and lasted for in laps. The buttes of Utah a
tin cup held up. Things only looked at first the first time well, then
named, slipped under the stack. The base of Pulpit Rock half quar-
ried away behind Silver Luck Lunch. The echo is seen in photo-
graphs, looking at what's still. Let's go only to movies on the moon.
A rental park with tobacco placements, aluminum bounds. A slight
lick of sun tween thin clanging intros, rust, bolt embers, knobs
with no returns. He turned on the radio to a sun patch. Caught his
own headache in slights of cliff, cured in the going bebop. What's
turning in the sand of pencil flashes. The detective knocking on
yet another door and somewhere what more can or will be said. All
the stories lost behind the story the phone was hung on. The sun
keeps him quiet, not even a desert, nor a tenement its walls. The
cats all have read the book of so what. The lines of sight on coffee
on the book of windows. Fleet, and worry down the valley brown
irons. This then the cost of potato carves, a milling tube. The
light's on the stick magnet. Obtain, and be round. Cirrus the auto
fits, a pack house, the pump fails to loom. A shack behind the pen
nib works, for to mull and stump on starlings. The flood shot the
tarmac down basalt to weld in municipal carparks. The mothers
all call for new crystals rather newsprint. And carbarns, all expose
to bright bugs make a fist. The mainline doppler has come a crop-
per, Fresno vernal outlook. We all live behind windows and shake

song from strain. Alluvial outwash to sink and grey matter glints. The lights of Albany, a hole in the thunder cover. Eggs over curbs under arc-vapor. I must turn this record to eyeless amalgamates. That this light has come on the zoo, the whistles there. Cauliflower ointments, the books on rodeo stand, and fall repeats. Go to the bark, mirror, and settle for Thoreau. The removes are in funny waves, like Creeley in Bolinas, missionary neons, cork as a saddle. The lines are drawn creaking, the muscling swans. The bellflower lands by its rope. We go off on Soda Surface Avenue, never to bend car eyes. Petaluma in light of allergy, railtrack, and sandwiches. Rimshot burns a warp and repeats, within a clever tacit. The postcards are arrayed, a Civil War mist of past hills. The detective files in his district, and amber compass of sockets are home. The light on the snow is a salt squeaking its flanges. If I could believe in Jackie & Roy I'd have less of a trip to Las Vegas. They hummed like bananas in the charred arms of the grotto portal. All that singing comes to, a pinch between the cheek and gum. And I'd rather a peak near to Boston basin for some tea. Uncrated, and signing the instructions. Typing some notes on a berry. A munch that caught in the shuttling radio. I would read a book, but the highway. The tomes elastic out a bolas all the way from school, an appletree. Scowled down below in the darkening Everest. Mounties crying alarming over the pears, their trug boots, the notches in Olympia beerwall. I have managed to start the car before Edgar Allan Poe. The country all a kicky sump of speech, slats before sundown, a tunic, a Mars Bar. Caver visits watercloset, totting in his membership pipes. One herringgull one roadrunner, all the parkingflats between. One sip of exploration, one of preparatory illusory parliamentary cooling sidewalk gumdrop. The tubes come on in Jack Benny. A hoopsnake rolls into an old wive. Beeves in pandemonium circuitry, a picture of your mother sitting on a whelk stammering. The laces come rooting out of the pigskin. On the attack, a band of mumps, smoke-hangers that Burlap Sam provides, Slim Pickens drying at sundown creekside. And back to the buttes, sans lights, lacking lunch, picking out a stack to end all durational chemistry. I have parked, and never found it straitening, pink down light on a birch side. Live in chickadee haunts and pick your words from snow snooze. Ketchup on the radio. If only voles, and then piano movers, and at last drawers to hide punk in. Signaled with honky marbles to the last man to pen marches in his teen streets. This the overture to Hula Bear, let's leave off all these roses. Keep boulders by your desk to whack when words trail off. Coming on, the night of the pumpkin pin. Take the dog waste from your shark skin and classify rootbeers. Pin up the cave link on your beaverboard wa-tertable. Tattoo your knuckles to hold fast without music. Shy at a cardinal and knock off bark dust. Say thimble rattle, say water ouzel, say pedestrian darkness laughless and past auto. Let's say Thelonious Monk.

IV.

"obtains from the creek"
—*Robert Grenier*

It goes on in tubes, away in globes, comes back in bulbs. Snow-storm, clearing and fair but seasonably cold. Thaw, moderate to heavy rain, center and south. Snow, north. Mild, rain center and south. Snow, north. Clearing and colder. It rain and snow. It snow mountains. Generally sunny and cold. Cold snap, mostly sunny and dry, some flurries mountains. Partly cloudy and seasonably cold, some snow flurries. Sunny, cold center and south. Some snow north and mountains. Light snow and very cold, north and mountains. Snow, north and mountains. A secret method for enduring mastery of life with pyramids. The top cake, the bottom chowder. How many things without witness, plain as noses, or crested away. The fire tower behind the candy bar. The bird strips to no applause. The century has handed the photos back, drypoint and rimless. Left stoking an orange and glaring. The pirate heads blinded for Hollywood, antique particulars (chairs for instance) with portfolio. Live as a Pontiac and just as sun-burnished purple. Now the parks have let out, where will all that stored math get one. The sign stated pickles, bricks to be examined. Novels full of pen points, slippery as a few hairs. And then the fluorites, with which such as Pound did not deal. Halogens coming public, issue of reservoirs. And yet, the word yet, pendulum of hope's reclasp. Black Holes in breakfast nooks. The state of the building starling requiring map-page. The high bush is sensible, such sense being verb, to inches to cut swinging, both to each. And the light goes out in the cab, under bolts. A city is vertical, list of itself. Spend some sun patching a darning needle and see. The bark canoe slides under the china turrets. The record spins the air of dust. The book once read, comes blank. As mesa river forks, can you hear them. If snow, can winter be far. Can plaster have. Just like the sting of a bee, turned the tables on me.

IX.

> "Names are the colored barrels
> we trip over inside."
> —*Charles Olson*

But it's apparent, that. Self night of the ticking idiot. True that Johnny Carson created carlots. Abbot & Costello launched first Liberty Ship. Charles Olson & Ben Johnson have the formula for toes. We have seen how Farley Granger ruled the ridge and brought it home. Joseph Cotten raised a stable for tanks. And the lights come on in Ray Milland. Floyd Collins invented disaster competition on the nightly news well before the stock crash and watered some Pulitzers too. Just so Lovecraft kept his hands from the horn button. Jackie McLean stacked apples all night long. And Peter Lorre came up with staples from the ebony panel piano. As Dalí iced his clams for to line a dome. Comes in Chuck Wayne combing his teeth with a match. And Errol Flynn as Captain Doodad. The light in the aviation bulbs of Eddie "Rochester" Anderson (put in a trailer is really Bobby Darin?). Louis Kahn sat in the salt and thinned his sheet lists. And David McCallum is from Glasgow Scotland. As Walter Gropius, he lit the wands but it wouldn't fly. Claire Chennault sat somberly before the box camera. And you saw the violet straws of Milt Buckner? Names only details of worlds in the world of detail. Michael Ansara, Bette Davis, and Jack Kerouac, all born in Lowell Massachusetts. This is information so so disembodied it doesn't admit of slowing down. Mickey Rooney's real name is Joe Yule. As an ice jam creaks outside of Albany, stays still, sit down. "Electricity, the high priest of false security," Basil Rathbone, an attribute of Sherlock Holmes. Refusing to be an attribute, so I am a departure (Cecil Taylor). No one is original and everyone differs. Scanning the table, picking a name from anything. The painter is drawing: still, there. Fish so small they don't. A whole snow in the dark. Chair of cadmium red, call it Muscovite. Rouben Mamoulian's first production was Beating on the Door (London). And Janet Leigh's real name is (was?) Jeanette Helen Morrison from Merced (clearest voice). And Peggy Lee was Norma Egstrom from North Dakota (muffled). And Pinky Lee (as a child forgot), Pincus Leff (passed on the tube). And Clint Walker went to Vegas to make contacts and landed a contract to star in Cheyenne (collects rocks)

TO THE CAPITAL

The certain old
pipe heaps and rust
buildings of America
Gravel car bustle
on the three-wide
Shirts
pants
aluminum mars
the overall
Frizzle girl under a
wading bull waits with
taped thighs to visit
Guernica (America)
but the day is large and
nobody prepared for cement
the load of buds and fender tassle
The Mystery of Trenton Station
and Hotel Petrol
Tunnels grow too close
and carbonaceous
Girders go up in a film
on blue
River wide
Trenton Makes
The World Takes
over local Huck in a
trout skiff
Scotch coats in here
contrail blades there
Do you believe bushes will hide
the shack of the thief

who left these woods '25
and rode a hurled ingot
to wagon-nod glory
missing the watered earth pits
and his girl's duck at the shout
of a pea, nights?
Too much smirch
in the panic wash
A whole cemetery plotted
to display his stones
Behind the tenements a
baseball wheat wreck
Roadbed ties my plants
to my autos
(maraudings of
the Highway Gar)
Glass box blasted out of the
back of the rust alley of
the barrel cue
and lapsed
as the prison stuns
your wrist
and a peculiar wall
chemical blue
resists the sky
Baseball is
played right out
at night
in front of your
bedrooms
Prestolite
McUgh

As old blue-wrap tin pop
sifts the brickside in stride
seedless
and I blacken above
racket-coated walls
R/R Sucks Dick
Amazing Constructions
of open sky girder
condenser boxes
"Watch your step
even if lame"
Flames behind green panes
at the baking soda halt ramps
Kilns
collapses
Eking scrap rust
through relic heaps
behind Intention Spur
and a high wide white
cannisters Waldman Fuels
Grey juice closets under
bunion stacks of North Philly
where bricks rose out
and the Alamos roam
and play-yard ball 'gainst
a vermiculite backboard
(shredded)
There is the bunting plant
of the inlay windows
where the ballpoints get washed
Train roll backwards at stops
the very essence of "seem"

Roaring station seats
peck at the flatiron background
and we bowl off, fleet
as a papal bull
and there's always some girl
in the aisle with
yard tits and a spare face
"Copper" on a white wall
below the green air burners
Fun with stoops
and black ledge crayon
lodgements
Wart on your
pin is brick
in trouble
and we pass the duck river
of glassed-in wind gardens
"Change for
Peyote Courtsville"
Copter plus derrick equals
domicile erased
You blank too much in
blot star switches
and braces
hefted marine or
ultramundane
the Roman arches and the
water-bearing train
and let me see you smoke
stop green stem signs
calcified to food
in the laughter yards

where evening is red pants
These guys shell here
underground in the
self-improvement bins
Would you rivet a leaf
of icecream on the sky?
(Breyers)
but uphill the trash rose
to the fort
and mica supply
and there are sleeps in the river
(filled-in cars topped-up)
Train passes you by
everyone's place in this
Tap me when we're out of
sand hills
But there's too much
sash, hem and bugle
we'll have to half-mast our
hemisphere and smart
over the ore barrel to the brim
(versatiles join
the tug-wash
in backyards)
Train is lowest plane
awash in backyards
and oil heat and Acme and
grimace bushes and well tongues
light standards and all
the garage that fits
The ad-boards are ripped
and the trailers sallow

there is a belch of dogs
over the Hazleton Systems
as coins jiggle in the
Astro Subway for a
"shipshape future anyone
can bolt"   tongs
meet electric buds at
the "Hut Hut"
but who shines the foliage
behind bricked-in grease jobs?
Who will roll the no
smoking cylinders?
Last year's corn row
sticks're angled okay
and we passed up a whole town
made of shiny beads
Those golf towers are
plumptions
Woods gain rust
before the greens burst
Water towers echo each other
over miles of swallow-miss
and here's a whole apparel pit
of conked maroon rims
and ankle pants of concrete tin
Why should
then not
connections be
me?
Chimneys loom up into
lamp air
In that boxhut

is the very large
dog
A man with the face of
an eagle raised by nuns
occupied the aisle a minute with
beers
In ceramic pot on pole
is not bees but hums
a canning jar of electrons
not loose above the yellow
reaches (forsythia)
Train stops and "it looks like
we're in a jellyroll" (Celia)
"Amtrak" sounds like
mongrel breeding of
subway and airplane
and turns out so
Stalled on a siding
of Mudwave Bay . . .
Here bodies
of truth are stored
in beached
refrigerator hulks
(entry up)
and over there they've
fenced alarming
dog hoards
'Least the trees
are still
allowed out
nights
(not neat

or in rows)
Bulk yards
in which
horses dive
The Popeye in which
for a second
we saw Olive's tits
as she's a riveter
Wartime conveyor
belt dangers and
"the feeling is mucilage"
Never thought I'd come to see
such piles of ties
cottage sinks and
well-thumbed waters
Every side of the
train wheels by
yellow center lines
of the very element
The sense there's
too much soap
in those homes
No tremendous eats but
tremendous lumps
of rose coal
cemetery to a fairway
But I don't believe in
the collapse of cement
furniture barns, flagwell
and the oil on the owl
Then a fear-red car
patches it all up

All calmed to a mint freeway
then the light came out
in back of the tidal train
and lured the housed-ones out
bannerly to moistness and
thong duty
When you join the government
you gain a glimpse of the
back of your own neat head
and the green signs all point
to ballyards sundays
"Magic Mushrooms"
on a B&O abutment
An egg-blue "New Motel"
(old)
next to "Tex's Welding Meats"
and a block of "Maryland
Chicken"
Here they rivet dark
in interior hoistments
and backs of tenement moil
like insides of wreckage icebox
Pebbles on corrugate
aluminum flats
and tarpaulin maps
at the mismatch battlery
(Baltimore)
"After every meal
Wrigley's
BETHONE"
As the interior shovelers
shoot dust from every

rose brick window black
block
and hands raising breads
above the rail and the pave
Abe has a headache
on this bogus bill
over red flags
and
Heinz
Realistic
Auto
Repairs
as Thelonious Monk strolls past
In pester of
the unknown smokes
In tunnel hell
washtub stopper dangles
next naked bulb
in alcove
and train begins to swim . . .
Mystery of bulbs and chains
deadens nerves along the train
Two bulbs and then tiny
bulbs of a luke wattage
keep the earth from tilt
LEAVE
AUTOMATIC
BLOCK
The cartons line up and
the avenue says goodbye
We
Wear

Orioles
The
Nationwide
Boxcar
Pool
Empty airbottles
lie around girders
and cemeteries
but steps still lead up
to the porched seat
and Read The Watchtower
Arbutus
Volunteer
Fire Department
(brick)
"I said I said
and the guy said
we made two trips"
The whole rail trip long
we dine on fender watches
and drain below the feathers
jet-in-the-pocket wide
I'm wise, said Tendril Snake,
I lynch copseable pennies
But a mercuric toot
above the metric noon
'll crest your rest
chamber to rust
and a ruby parry
and I like dot-holes
in an accordion pattern
adjacent to the glass

and its flatter outsides
What clues in these woods?
Maybe giant skinks
with auto-barrel toe-caps?
or the hatch to the
concertina mine
of the festever!
(and subsequent
feldspar palaver)
But why are we all sandy now
a swamp's nearing?
Sand roads, agh . . .
Nothing'll come of this
suet hook
outback ramp to the
semaphore banded
tossables
I want to live in a
mint woods and
fossil my bandages
No stacks to crimp me
or cleat horizon
When Sax rises from his
andiron shaft with a
glow-stint variant on There
Will Never Be Another You
Aisles of black doll
pennied with coppers
on CottonClub blue
reaches the silver chest
of the brittle bees
and Mainstem breaks out

all over Bowie
With hunk device
wrapped in oilcloths
these are Devil Backyards
Give it
a glance, give it
forty or fifty
lines with embellishments
till the very
couch breaks out in hives
clad as a swung bell
How to sketch red
slat sides that
don't look either real
wood or paint?
That backyard's caught up
with the neighbor's pool
That one with the snails
Beer
Drinkers
Hell
Raid
Steppenwolf
on Esther Williams' Pool
Bureau
There's Michael McClure
the Train Driver!
The thrill is gone . . .
The sky has grown . . .
etc.
and somebody lost his flam pants
down the back of the

brack ash post and
durable litmus mast
ClabberGirl flotsam adit
Let's so see
Dawn of the Staid
(Stayed)
(Said?)
Why that man's three-four
bars into the Bricabrac
Waltz!
and honors the close apes
of the brass pantaloon
Close the Book on Rail

from MELENCOLIA

A great block of wedge wood stint
stays at the star of its corner which.
A divider in pierces depends, wans.
For is what I have made be only salvage?
Sat in my robes, folds. Decomposed, fled.
The world a height now brine, estuaries drained to the very pole.
Geometrics, a lingual dent? Drainage, albany. Where at the last
stand all this sphere that herded me? My cell a corner on the
filtering world, all out there herein my belts. Things in trim they
belt me, beg me, array my coined veils. Brass, copse of my trends
to needles never suffered their pricks. The world in anger
is an angled hole? Drop my pliers, sit hemmed in, which have made
has clad me in. Meld thought as is droop. But the classed
claustrophobe as is mold of engines, their great cupboard strikes.
How many facets to the pear in mind? All uneaten what will rest?
Will it cog to the lagoon of black dust all clogs? My clothes
a bitumen in semblances, back of the sphere is a dome. Pends,
draping what thought to be, hung dwindles in apparence height storm
off sauce crystal in pickles. These ledges of the lids are calipers,
wrought off standard and coiling valise. I have brought down the
world in a cloistering pelt. It maketh wedge, to all the sameness
joints a bridge. What choice of thing for silence, sheer of
point and unencroached of plot. Onions are dim till the lights
in the ice surround are trimmed. A mind mine to bare but till dust
all is lodged. There are no lights in absolute thing? This room
the brain of beveled thinks. Rock spall till it gain meat heights?
A rim of stench, name of thing till it eat away in twining fade,
all go gold in the flats of drop. An andiron, a hand urging.
A monad, a pleistocene of gum. A crystal, third foot to each
standing man of quitest thought. A knuckle, brass and wheat wrap

of stillness. A quoit and no plating sky of semblance. Quick-freeze python, brim raider, elephant standard, notch of whelm quease, fronds of forks the coin of needles await and wearing brine moon to quietest frieze the disc. House not to live but collect the magnet fronds. My hands not to measure with they throw.
Do they see the amber will not allow but a scan to escape but alleys the arch of dusk a mat to play and in rubber prevent all musk and larded the stupors stand at. Musculant starers boil me ledge and encase the crisp but mum. The rose is a jape of stone. The animals follow to honor the sediments. I emboss when I pen but still they escape. I lie in my cell and draw all wheat from the marrows are a stone. The birds fly from ringing on their axes, a whole sphere from their tones. The crash as a whole, things in their rates mounting strains and piping extents of char and chased in tune. My wrist here stands for a brace of coffee, I lie it all out to be. For my lies of bronze will be stone. My laps stints of coldest collide the shards brim to in furthest flung design. My arm strands plumb to the deepest wells, for what are eyes. Eyes for which whelms bend what in reachest stare. Eyes are oakness, eyes are must, pierce in sleep, lag in ironing the pig iron pierced. The meteoric, the thrashed in fieries, the bleated rug, the mission pipe. Stubbed in matrix the we does not see but stuns itself coiled and revolving they make pole of solid dome. I will laugh at my polygonal shoes, but not now they are wastes. I will trim my dome from walls of gut iron. Little beveled cornice irons strapped in their tumbling ring so well I shout I might. Chair, be newel and anoint my back. Sled of butters, stack these hills. Polecat shunt. The lion will lie at the foot of my table I array my brains in a lie to draw. The fluids defeat and they ring. I arrange such measly to what mere foot of the slotting heights. And what stares back in the rings I may sound. All my things scattered in the rinse of a lamp they are hoarded feeble. I list and weak display my

seeming part strongs, iron lemons, painted burning skulls mathematic tip, a metal was a jelly to my thought raided past, ruler long stunned. Whose names throttle this cupboard but are mine? A stirring wends its apple way, its birdy throat, its muscles roar from wood stung strain and cellish hung. Arranged, stuck-hinged, the plutonists deny, the hailers of planet as a poorboy shrub. I have stopped them all a moment in my sad, my plaited noun a cramp so dense the climbing worms will not worry it. Seal my death here. Sky shrunk to a pin no rolling voids in a boil will scout. Light stay enough to dim my scowl, my things to congeal no collision no array but edge in grace.

ON INDUCTION OF THE HAND

Perhaps I've got to write better longer thinking of it as
grown up out of the same singular lost. The pattern is in, or is it
under, the hands? Better be in or it's gone from the brain
choking on airless. The outside leaves stain the sands of my
sleep even through glass and alerted in this very chair as I
thought I snoozed by the strings of this world. What world?,
evening of syntax brought full over the mounds of these what
lives but hopes. There is a wrench that a certain staring at
while balancing humours we call words in state pours wings
of edgy fondness bound useless in calm of lucidity down the
chute of the sentence. So-called duty roster activity when
typing at the seeming to be nodded at by trees. They yearn?
Saying that I am out there, with a loop I hope carries me
swaying back to here by means of them there. A tree could even
be a monad to this use, though never is it held in my heat to
be even. I let myself off myself never, no dope again trembling
my attic wires loose from their packets. Containments of such
that I never think them sendable. A poet used the word
"lozenge", he didn't write it. Some other and more careless
scribe wanted me to write one of those but the hell with what lies off
him. I remain stormy in paradise. I pull up my pants when
the itch takes me, drops hitting page. Writing *is* a prayer for
always it starts at the portal lockless to me at last leads
to the mystery of everything that has always been written.
The state of that, trembles and then fades back in leaving
the hole where it's gone. But I pout instead of kneel. I
would rather confess, but there's no mouth to pour toward at
the poem. Perhaps it's just that the words have all been said
but not by me, and the process *is* a trial. What those leaves
are awaiting, every day my burden's finality in hand. Beneath

it are the faces I've yet to replace in a rock as stern and fluid as Piero's Christless blue. But all the while I eye you, demon, your bird hoards are clustering here. Sent for calm and brought crazy still.

ONE OF ESSENCE'S ENTRANCES

The blame of the day comes knotted in the pad of night
Sieves of the blotters we obey are throttled in copy
Are they standards these holes of boast in slanted rhyme
Strident forth that lets the lips and frees the core from care

A lap I have seized on tongs arcaded acts in turn
Such gaff that the throat is bent and strings with harm
Drop over the decimal fence come felt to true
Make of chime in the chalked-up trailings avoided

A liver beats too in this brain rose
Thrown back in shivers on the launch of song
A twisted thus married burn that leaves that touch
Hauled off in brace of themes that break before

I head no solid avenue braves the flood
I sign no echo of conduits sieve my blood

HPL

Those streets were not his
so he kept them in the dark to himself
knowing age for a solid pent in mind
he turned out volumes of locked domed hills

Penciled purples in the daylit dreams
wore wool humid and apology bright
letters in the doorway, arabic at the edges
the colors of science turned jagged at his cease

He was not Poe, he lived on a hill
dreamed afternoons and woke to write
icecream from ivory, an undersea
crystallized Providence cats broke
out of the past and Fomalhaut speaking

DARKLING THRUMS

What so true as night come fused
So shown to glance the brain off plumb
It lights the well dull thought enthused
Envelops dim a light to sum

I hold it throttled to engage
The world in shadow state as bend
The threading things the sight enrage
The climbers inch in scorn to end

So this has passed, this shuttered heat
That cluttered nightscape at the heart
A shade mere memory of the start
The brain erases to complete
As shells then buckle in their rate
All night rings lurkful rage contort

BRASS LAND I LIVE IN

The avenue's too long for howsoever phased a song
rather a truncheon the thing that eats by itself is eaten
by the very one the gables are lit in a teething monsoon
sorted and vented in a happenstance cribbage
you take your time with, lose no matter

The water the rhythm, rooted in a kilter
an exit over which no red spot hangs
I'll steep you boys some tea, diluted far from harm
a dilemma of loading you'll label as language
and farm off all boats in one leakproof lot

Stark as mention, at all at trying-out wall
all that's either bricked or soapy dries
and neckties act in a pinch as throttles
will guard you off a sky too thin a ground too slow

I've come to the tiniest of conclusions: rice
and you keep putting your first foot forward
perhaps to cancel the phosphorous forest faster than a breeze
we'll coil all hell into a forcing hand and head

OUT TO BUSINESS

All winds up on Diamond precarious
we stubble among youth hulk heaps
a keen hoot at ledge top
   the blue spin cancels
     shrugged sample dome top
still spine of Rhode Island to me
though plaster face now and written on

To see from far away high up behind
   how the state locks its waters
     and otherwise flatten environs
another spill of kids with us now
   nosy and risky so openhand hilarious
     new to all that rose hard flight

for Celia & Kristina

WHAT SAW?

I saw Donald Mouse
move in an attic
together with a set of water exciters
tuned to the beams of his brash abode
shocking a bore, the whom
no one can slap me the blame

For whatever turns to a soldier of lead
whose skill on the sky saw threads in key of perfect
knows the trees lead to nothing plain in backing 'round
he'd give doubt the slip liquid afternoons correct
the moon down to a quill with a further quill

With a little luck train
with a little luck change with a little luck the name
                            with a little luck
he can shake this whole
a plenty the heavens withdraw from

Donald Mouse

FORTH POEM

I want to go climbing in an elephant house
   and what would stick to me there
I couldn't grow up to a washed down pace in my cube
   the one with the tangerine flashlights at its pig-iron angles
Stop slopping California into the backrooms of California
   all you ineligible planet shed malingerers!
My voice has grown green under the white wash of my hand
   the only blade I'll learn to strong
There are magnesiums to this page, line up at
   the bridges of the only pianist not a hermit
One long unlisted time now I'll have to see the world
   goodbye, salute it tight
As no one any longer runs brainstorms late
   you could set your sleep by till the exit colors
Did the elephant hone a battleship on his
   baggage of canvas maps?
Yes, as the world steeps away, derricks and all
   without saying
Send me a stiller postcard of the Island of
   Thrown Curtains

for Peter O's Collected

A WALK

The light wavers in the glass and the world turns over ends
as people talk they take our breath away, in firefly storms
"It's got to go down, do you want your tire to fall off?"
the avenue drains, the stars peel off, the coast down further
"am of opinion might get car," barber pole past the barley fields

Skull's steel trap a lace of epidotes
the bed held up on bandaids lumpy
my back disapproves its own lie
a mock-jerk sings Ab-sur dity in the street
following tape deck roars down the main drag
while backstreets are still a century ago
mind mist of parlor and cellar and back attic dusk stoop garage

Yard of vast trees that darken the lawns' surround
here such as Linda Ronstadt will not fit
the specific light of the domestic angles wrong for that
star pins must strand the music wend
trellis of roses bank the family's minds
the attendant cat larger than a statue

Lessons on Snow Beer, and here is the coronary ukulele
Winstone & Thorn, vintners of the rapelling magnet
a housing that snakes avoid, Tarbacco
Tin Cup Pentimento of Horace Silver in flames
on dog-painted shores of Cape Verdean New Bedford
when the beacons tune out and Moby Dick comes due

HOMAGE TO MELVILLE

Tiny rooms set in deceit such a way
that their very appearances were at fault
with all reality.

He arrived he knew not how, spending
his first hour on the new land
gazing over an ever-changing but
featureless sea for the craft he
felt less and less sure must have
delivered him.

The sea was all set as the sun had
spread it.

If a man must ride the wavering deep,
he should keep his hands away from
the buckles, axial pins, the angles of
the interior cabinets.

Setting out, putting forth, dawning down,
toppling measure, drawing on, escaping
the yard, unfurling the tooth,
having a go, leaving off, launching
sentence. The land sheers away
in piles, negative passages, inroads
and summits and parlays. Dipping
from the bows, he takes stock
of amidships, steeps himself in airs
of another stripe, descends below.
The horizon, the horizon even when
unseen.

Even the smallest things are visible
on the sea.

At sea, taking a sighting.
Every vessel should display a specimen
of rock, preferably attached to
mast amidships.

Trying out the oil, bringing in the light,
struggling in the black.

These were not easy things to learn, nor
could one every truly know them, for they
lay well outside the province of luck
and lucidity.

He averted his head, and gazed back
beyond all humanity.

NOON POINT

I think I wrote a poem today but I don't know well.
Though well do I seize the trees shake but am not given pause.
The lights are every one of them out, we see it all so well.
Nothing is taken care of, everything lies.
Everyone rise.

THE END

And that whole sun afternoon I drove through
vast rockpile room of Wyoming worrying
I'd never see another signboard nevermind
a single human again and just keep on steering
off the edge into further and more wild rooms of
same stone and sun. Everybody else slept
throughout, dreamlessly aback. It was a
stroke of The Fear come on me, all in
what I now know was normal bluesky
sunshine somehow making it all worse
and lone and racing loss of finitude until
the light lowered to sundown and with it
came a town. Sometimes you just sheer get lost
in bright time of day. But those rocks
on the floor of that sizeless room . . .

RADIATIONAL BOWLING

The statue of Wynonie Harris out of Bakelite
in the center of the passage, Gothic Avenue.
It glows like steel in salt.
Hums so far too much like a bee.

Wears and then smokes Chesterfield Parletons.
Lands his foot in a Berber. But the statue
is not, is a hydrant of lime, and stalls
all singing cast by lamplight.

There in the garbage passage standing by a towel
the whole next rest of the lot gets forgotten
and we're apparelled further in yellow fat snails.

Is there a bleeder valve? Is there a smile
as slick as this sand is damp? How could
you forget the news when it's radiated to
your steambath via quail?

A lump formed in the horizon. It was the sundown.
The strives of the pedaled brothers would shove back in.
The formation of Wynonie Harris is reported
every once in a shortage of the moon.

A DALLIANCE WITH SALT SIDES

Gents bounce thoroughly around in turn-of-the-century
costumes, and cartwheels of parasols, primrose proportions.
Hulot there tampering with lids. He thinks
all this dally is a matter of fact. Like the chair
slat of the ship shape *should*
collapse into flats at this same point of
beach each time. But no one matters
about him. A cast of grey face
in the morning day. The flue cats smile.
Everyone is composed with striped pens.
Chattering at the seal of the umbrella bones.
As if Trouville were slotted Malibu
and the grey ghosts of its there. Boudin
dolloping by, in a sealing wax raiment.
Pardon, mon Boulevardier. Na beef, sah?
Close that thatched door! And the collies
drop rolling out of the hunt huts. Slow
revolving propeller beach, with the porch
at its knees. Got trouble bends? Send 'em
up in a kite balloon. Knowledge of the
nodular sort brine in Hulot's mind.
As he folds the stubble into a semblance picnic.
He parades the patrol in prepeppered lozenges.
Silly but ordered munching in larval but
sophisticate cupolas. I'd have the nerve if
I'd learned that word." Kings of Castles
loose in the sand mine, lighting orange
baboons at the sun. Cement has expressly
yet to be invented, or still not so pressed
into use. Carnivals can still be of sand alone,

and out of fog. Hulot discusses anchors with
the Trellis King. He has memorized his
glasses and laces them on the dog. Then
it is told that chickens need his permit.
Somebody ups and pastes a celluloid of monkeys
on the central sphere salt seller. Now
a biplane or elevated candy sack. An
entrance to the Told Elves' Pickets lining
any calibration of brain at all. Huzzah!
Dog dug hole under Hulot! Much marching
grain fun. His magic dives laughing inward.
Whose thought suspends his throat? Throngs
shocked at what the Dago ate. As gingered
as if he had whipped the Pimpernel.
A cast of cobras coiling back the dunes.
Hulot serves.

SUN SHINE ON A FOG HORN

after Don Van Vliet

Then he puts the dust all back
whole in strains that stun in
Then he potters, then he buckles
he manacles all his shutters
and the smile is that redness at the end of the treadles

While in stairs the toys are short streets
barcly enabling glares, top too neat
he clocks on his stars the shoes that meet
he clocks on his stars the too meant sharp sneak

In the closet in the rhythm of a ribbon on the snare
on a rickety tie and the shapes were there
pell treat
and the snores all a lair for encoupled sea
we bear, we peer, we buckle what we wear
allowing for alarms

This is the hem on the wrist of the harking plaid beast
we see the pleatest these, he sees the seas meet there
and the hoistments are scaling Remley
and the ceiling is missing a leg of me
scarp mast of tongue-alp battle

sculp mass when you owly scuttle
and the hums run
and a gum's it
of a coast rung
snake
the clung ache

THE MAN IN THE LIGHT OF THE CON ED TOWER

1.

Brodey's got it, and trees are of beauty when stripped
Ornette's tucked into his motor launch, and the breeze
is only strong between your teeth
Not to talk about the lips of lame land
possibly orpiment thread or paris vortex green
Brodey's shot the thousanded as if
those locks are scald

2.

Brodey's thrown the word, who will watch it light?
Ornette's throat, a radiator, birdy-lined with simples
See vernier of corn oil velocipede
or Ornette's thought, a parade unknown to Central Avenue
Ecstasy impossible to be memorized

3.

Stop being friendly, the studio is cold
where thought's grown in the background stops
G.G. gave up audience, but J.B. knows the Road backwards
the mystery of each period the carburetor of his start
When I grown up I want to be Rayette Dipesto

PERU EYE, THE HEART OF THE LAMP

There is a stone in the air
calls on me to quiet
all that moves and is not light

I sit on the solar spine
a stone so carved connects
to nothing but still
all the distance lights

And do you wander in a blue stone town,
plain linking own self to mountains, or
with others? Train signal of an anciency,
Jupiter and Saturn rise together. Bare round
powers. How did they lock the stones?

And I still stand cleaved between Incan walls,
stones hold. The harpman blind sings in the sand
that held his hand alert as cut corners.
The sun is out of line in the Indian past, settlings
of Mestizo stark wine. He whims and blends,
almost Appalachian latch, and the sun renders
a dolly racket on the Fanta fenders. Juice
neon green washes ash, and browning awning benders.
Still am in Peru, I doubt my start.

It was silent in the world with the voices
like soapstones. And in the yard the grass
we talked on they had sat on. Sun and
moon and on. Hats were trivets.

Stones that fit a leather sort of granite.
Since that homing on a ridge spine time
the humans have progressively retired. We had
to go there. We couldn't stop speaking so
we did.

.

She cried with grief that the boy would
   take her clasp as the walls tolled
There in overage Peru, under the
   powdered scrape of the Fanta sign
But we left the train, in the cloak of the soft
   ore bars returning to their stone
It was night, a night like a day that had
   not always returned

Where the light water flowered in spar streams
   not Greece, Peru, but the light was.
And the Indian girl ran down from the hill
   a lamb on her arm to be pictured for coin
But this taker was a mirror
   her spirit refused

We walked in single file along the shorn stones
the mists to recede and the mountains bump us
We could only imagine on their compass intentions
the sun an only part of their year

          If you walk up this height
          you will score the sky.

We sat there carefully and listened. It was a
park. It was not. Sometimes you feel you
are clinging up here. They have placed the stones
as little apart as possible. Perhaps they had no
concept of "on"? They had wanted to become
part of the ground.

"All the separate stones hunger to be once again
part of the great universal rock that they
came from. We have been at some pains
to oblige them."

We did not know where the sun was.
Different portions of stone and plant lit up
in pattern according to a mystery.

"The world is here. You have not come.
You will not go."

Mystery is valuable and must be preserved
Heart of the lock the sky
Stones a bread of the woven time
And on trails the vines lock up into lamps
Mystery is valuable and must be preserved

And the soul so light a dense weight
And the soul so light a dense weight
The ticking of the trees, the box of stabs
Shaken
The critical is the penetrant, sidereal, the mystery
The mystery is valuable and must be preserved

Come back from love to crystal lace penetrable
The latches are a moss and arrangement of cliffs
Mystery is valuable and must be preserved
The man on the rock is not there, shock of hair
The combinant rhymes a struck match of lamps
The lamps are a tongue in the eye of the mass
And arrivals are mere, the mocks of a mist
The mystery is valuable and must be preserved

What does it mean to capture any thing in a picture?
The Incas worshipped the rainbow. It is said that
their priests threw kisses to the rising sun.
The reasons for things, for coming and leaving.
When I began walking in Machu Picchu I
felt the desire to climb higher in the
ruins. Each time I found myself in
a cul-de-sac from which I could exit only by
retracing my steps. It is said that when no
written language survives "nobody knows." The Incas
are gone but their stones. Sometimes
their sun and their stars.

In the stone still lives the Incan night.
You can see it in the line between the
ridge and light. More than lives, is
always nigh. The stir.

I have the feeling I'm only partly here
that I'm slipping down behind the images in my mind
and behind them the lamp
that projects what's left of me here.

The green snake on the blue rock
The blue snake on the black rock
There is no black snake

Bee Odor

      thrumming turns of the trail
      sun dropped gorge

There is water in the alley.
There is a tang to the tongue.
The rocks ripped from the leather
of an almost perfect forgettal.
Where voice has been there should be
stone.

    Who *are* you?

    (repeated blurred into pure vocal tones)

I saw a man's universe at Machu Picchu and it was
not me. Nor the black millipede cut in two
by the staircase Ginsberg also noticed — there
is no repetition. Now I sit cold in a room
half under the ground in western Massachusetts and
imagine the density of the night, streets of Lima.
The impermeable black eyes, the darkness exhaled
from their noses, a palpable dark that stills things.
To enter on the endless walk that nobody owns.

The Dark Lamp of Peru

Then the Lamp of All the Colors. The blue
walls that are shirts of turquoise. The ore brown
of armed earth. The peaks lit but not warmed by the
sun. The lozenges of stone fit round
by Inca lips. Can't I forget, I can't
be all here.

And on the Andean Plain a railway lamp
winking at the high ice. One lone Indian
trudging to the terraced time star.

Machu Picchu is already an excavation in my life.

and became image-haunted afterwards.

GAB SHIFT

1.

I get a slice in my pocket, I feel the building move over
begin to tumble to the idea I might swing a better deal
rising out of swamps decked up in a charcoal Buick
care of Property Commission, fabric of whole racket U.S.A.

Guys they want to tell you, they got something they got
   to do first
some kind of downtown hubris set-up matter of chains
dents in heads without they fall from the top of insurance
towers on the quiet, meet you later, legs got a starch problem

This whole world, antic meat loops through Attica attics
girl plays with a guy found smoked out of the worth house
turns up lengthened, a lot of the Sure Day Troop'd best forget
eyesight to the pockets backed up, the lamp a large tool

Float back in largely for a brine stinger, no hope or
   a wrist to risk
seen down by the carbarn, used to be, now a lot, the girl
turned up finishing for the school with a crack

2.

And then she put it to him, she says "It's lost.
You talk all around it and pretty soon it's the same thing you up
   and lose it."
"No dime thing, just like the center of the street, daylight.
And it all comes back to me now, better than never past
   and forget it."

"You never did know about it and then you're missing it."
"Didn't need her to tell me about it either, or did I?, just plain
walking out on a thing in your head, you know?
There are times, and there's the one thing
'll hold you up forever and then she comes in and
tells you something and you missed it
plainer than loosened sin."

3.

Talkin' to me, are you?, then stop it awhile and see.
Bartender talk and some milk in the back
free as you please, diamonds to plant
a car around the side and some poppyseed juice
a regular plan for the future certified upright and dismal.

The reach. Then the tones.
Barbecue invasion of hustling twenties
he says paint the phone, then durenamel lives
pester thin lines around the car watch or plant fob
slot incursion of the edible fendable, then pipe tree
he sees what to do, then straightens
lying on demand, a magnetic bender

Sayable thing, sayable later but to be told now
mention it to what, him to me, the auto raises
pure span, lapse and dream, spot pan show
termination state to it then, and said how
a brand new snow thought out on the cuff

4.

The gun right to the head
the center does not
cold, had, not have
in the circular lot
and I do not think it lies

I reach something and just when I
the floor drops as if it almost
the pendulum is something that you guys would
a that or a broad, as if that state of soap
a living you do not make

It's like that building where the elevator doesn't quite
carbon gauntlet under all that you say
I walked out and he walked out but first
nothing and then
nothing and it matches

The rules were paid out under then the about to be limits
nothing more hopeless placement than the cage you saw him in
and firming up she turns just as you
stars were said on the sky
the roof was moveable, all of us
a tradeable malarkey

The lights came back once the deed was done
once the plot was taut and the window made
my hand her hand and the beat the band botherers
flakes caught in our flasks in our masks out the entry
world had stood enough pipe and 'flated confab
the toast then used up to its raisins
and the head pitched over to his left

OF WHAT   THE MUSIC TO ME

How can I say about the music, how can I
deal with all the musics, after they've lasted?
The linch pin is on the snare. And is When
the point?

Sessions in rooms, cardboard jackets, the imprint
tell of the wordless beam. Music loses you aim,
or the target's becoming a surrounding charm. But I
come to my feet as a tenor's blowing at me.
Black discs breeze in my dreams . . .

How could I have come to the deck in my life
where the music goes on even especially when I'm not
listening to it? Listening's maybe only
a matter of the time you think you're listening?
Once, on a demerol pill, I couldn't stop
a Coltrane solo inside my brain. Hours
while I strained to talk. Others in the room,
sun slant from autumn roof, Little Old Lady
and only I could hear. That's when I lost my
grip? and music told me it would be going
on, board sides bent with fog, no matter
my lean and time.

Lee Konitz is unframed. As if he went on
stooping in a litter lot while the notches appeared
on everybody else's weapons. By the arm of his
turn the unconcerned rest is kept. Bottles
go by on bicycles. And the head of the snare
is gleaming. Violet bars rise in the club

to a slotted sign of next week. Sessions.
Plans for overcomings. Horns unpacked and launched
in straddle. Lester winds his head on the beam
of his horn. And later will the cutters sigh.
No more time for tenor, the shrill purses in.

Location of boxcars one foot from your coat.
You go out to Hudson cement in the Half Note rain.
The changes are locked and Lennie's parallel to
no one's glasses. Horns steam had ranged high,
impeccable, if that word hadn't clicks
in it like key-pad goofs impossible to erase
from close-mike disc. All of me is the
stored-up world, astrain askim. We'll shake after that.
Even the ashtrays are collected by migrant botherers
at the shutting of sets. Mirrors that tell you
nothing but the back of the head. A tune of
such device it could collect all the chords.
Variation of crown a ring of the ultimate changes.
Evolution's logical and that's a tune too.

Nobody thought of it done, always to think of as
just begun. Nothing torpid 'bout N'Orleans pepper
rhymes. Sour sunday Chicago in the sun. Even sessions
on bridges (dropped my keys into the drink).
Nobody bothered on the turnaround. To think in
keys, Ornette thinks in all the keys at his kneehigh
window. It's like writing on a shelf, the full time of bop.

Sorry, shrugging listener, did I leave you out?
You'll have your time, a guide to bins you'll
wake up and not find. Impossible dates

with Kneecap on piano, or featuring guys
who never met in life. Maybe Twardzik
won't skip the next time you put him on.

And elbowing-aside Russ Freemans, imperturbable
in outskirt casuals repleat with sharkskin mantles.
Chet and Jeru with venetian blind lines across
their shadows stoop in jam with the outside L.A. sun
lawns stuck with hoses. Their first album session,
or anybody still hip's first date with open machine,
cigarette burns Rudy Van Gelder's piano ledge as he shouts
to fire them. Wide as early cuffs, the man is tipping,
How Deep Is the Ocean when Max is Making Wax?
A mere glance at the bar lines to turn around and
swear by. He's off on his Cherokee, he's
observant and sheer. Short the plating off his
axe and one change too near.

Damn, what haven't they played?
Is he as positive as I never heard that.
The music all over the lands as it is in hand?
Pausing length of poem on a moment with
Bird, prayer and stroll. Not a
gesture too old.

Not admonish, but to rear back to whole time heights.
Is the snare then near enough to the tom?
Has that jerk on box sapped the time?
Who would know easier than a tent roller?
Or the Baron of Cigarette? Who would hold
a nod for thoughtfulness? Walk up then and
deal! Got to the channel and the apartment

was missing. Cherry slept on his collarbone on stand.
Monk broke through the hum-away standard frame.
And they timed him the blame. Still he'll
arch his back at the reverse of noodling.
Stocks my thrill. Moon over Arbogast.
Pass that salt till the chicken flies.

I made it all up again, let's scribe down
the ointment. Follicle as Bud's Bubble (hallucination
with tuba). The man had ready hands. His time
inertial. And they raided his table to wrest
the gum blot Bird blew at. Unconscionable cog,
the brain of Bud. Dark as piano in a closed
deck. Humans learn at, if you take the time of day,
hum on the pass. Burst by in kilter leaps, clot caught
at the ankle. Play the bead game, mother, and you'll
lean behind. (Bud's double hurried his brother
to rubble of the pike) But I feel the glare
in his notes and scuffle.

How you could go on for liquid pages!
Fruitcake as hiring yourself a blues. A set-up
range of sessions shearing off a cake (not George).
The last one I heard was a Japanese session,
the piano buried in the mix. New bassmen
wire too many solos. The drummers amused.
No longer monikered "Stix" or "Kid Shots."
They raise their rims and fire the whole team (rhymes
with tire). The room is empty and the kid pads home.

I have the imagination of a briar. Where is
Frank Isola? (Ron Crotty? ears askance)

My whole lounge is gathering sidemen. Clear them
a gig! Tear them up those bum checks, they
never got anyway, hear them tell. So long, Unfair List!
Drop that hook, George Wein!

Come back, Joe Dodge, from the use of your car lot,
and drop kick your bassdrum down everybody's new hall.
Yeah, leave the bandages on. A Train's lonesome for you.
Bru's astray. The melody cap's lost. And Desmond
passed praying for your time. Even I want to make
my own disasters. Could you even
my horizon?

Bop never fell out of anybody's mind.
Once they faced up and trod those unfastened banisters.
And "the rooftop of the beatup, tenement, on 3rd &

                                                    Harrison,
had Belfast painted." (a Kerouac that Williams couldn't
                                                    hear?)

But creak the hinge and pall of opinion time
foolish as understandings penciled in at the bottom.
No sink to wait. Fervency strolls. And
we quake in the light of Good Bait, stripe and
perfect gate for a tenor. He's mumbling, but
Bird's attire chevrons his lines (squeak reed).
He ribs Bud for foolscap and the crisis is on.
Time's brawn limb bends horn, if not acicular
coughings in the stub of club. Bird's arrayed for
us to pass this point (if not all fell points)
as Lady leans back, curls lip with her weed.
Till even rocks in the street whisper Lester.

I haven't got the time, what's your name (at the least)?
Time for stock shortnesses, if not orients of the
on-go. He hitched up threads, one wife short of
his life and blew. Brew.

Meanwhile I sat back in a canvasback chair
on a Malibu deck and contemplated a map of
Greater L.A. I was looking for aberrances.
The clubs didn't show up. But a few cues did.
Soon I entered a Long Beach hotel to watch
Manne and Hawes move through time.
(Manne looked smaller) They seemed far from
Pacific jazz (or contemporary or fantasy or anything
familiar). They looped toward New York,
sounded as if they were far as Winnemucca
(this was '58). Shelly's crewcut blurted
against the seawalls in the watchcap night.
Hawaiian scenes might have buzzed in his drums.
But fascination faltered not, I wanted to grab
his wrists. Nowadays his swing seems hitched
to a nob, as if he foresaw less space within his beats.
Maybe it's his horses (?)

Which brings me to a widening of the arteries
(the artifice strengthens).
Free particle jazz. Hazy mist mid lot, hang the bars.
And they twin themselves in reverse benefaction.
How to style the stop of hands. The moon moves
down from the trunk. Ornette muse over rivalrics
and railleries in sway. No kind of dollar beeps.
He keeps his young ones aBlakey. The old man
up there wide but pressed right. More cymbals,

more dangles, and a room man to set them up
before the stroll. Ornette the curiouser and
came around. But the scribes had cackled over
more rimless buddies. Ornette and Chet
in their clickless reach.

But in Ascension the bits come therming down.
Even Elvin's teeth can't smile. The laces
in the runners are outer. The throng tends to tend to
its time. Plus two takes came without say so
you never knew which you might attach. Was this
the great big stand up leavening with nothing?
How many pennies in the head? At the john door
of the Five Spot the skimmers throttled. In which
end out which lighting human? Cold blows
everybody's nose, even the sifter's. Trane came in
blocked up the door with curious points. Ornette fiddled,
seemed of glee, but wasn't. Night thrown
very large then.

But what is this becoming, an excuse for inroads?
(possible definition of the music) When the pen
runs dry you sing. Then comes the trance, the
other life, the remainder. Nobody's mind is reissued.
It stands then slides past the roadpost marked
Striver's Row. Passing strange this elimination
of known parts. Once the preliminaries to set key,
tempo, and order of entrance, then the red light
and the curving of surfaces. From the top where your name
grants purchase. Summit Ridge Drive.
Grandpa's Spells. Bird Food.

Radio taken up and out? Tell it to Donna Lee.
Tell it on piano as is never in the background.
Music, bending different. Abrasions of amazing
pockets. Time to sit out in the ceiling. Meaning,
a parcel left for Parker at the Icehouse. Marvels
of the thermous oak, and sendings of the told back sound.
He's up there, I heard it through the service door.
Last bars, frantic postcards. Linings of the road.

HOMAGE

Rode cars in the second seat
and tried his eyes as the land grew lame
talked between but leanly
listened
and coiled it all down

He minded it all
home and true to the slant
of shape the fall sun
up and boarded at

His books all
one voice remains
without sum

Thus
Jack

Still
tell me

from MINE: THE ONE THAT ENTERS THE STORIES

I

The world looks like it's upside down today. I mean, by that, there's nothing to repeat, at last. But that's no doubt, not entirely true. The trees are all still standing there, no wind, and they're not at all like people as I saw somewhere the other day. Lots of what you read seems to go to make up one big anonymous voice, it's not really that you just can't remember exactly who said anything. Something in writing makes me want to get up, avoid, and walk around to no purpose. Perhaps this will be a big book of very little definition.

Where was I? Standing here sitting. Betwixt and bewhile. Turning around to see sun or moon on a last point of land. And could one make a sonnet of nothing but trees. No doubt later there would at least be a window somewhere. Trees are like clothes, they . . . No. From the point of a pen things stand for a time. As long as one goes on with it, going on being eventually to forget what one started out to do. I think of soap, alone, no use, for no reason in the world I can tell. Secrets are locked up everywhere in procedure. Tell me the time and I'll tell you an unkempt joke. The hours are like clouds, their coming and going directions obvious. But, as far as I can tell, writing, like its poor cousin speech, has no beginning.

Knowledge is useless, unless it is aggressive, using its secrets like swords. I have often seen the hacking variety, unclean, unstable, useful only for starting backfires. My palms itch and my back has been strained and she asks me where is the saw and I tell her I put it on the red settee on the porch. An epithet is a denying use of somebody's name.

But didn't I start out here to tell a story? Perhaps, the central start of any tale, as Beckett says. Mine is a shadow of tar boiled in thought till it is a horse approaching to kill you. Don't call up what you can't put down, as the old darker magic had it. But often enough mind and world get together on the old walling-off-of-choice operation and whatever could you have been thinking of. The light of day, the trees in lines, the recurring of dark as a solving.

I hate glancing across spines of books in rows. What they are is not so easily contained. I should dig a sub-basement here and make them all live down there in the dark. Deep in the world is pitless pear, surrounded by cities of airless stone. How are the people there, and how do they view the pear. Do they ensure that any account of their life and bounds must rhyme? The steady congealing of losing one's way into frictionless art. Viewed by life on a float.

All books live in the dark anyway. Then they await the opening light of an eye, as in a child's garden movie? I can only take heart if pickled, of an artichoke that is. Is what true? The dreams in which I go about my same life as awake, the only thing different and of interest being the room it's all taking place in. Sometimes I suppose that my empathy is more with things than people anyway. Supposedly a terrible thing to say, think to admit. Perhaps of a day I'll take the right side. The night side in which all seems rightside up.

Chimneys seem more reputable in the mornings, therefore they are the property of dreams. You see birds come out of them sometimes. At nightfall they pour back in. Topless chimneys of my childhood, and vast vertical thundercloud masses turreted directly above my backyard. No sky has ever seemed so upwards since. Nor have I ever lain so planked down flat on my back in the grass of the absolute bottom floor of the world. Well, it's all too much, so much above me, as they said. And the world keeps consuming 'round, turning rind.

Bloody tigers and fang-high fences in my dreams. Horses with baggy pockets and rhymes for cast-away things. Iron laundry poles as the center of the earth. And when the mail got handed it would be warm in your hand. Nobody lived past their role in life. Movies so dark it seemed impossible you could see a thing. Or anywhere a place to think. I pretended I knew my name and they never forgot my seeming knowledge. The windows either blue, grey, or an absolute black.

To tell the tale, to wax unrepentant, to overlook the middle for all its ends, to form all cast out on the sea a lining, to wait until the glance all sufficiently watches. He lost the key with only the first name attached, all resultant pursuits for the nonce baseless. The agent assuming the guise leadless or is it pointless. How ever the threading I can well imagine. Battersea Bridge in the morning star.

Too often I worry about the world, I worry about a window. The world now as a blanket of thoughts blank. What do I think of what I do think blank. Or is it thought that strews the trees then returns to shake them. Not of persons. The liver and the gingerale and the poreless packages in passages awaiting trammel. the people that seem to walk in tune with lag notions, that cancel the brightness of the blue sky with blueness, that age things beyond their term with speech. Will I have to think about or further work my dreams if I turn to the next item of apparel. How did Henry James hold to all the crevices of his sentences, and how did he stand by what he thought to be his shortcomings. As Proust, to my mind, no need to, didn't.

The lights are on the fairway, the lines are teeming up to naught. The Labor Relation Squad grinds down the marble stairs of Fiddle-Gut Canal. The three cats pausing there, each by its hand-dipped candle. The iron claw in the bone-and-plaster mansionside. Perhaps the Sirens had no notion of Ulysses' passing. Only an error in repeating verse. The time it takes for things set together to adhere, said Joyce. But today the bones ring with air, only air.

Yesterday I painted the ceiling, today it's as bare as ever. When notion's focused close what's aligned and what gives. The rocks that were brought in the house proved short one. The shirt off my back made still. Turn on the radio, listen to the hours that hover in a caution of steel brads. The horse came over the bridge, why does that ring with a moon. And I take my hand off the switch and light the lamps. I'm not careful enough and I talk. That I bolt my food. I cough up what loosens. I learn spelling and I smell. I lap up the lightning by a water that's loosening. I call the wall Latin, a pinball that's flat.

Apple towers. That's firm enough for a possible daytime. Then I examine my shit in the rock bowl for reddish trails. Then I think of Allen Ginsberg, the constant millions of poems. But the longer the work grows nameless. An astronomic ukulele. Ah, the venerable poet laughing all over the leaning place of yellow objects. He doesn't want to throttle the basket weave, he wants to bare the glass, attend the boring plectrums, seat all the peering trains in lead-bottom world. The standpoint is ever the period, says Creeley. The coins in the cashbox appointing blurry world. Enough of the word world, enough of seem and as if phrases, enough of the sermon on the mount no one heard clearly in the yellow gum wind anyway. Enough of anyway. Stop poetry and stuff candlesticks. Green back dollar bill of croaking cerebral Ray Charles on a cocked electric joystick. Better Stevie Wonder on skyshard chainsaw? Poetry without music another court of bliss. Don't stitch the numbers on the wetted side of your choppy plans.

Chainsaw blatter clogs the gunked up anyway mind today, old folks rolling the mildew log. Would my thoughts would come to a pretty pass, exact cobalt breezeway image of tooth among mesas blaring crimson. If I coil such glassy data enough will it critical up to independent shock transform? I smoke too many transitions anyway, bubble on the burnside mind. Sounds turn flaps and the cigarette's active point is a hole. I think to myself all the things within reach on jammy typewriter fading tattoo. But there are things in this world undercooked beyond thought, the clearest view the underworld. but I don't link any thing enough to stop it. And I lie as I love it. I have thongs in my mouth stand in for teeth tie up the view for others. Noticing the flattened slug ring on Miles' horn hand. Inking into the blue sky of far away blade chains. There is no youth, only variously light-soaked ignorances. Next to the corn wall a thorium tube.

Fits of writing, but how will it all haul hollow out. The eastern sky aflame with pitch, the western at noon under knees. And the separate rocks are green from pressure of dreaming. Dreams they will spur their grains into wheels of a sibilance leaning. Core all lashed across the backforest lawn. The fire is in the spine. The door is open on blade of a tree take star ice. And all of my pages bead wooden. Then what be the story I was bound to tell?

When I started this and now, the morning is gone. There are ropes attached to the strained hips, haul on sonnets of Shakespeare. Must we heave our years along with our selves, Dalí's pianos? I bring to you understanding of the true cancellations long past forgetting. Everything not said here of everlasting import. Try yourself out in a blue pair of olden shoes. Sixties art the colors of product shelved, lips bruised at gearloose hands. But Billie Holiday caulks the window in blossoming eggplant. That I throat honks in the morning, but I place myself past too fast. Now I see roofs and have lost my youth aloft.

Now I'm going to once again drive past all the southern New England oat windows as in a spelling lesson. Where then those persons of arm loads will curve into snails and match. And underneath each television is a sample stone of this region. The poem that merely goes by is detectively simple. Three lines past one point and I lost my mind for a minute. Lost sight of birds, lost alphabet cards, lost subsidiary thing with the hole in the middle. The album car. A coining of wheat to spin in your ear. A factory lover, a lump to the giver. A whitewash down under the eerie loaves of the Rumpleskin Brewery. The walk back to the meal under the odd domed hill too late for weed.

Each time all the theories of poetry amount up to a lapse under the slick between every two words. More important the metallic ring at each tap says this typewriter may soon fall apart. And between those nothing but, as the piano player fingers, my heart. A lamp on the couch in the afternoon small. That poetry is a dwindle. But I do want to say something as a speaker, an alarming of masses, a cough in the corridor between cases. But these people are cramps, even to the heels of their volumes. As I march past across collided New England to gain smile at a winter-heated hay. The girlfriends' sizes have come in the post today, literal bumps. Each side of toast the beginning of a story. Story of scarcity bristlings.

Meanwhile I sat here coded. Stared off in the light a stranded apparition. And the guy says to me, he says, if you look down into this shaftway here you'll see the steely beckon of an orange coming. But I don't believe in the chance tattle, only in stationary dreams where the borders keep you edgy for news. As for instance, the salamander should report in the poem on fire. Would you see him sneer at any worry on housing? Your name is the precise settle of lights on anything spinning.

Today the sun is as wide as a blue car register, but the cat tray in the basement still smells of a recent movement. No matter the writing erratic long as it stays down. Made an error right in my face. Later the long cards were brought in ready for my filching, I mean my signature. They wanted the strokes rhymed to the timing of those violent tube lights. I couldn't though ended up I stubbed. The cat over again. The miles to go in one furl steering motion. Then I put on my clocks and went instairs.

In a word, the mercenary tweeds. That I possess the manifold poems of everybody sun-hot in the bright volumes of the weeds. It's true, but who wants to hum my stories to a pipefitter's tune? The poems have exploded from some subsoil growth on the rise there. And I end up with a handful of light-popped crayons. Why does this always short out in cupboarded poems, when all I wanted to do was orate in long strands my gemmy philosophy feelings? How did Shakespeare look when he wrote, let me see his hand positions. Or did he waste motions. And was there a cat in the room to go quiet with him, barely apparent scratchings. More apt a dog? Did he keep stopping, and then did he pace? Or did he run it all off quick spontaneous as Kerouac says in a sluice. The muffin jars . . . I have to remember to listen slowly to my lines or pay the price of thinking them wrong.

The light's avenue must be meltless, or risk rouge damage definition in the bargain. Subheading: Spalls. Between the gates of writing it grows hard to see. That's when we start the jokes of the two-handed pens. And crane to see the brains begin. And loft the yellow anklet over the tarn, lots past to see. The imagination is brought, now I view. Enough tattered and I won't swoon, over anything pictured cabbages huge on officialdom tar fire walls of recence in persiflage. The guy has got his door open and now he whistles rarely. Radio thoughtless provide backup of bebop harmonica. But why not then the clarinet? The meat marvels are cloistering buckle by vernal buckle.

It was as if a mystery tale in which the detective finally arrives back knocking at the same door as on the first page with the whole story to solve all over again. Art, Every Day, The Enigma of Bildungsroman Wick. I think it all back to when in the middle I didn't know a novel could be done. I thought it lasted and I was right, but in patches. The top of the mountain mirrored in the snow of its neighbor. And everything comes pilfering, allaying, exacerbating down. On the floor of this morning is the world thorn again. And I could bring another light or I could think, which?

Still the world moves on Beethoven. But the moil reverberates in its lighted car. There is a conflux reflex, you have to make sanity about if not out of. Whereoff the time of this window missing? The optics of data are arrows are thieves! And the music listens, as the painting pictures. But the glances cancel in too much move. I awake believing I know the exact fiberboard location in the basement of racks wherein the impossible to classify jam-date LP may be located. Those guys never even met in life. Which is why dual piano sessions never work out. It's a battle on the bridge for the cleft of the ship rocking out by all tissue spindle threat-lights encase you to harbor leaving thought. In as much as the paratroopers fall they mow the lawn. Then many tiny hats have fallen out the back of the radio residue of youth chorals. Belief though all an adolescence of fading lessons.

I live in Idaho. No, I live in Saint Paul. No, DerryWheat. No, a Placer Del Sol. Perhaps CleatRanch Western? Or a Marrywell, Delaware. Eventually the rosters fine down to Rhode Island, palace of brad arts and the costume brine resorts. Here I carefully casually placed each rock in its separation paperbox, thinking them all eggs. What did I know in peacefully grounded window with the sun going off the dog. Illimitable breakfastfood message packs. Whines behind the radiator. Lump seeded yard flats with vanilla. The car again had gone away on my poem. Once again wholly I was handed back, bright sun on nothing to do starring. Worry not, whatever of the past you've forgotten you have made up. Never go back to highschool, never recapped on fool stool. Evidently enough tests gone past. Lincoln Logs to Gabby Hayes. My trains went down the garbage, the cellar which is desire.

I have no reason having enough room today. It rhymed all small, versus the strain world. The pincers emerging from gelatin thingy horizons of a pall studied. Added to the end of my line am I scribbling dutifully. Kerouac thought he was the end of his, a river delta depositionally subsiding. I ring his name for all crawl time. Singer creams to the bandstand and lifts one lip to gramercy. Above you see the flute towers and the acicular budgings of an early Stan Kenton. He was thought to be as gaunt as he thought himself greeted, nodding through threatens of corrode-dome arrangements. No more of him but in the settling atomics of ode riffs. I focused one ring on one finger that night, flew the girl and avoided a fight. FlickCheck Towers, Forty-Nine.

Not only do the big bands not come back but do they even stack up? Resounding crannies of smack took the toll. Now take Kafka, he arose in the morning no matter the shape he was in. As long as his and my and everybody else's brain lives in darkness, you have trouble with the moment, call it flute or oboe. I sense an orange in the hands of a stranger to your life. Brief glimpse of cracking darkness in the dayfire. Andirons cored with onions. Litmus sheets in a tight glass vial robbed from lab hookies. A grail robber who only could come up with bread in nitred boxy loaves. This emerges near the beginning of the delve story.

I walked into the room, why won't that lay flat? I started my mouth to talking. See, that's the problem, interstitial ramifications within the outset. Each two words throats too deep. Forgettal is becoming a premium. We became desperate to find a place to make love in. And everyone heated us further by avoiding the issue. A snare is a delusion, said the fiend. We finally woke up to the hopefully temporary impossibility. There we were in bed with heads. There the thoughts deformed in the ease of anything coming up possible. Dalí put down his pistol and walked to the screen, pointing, "Theese is the Black Christ! And THEEEEESE is NAWTHEENK!!"

Or models of deuterium a heated delirium. The nacelle on a French aeroplane, bumping down the triste companionway. What did Franz Kline hold by all those char-broad hackings? Whatever it was, you lose it in color. The women each a veteran of the silver screen but in a pointed script they couldn't blend, each to her own angle of blouse over breast. The wing strut was iron. The paint stroke lost weight at the end and slumped to the floor. The words were not sufficiently wedded in time. The compartment was dry.

The unloading of the cars proceeded in a shipshape fashion. The men on the surface of the moon could find nothing, even lost purchase on their own names finally. Their faces became disturbing and they took to hiding from one another. At last the radio rested in static. Nothing seemingly had gone wrong. But you must expect a story to turn. They are still there and probably still alive, they brought along so much oxygen and food. One might hope that they have taken to writing poems.

The term "epic length" is a formation of noncommunicating closets. Reverberations change the scale. Proportions are storeable. And the mind go on to the ends of the world? Reading is a drag because you want to have finished it yourself. I once said I wanted to write a novel that would be here today. Amend that to read, written already three thousand years. No, I'd rather write it than read it. Or at least get to the point of not knowing whether I was writing or reading. Silliness in folderol? apparel? What was that Godard word? Dreadful? Betrayal? Forgetful? Tigress in Jeans, Redcap in Steam, SkiTrails on a Mountainside. This writing has succumbed to massed flinch.

I couldn't sleep, so I wrote . . . Someday You'll Be Sorry, said Louis Armstrong. And that's it, no big deal! Applause. Musicians. Scars on the belly of the Flying Boxcar. What I want now is smoke from my mouth to lie on the air like hair. See what happens? I do tell a story and right away I lose my grasp on the functions. The peak was heated on either side by a sun.

A sentence producing pronounced uneasiness. Smithson's compact mass in a dim passageway. Set loss of vagaries. Carbonate integers beneath the barks of oaks. Supersaturate sentences. All My Tomorrows. Punctuation seed. Superheroes versus fading laggards. The scent in the snout of the shoe. And the reason I could never find a decent insect book turns out to be that there are always too many species to ever reach classification. The novel has arrived, please send the key.

VI

The mice leave the box, continuing in a straight line. For sure they don't love the world. Pencil in answers at the bottom of each step, fade into again flat clay. We don't ask of the world anything left. Stung brains worshipping straightness practice. The musician lives for his shot at impassioned linear continuance. The sense of Every Day meaning not a passing second without the fire of it. The verse of everyday meeting, the log of a dance. But does the jerky bump cakes. The lights open on the water, valves of the harbor. Animate strains of night flat. The days slow in the palm of the mind. The hair itches the day long. I saw the mice remove a watch from the drawer, a concerted fact. Bow to the furling world.

> "to make gestures and long harangues"
> to divest oneself of strong meringues
> to lay the cliff on which it hangs
> and bind the ghosts dilemmas lift

The mice are insects and walk that way, strict legged. They answer the call of the flashlight, line up along its beam. But I keep on shifting its direction, switching on and off, laying my own pattern. Safe, it will not bother them to stand for a chaos. Chaos Narrows, Chaos Jumbles . . . What was the name of that vista spot? The slags of all time can be bounded by a map, the beings then tread oblivious. Let them wander in scarifying bands, fitting tin hats for danger. In time enough they will approach the pole. As I will never approach that window again. A kind of off-black ink at the lip of the page. Then the horror lurks at any opening? Perish the crossings.

I don't want to leave the mind's desk, but must escape the rule of mind's thumb. The supersonic plane reached its apex at such a height a whole range of distant clustered galaxies formerly unknown became visible. The pilot had not even pushed the special button, in fact, he had not even known which button to push. The one with the cap of blue felt. But the earth moves closer to other more impossible objects in our sleep. Bottles of crabbed sauce glued to the inside. The cat leaving tongue furrows in the butter left out on the counter. That huffy roaring of the air blower through the heat ducts, I'd rather were the sound of the clouds braising the sky. Or, the days when the clouds are the sky, was it O'Hara who said, Sometimes the sun doesn't set sometimes it just disappears. At the bottom of the year, right, the ills lurk, though they should be isolated in the cold? There should be and are alternates for every increment of speech, what a mad foul that would make up of the social. Would it were that I had gone out, if only I could have made up my mind to. The ossified conditional of relations. Wills that line up over the days only to just stand there resistant. The sandstone arch stood at the edge like a lock bolt, one foot forward to air the day out in the sun. That I shot it for its evident possession there, I now own. Ragged line of blue at the top will do for sky. But what made up the weight of it I left and left. The fortune of the other read: You will tread the soil of different countries.

But the man who wanted every thing in his home always in its place. The fly locked to the page, the cat to the table, etc. He considered buying actual tiny locks for the smallest things: brads or even motes of dust. Or Celia's thought of a beach where every grain of sand would come in its very own can, each to be opened before you even could lie there. Just another world heavy with intention. Hello to the man in the frictionfree suit. Alright, I do want to hear about it. Was or was not the beachhead achieved, and if not why not and if so how? At any rate, what became of the peculiar greenish bottle?

I am distracted by the neatness of the scatter. It really was the glacier, and not the "mountain-high tide," that produced the boulder train. Cataclysms are enclosed, sometimes to the point of invisibility, by the general all-over slowness of thing. If I can keep it continually wound the ticking of the clock will jar it over seventy-eight weeks to a position blocking my view of the Giotto. Then will I rage at the boundless ponderousness. The whole division seemed to come into view all at once, each member tugging his boots through the knee-high ocean. Any motion once started will come to be battered against.

Melville's Arrowhead, the second story so divided by a broad stairwell at the front, a narrow windowless corridor behind: his side, her side. That he sat writing at his table facing away from her, facing north, facing that window frame of Greylock, the double humped mountain white all winter lit with the sun behind him. That sun evidently hers and, as he said in a late poem, certainly Spring. The Winter of the Great Beast. The winter of my self come to get me. The putting of the head beneath the edge of the boulder and willing it to smash me, the balance being temporary anyway. Then the lights come on in the roof of the world and the writing continues under the whiteness of fingers. A willness of wonders. A shadeless contribution to the blurt of the art. The gallery an alleyway all crumpled in laughter.

Foghorn wants in here, and in addition wants the word versimilitude attached. But something scratches me, same root as verse?, so I check in the dictionary. Turns out it's verisimilitude, very. At home with the wrong root, all these years. Or one of those words that hang around, you even use without knowing the meaning of, having always been meaning to look up, and when you do. Wonderful when they turn out the opposite of all thought. As if love shared its birth with loaf.

The trees have been added to in sleep. Curious regional inches. Curts of bark. Escarpment swells. I didn't notice, I was being watched. Seems when I'm most myself I can't see. Bee seen to see, each at its time. Beyond the place of all seeing, a dream. Or the brass band I live in. The literature is tenacious but dull. You wander off among the stands in docile tremens. It is a Fourth of July with fireworks but by mistake at noon washing out the effects. You eat a rootbeer stick and tamp the ground of the former sparrows. A man is approaching with a hoop of a gelatin green. Turns out everyone is carrying objects they know not what to do with. Put them down or having done that with a fear of encroachment sit on them. The day whirls around in its picnic oranges and plastered ribbons as I find myself back on the lip of the orchestral parapet filled with a sudden inexplicable desire to orate. I fill my lungs and divest my brains of so many saved-up crossed-up messages, postage to the winds. But my band carries on and no one hears. The day goes down to silence finally, bland winds through soft leaves tucked in tiny lights. Graduation day of Charles Ives.

It's punk, that's all. Just punk, I think. The bald darts of occasions missed. A dreary world without coincidence. The whole of it stings without points of landing. Avoiding the dentist you'll be hurt anyway, conjuring fully the room and the pain. The lights occult in a two-minute egg, and the close enough movers of world push lame smiles. I could be wearing a pinstripe suit of gauze for all that attaches. The street is late today, and the ones who were to see to it far away. A giant billboard of barbell bicycle invention has replaced the natural store. Proximity machinery standing to repeat itself. The fade sun is an onion on a bridge. I confront myself and command.

He had no thought of what would come up, only the snow was falling. It was his own fault that he had left himself to live in a house whose only doors would open. There was a large grape on the plain or wall burning with a barium glare. Beyond was all women in coldcream raincoats milling in a skating fashion. Try to get a lock on this. All the windows in the city simultaneous, timed to the breathing of the light. The sun should be so lucky. Sheet glass on noiseless tracks. Pedestrians on shuttling rubber bands. Scoring by Harry "The Clasper" Barrage.

VIII

The blearier the men the more they stalked the black locomotive in the twilight. A parallel adventuring along backdrops of dull violet weed. They came to nothing, found out nothing, in the touchings of the outermost nerves of the brain to the dark shapes of the outside, shapes so dim they were filing themselves away. And the birds go up to the tops of the trees where no one will see them. As when sleep comes then the cat goes up and down. The links of all the branches threaten cracks to glow through from the other side of the fabric. And the men persist in their seek of the smudge locomotive. I have no further vision here except of men stumbling around a dim engine cellar in dirt pile dullness. All further endeavour strikes me plod. Tobacco light. He who is patient obtains . . . what? In certain cavern chambers I felt I was crawling inside a mind.

Under my life are the galleries of the circuit delves. And there is much there remains unraveled, if that word could come to mean unremembered. I walk forth on a thin shell surface I fear will increasingly crack through. My voice turns thin in the brevity of substance. I even fear to call. But so far I can still call it. And the smoke gains smile in its shelvings at the window sun. In all thus tensioned such murmurs are marbles, and the merest notion a rattle. Iced candle flamelets on the vanilla throttle. And there grows another mouth further down on the neck, through to the throat. It must become possible to speak with the lower animals through that one. Out in the slow light of the glacial top the day all the platinum stakes disappeared. With the sense that they had gone inward, behind the surface of all solidity. As in the silent dream I climbed down the abyss behind the radio in trying to fix it.

I come not to bad but to sorry. Nevertheless this all has a kind of linchpin severity. Swedenborg spoke of "correspondences," but perhaps this could be taken further and in another direction that that of the stratum of mystical glues. You write to friends and receive certain objects in return. These are then placed under glass in the collection hut or cabin high on the Schneealp. Returning to view and handle them again each summer the composer of bare intervals unburdened himself of the central coiled whisps of provocativity and at last arrived on the shoulder of lyric heat land. Here one summer I myself noticed a small ice cube that seemed to have fallen a long distance through a darkening shaft into the light of benchmark buds and drift wheat. Below planed the snow glacier, the one that had inspired Baudelaire to a coronal of IOUs. At the precise rate of thought these are the ordinary events. I picked up a pin in the sun, it couldn't wait.

I tried to watch that on a tube in the room. The thing? Oh, I saw that on the lathe of heaven. Did you . . . Did you mind? The circuit clicks off leaving the only motion to a pair of squirrels picking at the pie-plate covers over old pipe holes. The resultant heatlessness will not necessarily depress one. For the sun is out and the wind on things, the hairs on a bowler's head. Makes me speculate on the fur growing in the moist dark at the backs of paintings or even sculptures pushed back against walls. When I walk in the streets I see meters everywhere. I have not the change I fear. I hold not the risk of knocking here or there. I hear a ticking, always of other objects besides clocks. Must be their molecules are disarrayed at certain angles of the sun. Where is the man who will clasp to himself an icicle at the bottom of the year? I have often thought to take the time to watch things growing solid.

Grows itchy, grows straight away. Behind the barn lay an algaed green sump, whence rose the polished toads with veering eyes, thus the reference to "powdered frogs' legs" on the radio the following morning. But by that time no one alive within hearing, the end to another briefly far fetched story. The seeds developed unto death even before anyone could ascertain their existence. Thus does science develop ingrown hitches. The glass of water is always taken away before anyone is finished drinking from it. The album played through with a lead rod. The green flash beyond belief or exposure. The pin at the bottom of the pot. I have told you and told you.

Then the lights came on again, shortly but briefly, and the groaning hefters groped for their clothing and an equally ill-fitting consciousness. The barracks room was painted in a vegetable but nonetheless blinding Tahquitz orange. Perhaps the intention had been thereby to burst the men awake, however cratelike that notion. At any rate a line formed leading creakily from washroom to entryway to a dimlit outside standing around. They await. They attempt to read the type on their shoes. They watch the sunball rise behind a clanging rustiness. They see the treed squirrels eyeing them from variously acrobatic angles. They wonder just what is the work for them this day. Will it be more wheat to be aligned or a whelming despair at the ledge-sized fragments of iron to be whipped from the dells into place at the perimeter of the campgrounds so new to them. They had arrived over a numberless succession of nights entirely spent hurtling through tunnels, a veritable decalibration of the compass. Work was after all everywhere to be done and on time. Teeth had each to be tuned by a fork proper only to it, and cabinets of a greenish porcelain installed on every pole by the way. Gallons of wire had arrived at the camp, a sort of violet liquid that achieves tensile lengths when exposed to the least puff of air. There were these tasks and always more to be done, none of whose eventual functioning they would ever witness, for by the time the final adjustments, always made by others in their wake, had been made, they were always already on the move elsewhere. They were commonly known only as The Spiders.

And in the restaurant, a noise. The glass top of a medicine bottle, salt, had fallen against the chromium molding at the base of the counter. A slightest pause, following which the patrons ate on. The radio had been removed, since the uninterrupted talking thereon had been felt to constitute a confusion of the conversations amongst the eaters themselves. Thus the unfolding of the species proceeds further into self-containment. We will no longer admit to the possession of outsides. What's to fear? There is nothing out there. Meanwhile the diner, cradled in cables, was being lowered gently to a spot on the tundra by helicopter. Standing room only, for further thoughts on this matter. Emblems of personality will not be returned. The cruciform piece from the base of the stem continues to be kicked from foot to foot at random.

Then came again the animals. The aloof snort snail, strumming his glass ear rods to good effect as tweezers. Through the agency of this one, odors could be perceived purely visually. he disappears down the carbon lane, as if a gruff rug were tucked at the edge of town. Next comes a lion whose torso is composed of a trembling peach bag, from which bellows a report like audible parsnips. He is erased at the edge of a weed space by a passing glazier hefting his sign. On the three hinged panels are shown: an oval pile, seen as from above, of assorted dark greenish substances thought to represent a theory of magnetism; a bald man in shiny black uniform with a sawblade, toothed on each edge, in the form of the Xtian symbol for fish depending from his horizontal left arm; and furthest to the right, in fact pushed right up against the border as if by a great but invisible force, the pink palm of a human hand on which has been scattered an arrangement of thistle seeds, to all appearances the metallic punctuations for sentences of words which have vanished. Now comes a flight of pinpoint-sized beings able to raise and lower the surrounding temperature by varying the frequency of their buzzing. These seem drawn to the point of a distant peak whence they are heard to disappear with the sound of a large angel cake dropped to the pavement. Then the lime worms, borrowed from the neighboring town, short themselves into the ground at any point, eking out a labyrinth of passageways of complex extent but such narrowness as to prevent human investigation. Knowing these worms to be tireless in their excavations, and so fearing the collapse of the very earth beneath their feet, the remaining animals hiding in the wings, and there are some fascinating examples such as the Zeppelin Spaniel or the Cleat Hog, have announced their unconditional refusal to appear here on this day. Thus comes to its end yet another world.

from RESEARCH

The snow is falling on the vines, the barbs, the aerials
The snow is falls
The air be
The light snap
The vowels are independent
Consonants cross
The lowness of divulge is opening as a shore
The room is cress
The provoke are tines
There is too much space and there is no time
Handwriting a fault, a wave of faults
The hour is a clock
Streets are witness
The mind contains a bulb
Sky of waters
Numbness of crossed hands, the skin an itch
Research, research and drone
Water turns differently in hemispheres
Your thoughts are your worry
You live in a house of the thoughts of the ghosts of the deeds of hands
Fire hides
The road is longer than a treatise on the thistle
The road is not linger
A handgun, a sunflower and a pound
You set the reef on automatic and you stay
There are thumbs
Rests and rhymes and throttles
The airplane is a container
The life a bare
The role of things is raveling

The department of defense, the stump
The march will lead the president to drill
But one of the snows is a seed
I peed by the red bra
I went to bed accidentally
Who is "Remley"?
Whose tongue is blond?
The shots of the ghost
In the glass
In the glass a parable, a plumb, a problem and a paramecium
The trails of living beings strike the town
It was fair, the edging fringed with hair
The pause in the hammer, it was a witness
The water above a whiteness
The car turned arrow
And in striking the frown the trees whined
They were a marble, an agate, a barrel
In an album, the strain
In the town, the doubles
The permission without pass

How do you open your mouth?
There is nothing in poetry that will remind me about the world
There is a constant retrogression, and this is not memory
The hand writing is the feeling of the skin
In my skull is an avenue that I stroke with the anthems of my sex
Coming to the end of a word at a period, a brightness
A whistling of silence over the board of storms
In the words of which there is no eye
A patter of small edgy matters drawing up the map
The cancellations are the poetry
The nothing to be seen in an undertongue declare

They could not hear Whitman in the hall of the century
The engines were too pat
Doing what we do best
For a joke someone brought a bare finger to the bottom of the steps
There was a quarry opening there of pure cement
The poet did not take on the job

from THE CRYSTAL TEXT

The crystal is always showing a world
that does not exist except in remission.
It does not contain but transposes.

The whole point of this
house is to change the light.
No one is to live there in fact
its precise location is not known.
Everything goes on around it
changes within it, beyond help
beyond hope beyond the very name of heart.
Yes, the crystal is a house
one is inhabited by.

I crystallized myself out of flesh
but this is wrong. I learned to scratch
down words on paper by tendency of crystal
adjacent to sleeping aura. When I was home.
When I was even a noun.

(The monkeys want in here but I parry them)
The books are arranged shelf
by crystal shelf. The numbers I have given them
give me sleep. An age at which
I replaced the crystals with printed words.
Now I am come of age.
Now I can no longer lie.

Infinity exists, therefore impossibility does.

(Q.E.D.)

An antipython spelling its life through miles
of dusting page. Searching through aisles
of collapsing volume for the spine of a single creature.
It lives near the square of the concrete church and
this is its address: Forgotten Routes.
I sat on a chair there and waited for
the papers to near.
In that basement would be
rubber waves and chocolate volumes.
In that air would come
worth and stress.
The woman would reject no clothing.
She herself in a form of remission.
My hand is on the stair though I am
comfortably seated. My only fear
that I will not forget.
The crystal to remember.

Chocolate cake, rubber wands, calypso in plaster,
a static emitter, a length of butter, the stage
in darkness, a crumpled-up tongue mess, Blake's
compass, the golden rectangle, body by Fisher,
a Balthus land letter, all my tomorrows in a
single vein of sand, or sound, or stilled light.
Better you reach out and grasp it and touch it to
your mask.
It coils your days to a certain same.

•   •   •

Slot talk. A certain tone, whatever. I have
my worries and I have my names. Sometimes all
the words. Could you say, What's his word?
The word of whom? Do they all jam toward voice?
Toward question? All writing a call in
darkness: Word?

Stop the shop talk. What if you only had an hour
to live? Too little time to think more than
about how there was only a little more time.
Is it always the middle of the night when you think
about time ending? What is the exact mid-point
of the darkness? This time of year (November)
it must be nearly midnight. But I always think it
2 or 4 in the morning. I remember mornings
when I saw the sun come up, the first false dawn
glow then the full thing, over a green bedstead.
And others in my father's room, in bed with
Fred, Long John's Party Line just going off the
air at 5:30 with those slow Manhattan strings
and crystal dew-air celeste notes ringing and clinging
and wafting, hot sun in the cool air of summer
dawn coming up over the Bullock hedges and
backyard trees across the street. Fine feeling.
Early in life all over again and whatever you had
to do today was new.

Going over tales of flying saucers in the
sunrise. Everything everybody could have thought
to say said. Morning, go to sleep.
A prime point. The sun is an unmarked
flying celeste . . .

Me alone, I wonder if I have any
true idea who. Certainly not an image.
But something else one could write?
I'll never actually recognize it but it's all
in here somewhere? By-product of
the writing addiction?

The crystal seems to contain tiny wire snips.
Catching in the light. Throwing the tiny messages
itself can't use? Kerouac stares at me
from the yellow button.
Tell it well and truly, Go moan for man, etc.
Writing noises in the night instead.
Scratching minutes. Companion apparel of
the long sentence.

•   •   •

The ways in which I didn't think of it as literature.
A chair that could read. I put the words there
in those ways, excitement, doubt, in a moment
I could see it all differently. It would look
doubtful in mornings, as if written by someone else
better late nights. It took me a long time
(years) to think of myself as a person who would write
these things. Things . . . I still don't know
wholly what they are, any exact response. But I think
I always thought of myself as someone who improvises.
I didn't think of myself. I said to myself
I will make something up in a moment. Then
I will look at it, perhaps I will dispose of it
by writing something further.

I still don't easily think of myself as a writer.
I still don't think of myself. I look at the writing
and sometimes see the self in there, out there, and wonder
how I was somehow that self being written, writing
itself out as if unwinding a spool of . . .
I only see certain strands.

There are great lakes, but not in the Casbah.
The foot often slips, off what?, and I pay
out more lengths, I follow with an unrecorded eye.
The ear has no problem following. I often wonder if
it is in fact leading. It will always be the
mystery, that self end up out there as those words,
a mirror impossibly deep. Never enough words
to the bottom of the distance. Sometimes voices
that echo from nothing ever visible. If I am
asked what I am doing I look and make up
for that person.

All the words make sense. As I often do not.
To what I often hear I can hardly hold the pen.
Don't talk to me of mechanisms.
None of them work enough to please my solace.
Sometimes there is a far response and I catch a
glimpse of my death. Keep moving, I tell
that self the words have come to me to be.
This is all becoming a scrawl I will hardly hold
to read.

Tell someone who you are. I did it.
I did it. I did it at every point.

The private pen has inked a vast presence
in the public silence. Writing has never been as
solitary as now, I feel. I feel tense.
I feel huge.

Memory blocks me with every problem in the book.
Forgetfulness allows me to move. What do I know?
That I do not, I do not want. To know I
would have to read nothing but my own words past.
I haven't the time. I only *have* time when I
move off each mark. Don't think of,
somebody said, I am thought. The odd way
that my own past words are never things remembered.

The way thought about writing is always afterthought.
He waited behind the empty car to think of what
he might have done. The voices always passing me
until I find the way to link on and inhabit. You must
say the words until they say me, Beckett said that.

• • •

And is this the same thing?
Nodded while doubting, and hauled it out into the yard.
Knowledge of squirrels, minimal, standing though hoisted,
spread out over a carpet of beads, close the door, squirrel.
He had stepped beyond his last. And then appeared at
the first. No known letters to impede his progress.
Oregano, stout. Loud voices though only on album.
The blood cells were repeated, as the trees the sky.
No erasures, no nothing pending. Entrance through
the hoarding, the penciling betrayal of stiffness.

Monkeys under the limit, the ground full of dirts.
Blank face, black avenue. The light rang
as he lifted his hand.

The crystal was white, yellow, silver, blank.
Transparence a matter of slowly mattering, coming
to focus under sun under thumb. You never
see beyond but through. Milky, blustery,
sheerly, coughs off down an oiled hallway.
Anything is possible, anything is undersung. Held to
be an oxide, held down under being lower. A
double one that repeats its index. Carted off
in chair, squirrel watching. Album bending,
match unlit. We see, and its mother,
the father of all hymns.

Marked cards, enablements to attach comment
or an elastic candle in firm disregard.
Cattle car mottled with starlings, fire truck
gilding out of harm's way a vote for fog.
And the amphibians we will all admit to being.
The crystal apparently on fire. The water
immediately on tap. The light. The light. The light
of its stone enclosure. She spoke, but
we listened.

There continues to be and has been lost, lost of
literary activity around town. But words or notes
or strokes or steps are not objects. But then
what is one? Something that backed into, or was
backed into by, the light and thus at first missed.
Now everything is missed and still standing around.

How can one speak from within the thought
of the thing, from the standing on the floor, from
the heart? Where is the source of the center?
How are the dreams connected, and where and
how weighty is their index? When I put it
like that all out of myself I perform a useless
repetition. Where bend the cards so they may be
listed in their shuffle? And how remember
exactly the leanings? Washfulness connected
to orange leggings.

I lost the mystery novel but caught the meaning
just as it was leaving. We have focused so much
on meanings we are left with maybes. And all
the structures have been left up, for the view if
not the hand. Perhaps the eye is beginning to leave
and the ear coming into its own. Perhaps neither or
both in the sense, what center of the mind between
them. The object, after all, is never just
red or cold. I took the mike out of the box
and played awhile with its alphabet. That I was
never out of my mind of the window. And how the
car comes.

Then dogs bark and the walls come true. The redness
was that of text but not of wall. Two things
occupying the same space of different sizes.
A thing occupying two shapes. Shape Master lifted his
hand from the sodden sign. Immediately thought
and put away. Immediately again. Immediately thrown
open to the glare and shut. The words in the cabled
message shut themselves off like beads on a plate.

The heads were still in bed in every frame of the Cadmium
News. Heads outlined in a reddish motion.
A not knowing anything by the saying. A largeness of
unspoken space for the taking, for the walking out, for
the wrecking after much intense building, for the openers,
for the nonce and the apple.

A wobble amongst three sentences. The church lived half
on its own land and half by the livers of its parishioners.
The walk by the way had been decided, by the waterfall
and its careful placement in cups, by the hand not needed
for a final allotment. The half-polluted cigars were
stacked by the river drained into. And another one,
a one of sod and limes and musical bracketing.
The one gone.

He docked by the crystal, pulled in all ropes and the book
could not be read. The crystal could not be white
for it was not seen. Sounds as if it was through.
But never finished like the unread book, the off-center
orange, the duck below.

And what is one's own death, locked as firmly as
a bubble in a crystal? A darker line I had
not seen before, product of facet angles, a
more condensed clarity, is these questions?
A question is a hand reaching. The crystal.

THE GREAT

The greatness of music
    and it won't hold still since only you heard it
        that mind doubles itself faster than seconds
Perfect rate
    brightening wasting ears that nothing will disturb it
        brains are burnished on what Bud threw away
Better sea and he heard it
    laughing in the teeth on the edge of shuddered building
        a straight shaft as shunt as Monk draped in the belows
I only want to make midnight mast to my song
    in shivered and tracing words in other words
        the Miles off further from the phantom he is blow back
And I preach to January, that's who, that's all, a
    Webcor Holiday floating ice
We Reach, a new anthem, as Carla's in minor
    better than whether and snatch back the coat
        Lester laid down, so pulled
Music not to stain you but never escape its frame
    there are windows in it all the copey while, oh yeah
Blues in a muscle fit, such strain goad mind that it'll fit
        no nod off fray of Blessing Ridge
Two dates of pound cake and one of fray horn
    that missing sunspot, period of Ornette
I see a great skully sea afringe with horn
    and missing dice and house grace of stub hands, Tatum there
And I hear
    what's missing there
        music is core of the missing
          the code of fly time

On Parchman's floor there are sendings
    and at Cecil's bar the heights
In all the sections the cats drop their mutes
    aghast at robey sky appear in ceiling tile dive
Confirmation
    of Bud's Bubble
        when Bird Food
          and Blue Aria in a Brewing Luminous
I turn over my hands more times than are thought
    and sheathe of the all
        the seething things
          a breathing star

THE ONCE HELD

There are substances that are
full meaning held from beneath
nothing meaning told
forever and a dance

If I live I shift
in a hold for myself
and wonder in and the wand
plies itself from my tellings
the hold of short
and the stifle of still things
as if time were down
and to live were to sliver
the vertical sun

Nine times zero
is an acted thing plying
an organ dream of walls
as if thickness were a song
all curled to the once
thought, full stalled

Numbers in tune to a plasm
of all things known
to site and sign the ball whole
no waking from
stops in a minute

Known is the tone of a number full
that nothing thought will follow further
a hall of substance shine and stern
the star call and no other

Furls this over in my whole
my want my apted need
enlaced in trace more shining
and nothing hollowed from this binding

The world comes into hex
and pearls in showing

TWO OR THREE THINGS

I.

the car goes along her face and we see
the rising horizon of structures
numbers blaze that are thought as technique
                    dropping sense
   down in the hallways of the proceeding producing comments
      samewise launch the cinemascope bar
   curvings, curbings, railings that cement
         overpass lodge construct and break
            for a wagon of tar dirt rough line
                  standing to its shadow gleam organization of region
I would walk along and say, under a mass at large
   and upper discrete a tiny wait, which will you take?
blocks of city wire that are flats of construe, cubes
   contain the blocking in of ventures, outward choice, fixture
out of the shadow comes the pole, unlit, a viable or not block
   of building landing vista or trouble with the lamps in
      an apartment block
they walk, steps as courageous as bicycle wheels still
   in a made mall the place of hanging, squares to stalk, partings
late light leak, a novel endowed with structures, limit
   parse, word go on
she sees, we see her not talk, venture front of
   blended dim, the reach is back, her back a curl
      the comb a box for sound and not folk to inhabit
         strew range, dim build
or other, angle off, sidling profile of the isn't turning sees
   what could or not maintain money or a month
      be maintained for money a month, a mouth

a blank that is being erected by, turning winds
    into living room chairs, a desk a dock, the ladder
        that horizons, steeply motor running out
and azure essence is gasoline in bright sun, the girders
    styling over the children's polish and streaming wind wings
        waterglass of light through chairs empty spindles
            salts that amortize and big capitalism
see that the top of the window pump is a radio
    dials loose of the Canada Colas, parchment fins of
        public gate hack-made skies
still more than the everyday cells overlying it
    undertone emittence, parallel Juliette system

2.

rightness of words, fabric to floor, serving
    a blackening of the shining innards, positive vender
        all gone lost on the wall in the smoke
we are parallel when we both reach for the object
    an argument, an automat, a frying of the children
        after watering the flowers, fastening the floors
I hear china installed in my already heavy heart
    needing more heat being too impressive to be
        taken for repressive, loafing, clicking things in with belts
the name of a man as a cheesemaker, draper of
    fronds, lick impresser, chain vender, lowerer
        of visible tan roads
conversing with objects, funny and stymied, lost in
    the loft of a geographic and baffling tongue
dental crosscut to American genitals now
    crossout as the avenue of a mistake, pear
        taken as Pierre, George as gorge

forced to view aerials of condensation industrial
   on a tabletop, plan of the corpus, innate wants
      brought to free heats
I can not read parallel to gas plants, I make
   soap into soda and launch frets, my acted-out
      confederacy, decor with young girl, swivel
do you enter the kitchen interior with Beethoven
   almost not turning to a smile, a road to hold
      preferable as to a dish
a region certain to develop no ideas, freeness
   from focus, sitting down next to flowers that
      bend, penal in its inhabitant limits
        a scope as moving as its glass

3.

my eyes are
the body when closed
close to all pictures are cartoons
   for what later and larger
      plan wholly unfilled

4.

naked and not at home
  in this
    plain of dishes
it doesn't make any absence, this joining of dice
   the woman remains, knocking in the water
I beg to differ, how can you read the meter when
broken signs, glass plates, faces that stub on
   fossil fade of the plan incommunicado

5.

would wish you to wait to go through, while you
    go
        anywhere at all, Bangkok or a door
            metal flats unfurnished but with pickle
                and nose drops, seen to be entreaty that
                    is nodded not to answer
go, and the door, and the question of the hand is raised
we live for minutes where nobody
    ties and the humidor for kelp
        the large egg barge out the window lodge
inside is a story, outside is the story of
        waiting, mechanical and large in tensive fit
            for whatever will rise, turn, horizontal
            and stain for days

6.

empty room, empty saddle
empty room, full of shelves
    known of everybody
movements back to the lap of the sense dissolve
to see she by
    parcels
        the name of you look at me speak
            type
                restlessness
                    topiary underpass
                      the stalled flare-up
to see past
    she environs
        to wire

to buy what has faded to focus
            involved hair and green eyes
the psychology of form is to box it
    apparently largely deliberately
    absently passing terminant
            gilding the sense of a drink to speak with
heads, clothing pink, vowels to put aside
desire's example of the too framed head

7.

parthenogenesis
    the opening bars
        state that the city will rise, meaning spread
                include, meaning close scrutiny
                breathe, meaning doubt
                watch, meaning death
we do not understand the noise in construction
    while crossing our minds

8.

but why is glass made to seem a difference?
nothing during
the light in the eyes one is hastened to drop
    waiting on the phone
            it's normal and besides
I say this and my look left
    shadows of leaves and heads in the music, the
    drift of glass, the long hall of the automotive wait
notes and percentages of breasts
not clear whether the man is primarily, predominantly
    sitting or reading

notices the glass or not
    drinks the liquid, dark
  pictures
    without which the voice comments
    on which the voice construes
      clouds
    the other human who is a woman
    does not stand, the music, the waiting
at the counter a long time
  we look down into
    the deep flattening of desire
      universe to face
      grit of all the other that exists, flows
      floats, controls beyond the hand's eye
look
  out of the flow into the self
    of the self
      the flow that locks the hand
  the closing cells of capitalism
  a collision without drainage
above hope, smoke
  ripples on the pen at land
    self chews up and fuzzes, bolts
    on into the music which day glares
I don't know, I don't street
  wheels of skies, shoe dare and uncoupled avenue
  cement face

9.

glasses to only reflect her
  the woman from behind
but how see when take is what

knowledge is backing
    picture and wall, not the same
she will remove
    I will twin my, her
pacing the routes of small space, hair
    sweater to the skin, to the shoulders and eyes
why are you reddening
cigarettes at noon
and words in reverse not out of the question
    whatever join the question

10.

I want my building to appear
shuffled through the cards of fucking for
art for pay
for alter and what comes after

11.

signs that are not telling
    handling the head wall
        precious cast of curtains, unconsidered, lumiere
you don't see unless it's broken against black
    me I wouldn't know all right
        my hair, the telephone
            walking slowly forward, raising room
the French language was earlier again spent this evening
column of pressed pictures there is no evening
    yes, but turns and crosses
        pumps
            can't you wait
                for streets

or the black cap of hair against wall of bottles that is my name
raising a finger of the left hand to reverse the music
    music is not to be read

12.

but I don't see why wreckage of buildings and the image lapse
you could almost say that society today is threatened
    by the extended letter M
that language overhangs
a garage for precision images
going
    examples are parallel, phantom
at the front the husband works though wrecked
    a bend in time and very loud noise
        the circle is automatic
        the blend a reversal
walking backwards to keep step with time
the sentence completes its shunt with silence
they talk though loud as what do they say
    signs, proof, repel
nature as purple as green loud, this avenue
    as if leaves could hold the cars
        from the sky a straining after mobs
            temperature tacks and unknown girls
I have a habit after autos
spin and repeat their horns, a solution
    a change of fix
    a return to the stable
but why pretend that language means what is said
    not to have one speak in the street
    or on walls a leveling of heads

object exits
objects exist, smiles, mist
    on the broken step the worker's head, adjusted
      and thoughtfully in camera
she is precisely more than object to
little more than dwindling as a button pushed
auto pushed red out front into searching reason
    reflection, reverse geography, plectrum
and the leaves recede to present a bill
you talk to through the auto window
plain day of France in the sun
windows and husbands to react through and to
    in specific, factor of distance, sky is metal
      and is counted on as moves are not
we could blend or we could blush
we could study leaves as factor of strings
back to the music

13.

it is of no help that the feet are shown, the
    cars opening, the arch down the tree-lined
      overpark vista of lumping vast
return to the music, cranes that are shot
    as they're shot
numbers of and then descending phrases
thoughts as are centuries jockeying for position or not
    we were late at the site
    announced in an algebra of reflections
    where you are from
    where no is oh backwards
the machine fails, fades to amber

the account given the cunt will be covered
it's a hazard, a television, a twirling

a titling and a hold on the civilized
backup a magnifying glass or mirror
    nearer or error

14.

you go overboard in corridor for money to count or
    for the whole night
        approaches, combs, camouflages
they are building the car into a cemetery by aerial means
    door to the interior close as a laugh
but the thought agrees with another night
a night like just any other like this
    whole guy of doubt
together, closing, smoking, canceling
    hello, eh?
but given the decorative clothing and a camera to cover it
    what did he say?
is so, that's all I knew
    she, pursed by the red bra
there are some acts I will not care
    hair black, skin soft as the light it
        rose occulted by itself
clarity that is that and the light that gives it
    semblable head for the dark light acts
give her one too, put it on, let it extinguish
    better to outline, transport between her legs
    her eyes, lift up and right out of the room
the containing head loose from its landscape, a portrait

draining, no clock, not like that
    as me you, far away, greet just to see
    meetings that knive
    burn and the shots that tilt, say
    meeting on the landing, the loose leaf light to construe
to try now to think means
to say without words

15.

scenes comparable to nothing but possibility, you're waiting
    for no one but, side by side, in a nod a drink
    is it she? it is not who
    a note, no it's for myself
        a proper match in the rain
for exigency, sound just inches from its background
    harshness, boredom, questions
    will not be answered but by hazard
        from the most varied volumes words that angle away
we were stacked up then dipped in water
I was frightened by pure mouth of dog that never laughs
    Khrushchev, bring me some food, an egg
        perhaps discredit bring on the whole
she, I am doing the writing but, he, it's the rain
    that's made me sad
I am over banal but it's the radio brings me words
    of solvency, the sex between, mystery
increasingly glances, cigarette and is scared
just as you have the eyes, the shoulders for
    in case it looks a lot, makeup
        give a damn, a beer, poetry and a sister
            written down by the jukebox list

and you, a necessity, light the pipe
    they explain with arrows
        morning that worked
weighted, and written over itself, poetry
notes that that garage is not part of a hotel
    pool, pencil, the pronoun "my"
the dictionary providing such things as pet cocks
but then going outward might it not cancel
    out into the area of stacked texts
        in spite of myself, mystery
        a being without a stare

16.

a novel silence
coming? off in some dumb basement or other
slow to remove the camera, other things
through a door and by a pipe to do
and the car that follows with its noise
with its repetition, an accounting of colors
loudness colors and the pictures will not be taken
across No Man's Lands of the drive past edges
proceeds that I have no sense of preceding
    tilted on arrival and into the sonic
        shunts of an alphabet
          that will refuse to start
but her thought is the circle of her present locale
    shelving blocks, window book expression similar to a face
a peculiar connection with world a noun face
    lapse face, face now disappeared from facade
        and all entrance when it's free from fatigue
and passing strips but what

are we going
    to do
faces are bombs

17.

problem of who is it
now how am I going to
what
hold as there where you are
    notebook by a chain gate
        in tongucs rclatc
        the more serious "uh"
calm friend of a child with worries beyond the inside
we see you're impossible
you give sound a chance, felt breasts
what's gotten into you after sleep
glasses in time being folded
for the example of a sentence
    its numbers advanced to the start
but knowing they're not knees because told that
    by radio sleep in the camera of Hitler
        he never looks at the camera
and thought is radio of the real

18.

at finally the most promised rates
a book in bed that squeezes the stem
interior lighting of the forgotten undress
a storm, I don't know, is changed
is born blonde and then dyed
is an operator and thumbs through

changing promise of problems and mistakes
the rock for the flame
the cinder for a hold in space
coming forward, a shift construe
missed my word by the turn of your page
ideas bridges on the road of forgettal
I lost it all hot on the grass, the silence

ON THE ROAD

Well, you just have to read and get involved
with things and scribble. The letters
under the mountain, and the wrath that
turns auto. We'll never sour up any
plans by jabbering on. We'll whittle
while we run. And in back of it all
the spiral ramp of conversations, higgly-
piggling over hours and starts and landings.
Nobody digs it all better than in
comminglings of flowage, hot off the rocks
back of the batter pen where dimers stand.
And the flash floats out of the stars into
our upraised tips. Writing means motion.
The hover left behind in the lever jacket,
the car park flap, the inhabited sever.
I was ready to take up amazement and
follow the words.

BACK AWAYS

— A Twist of Childhood —

In wizened old terminal birth
I hold up a spalding lemon
is a pearl, is a whizzing point of land's end
laughing at me, and whirling me up
a lap of the goodness

This the beginning of the toil term
the load of ingot and bland
the silly heave on the tip of turn it to true
whatever the collecting of lighthouses be saved as
the saintliness meditating on sand spits
the youth ope of eye on a bitter pear
oval of room on rectangular you

I stared at pencil edges, knowing them not
to be a parcel of see-you in doorspace
and who's edging there, the two
that misted you into frontal lobotomy, cheering
for free linger tootness blossoms
apparent to the bottom of the dare the glade
all in hoot buckets pointed
the sea, that amuses and frosts
the brink of allotment, one toy

Eyes that silent the bright band stripers
a later knowledge of snakey pens and men
standing bag-baggage back in shadow storm
rotters and kelpish standages near basement

clot and ravage
but I didn't know
nor note to fend

The passing out of all clean care
and blond muscles in the cave
of name dare and rave
coddling under a stare, a gravid
pottled grounding of chondrules
sited before your muzzled beak
  lip light and hair
you wake to the finding of stains

And what did I see all plaining in my hand
  but the finer geckos
the ones with plans, and sheltered avenue gainfulness
  hovered about the spite long nose
longer than the spoon around the bottle in space
my siftiness of premeditative prolonged intent
when mystery is a whisper in the candy heart
nobody knows but nobody me

The glass nobody
the me without handles
the back-of-the-door infusion of placky particles
  borrowed from neighbors of the weighty adult
sun on and waiting for nothing
seeing the blend in motes of serious
  and universal smear of no intent
  pocketless and on the smile

the empty blast of regal fear
I lost my spoon
but pestiness lasted

Did I know heart when I wiggled in trees?
what did I tent within windows' glasses?
Weighted Monster of the Wiggle During
I saved a cap for my mate and tipped it never
hurled holes in the ground to sever
and berries of no choice in the loam deck chested
I made them war for my manned tomorrows
   which never were plurals
merely white glance in tendon gloom glade
under hawsers of parental distemper
notched a common in my beckons
powdered all stare

Mere underwear
I make the sign of the sun peck
and remark alert at its hybrid
no central palm in the mind
so sorry wider
the lengthen, clothesbody
you got to reach
by screen means to apple sturdy
no matter the hook bulb
   and closet study

The it bib
in avanti letter
capsulates the puke mule
his roentgen itch and fodder buried

alp to the hilt
and in flinch
a whole palm of parent
   in dauby door
in rate of cloud, clown sediment
and a corpuscle muscle
clads you in delve
   age stem
you rise, but you don't
lacking swerve
and a litter-daze bulb-clot eventuation lesson

And make it be your name, make that pumpkin disturb
he's lying on candy, says the satisfied doorway
oof of clad and rumple to the itch
baffled at tune glands and the grapple
seems as if it's trade hoot clear to the door
miles trumpet from the grassine lane
name was hoot bucket and traipsed on in
pajama clout out of minerals frangible
nape of Bucky Bug, it's possible . . .

In the doorways there are nothing.

Sad saw of afternoon in the edge lace of cryable ledge
under awnings of tree pots and crystal case
where ice is housed for your lemon leg
and care'll go over your day like a wheeled derrick
denying mystico printings of pad whelks
and the tin on the door
of Grandness Little, the portico of these pictures

Adds up the icemen loafing
and leans from dormers the stories of them
as if you couldn't have tea
   with your head in a drizzle
cone pad of cough ladings
accoutrement to the phone
no illness head has ever so violet varied
and carps all violent in a copsey stir cap
the cartoons of Mister Pond, the shave

And coffee rose morn over all city breathe
was incinerator actual
as I giggled into my brain to feel who
was I to dare there, ectoplasmic in my walk
to loaf school and hair up to my witness lessons

Chucklewise of those I knew there
sharp feeted by wall and wire and cokey delvings
housings gigantic of volumes, romantic of sheaf
festering through boilers of raretism day
level hope on the scald, and the run time of pirates
experiating at the love of fence broughten trees
and girls in parks, girls of the alum car

You see what I do, everytime I miss you
whole cold parting gyzm polluting roentgens
would stop by where my father parked
   and level his fold head
   and mystery up my dead
                    bowed deed

Shambling off ramps, with half a cone to my fasten
the rooves of those blinds were flatten
but I lasted

          pottery blue boots
          in the chisel dawn

And your hone hours, tonguing tips the tooth
but rain off barn end I am loath
back to
      the snakes the walls to my chisel dare
      and apey stave

This is all a fizzing but has lasted
has made me full dare again the indigenous sud
New England of apple of harm and raid weathers

Putting the pages together in the hairy wetness
of stove bolts in rumple fights
you know, but I don't
being young
ink applied
spending the day in
bending try
  to remember
the hoses made my horses
my rug oval of train chug minute

But you'll all go off in a candle
and never fasten me again
and I'll sight stars never set
and remember gates shutless but on the lock

and trend myself back to barry baiters
and relegate my sadness to a yurl
and lemon the shadows
and kiss the migrant bat
and wait tight wait
for waters to witness my losted
                    (told fist)
   (adults are all relegators)

No knowledge!
all blows off in blues of furls
of slow dates so fast they smart
and cool banyan angles of the heart
my age
and another stage
all others
penitent partners
of the snake
whose sign is wall blank

Pushed grain past frond
   and knew it
   more than wait
assemblies of the slipping guard
remiss in its berry pebble clashness
things must shine themselves separate
from mass, from buttled arbiters
honings of the glove
and wait water white
blessing the nod and the dim open
to coin myself back to initial tip
and load loss with fume

meditant hung stepping
drapings the world let down

Displays
a grab at from my carey cage
all carried down like a case of my witness lessons

You'll be afraid of your own self I will
and tremble in destined plick of ghost coat avenue
recalling the nothing from the nothing gate

HOMMAGE À RON PADGETT

If there be a love for my poems I insist on
it will turn up dented in the mind by the dust
they attract to themselves, as then I am dubbed a fool
but only from the inside, so clocked, so wadding

Such is an example of the subjects I have never
to search for, they make here a rattle, one
with no handle, but available at many's
the absent moment, subject to matter, friable
and coming to pieces, the pieces always on hand
and cut to mind

As never do I mind this, but will you?
there is always room for a new scent and it seems
these rooms come equipped with them, there's
one now, the lotion odor of an order of washing
the hands last week just arrived at this cell
where I write but I forgot
that

I handed it in, crawling back to
my breath-honed mirror in the Palace of Forgettal
where I stopped by chance to write
the further adventures of a never
gone by the books life and later
continued my reading in biography of a Lowell
the one with the floral subservience and
an underchair Dentine

FOR LARRY FAGIN, AS HE PASSES ME UNKNOWING

Great spots of light, which are never empty of sound
you dream of in needles pressing down
they call 'em those "cat things"
listing at the table, with simultaneous knees

"I have the thought argueless for all time
that *blank* is the greatest alto
of all the rigid spines"
(take *that* to the coast and sun it)
my mind to me a master list is, as
long as it's end-of-the-week
done (these solos tend to spoil)

Give me a break, as Lacy said to Monk
but how does anyone get together, you one
and me negative one?, but first
come here and open this jar, audition
this open door, for
all the sessions of all the clubs

Of maybeless time wouldn't add up, but
still I wanta be surprised, like
at the end of the world really
the top of the spine
as you eye me over the endlessness question, a
chordal suspension, and all the fretful bins

There's roller. He's out. Stops, goes up the steps.
He knows he's a cat. Has the eyes for it.
Stopped circles. He's absolutely in the world and
on the cement, under the blue sky's light, follows
own paths where no paths, his devices.
I only know where he is a very small amount of
the time. Just sudden sights of him,
unquestionable. Does he see me, he lets me in
for a moment to solid eyes. We are
inhabitants and as inhabitants, pass.
No one sees all the cats at the pretty points of all
their routes through city for only a moment and all
at once from above.
He got out and he's standing on the step, one from the top.
How's about it, Roller, shall we try and go away?
He will stay, sure, and one day I will go. And
he'll not be aware of the "will" with that "go."
He is straight. He is eyes. He makes his way, up
and daily. He has captured whatever of the world
all he wants. Just what, his wants? He looks
a Pure Being of Receiving. And not one thing
to be reviewed. His thoughts are his ways.
His whole procedure in step. In eyes so opaque,
not even sun on a dare. I only trespass here,
where he is being. Roller, bring back your tongue
to this Planet All Eyes.

MOTEL

Motel is in love.
And if that was a person, what was that person
doing banging on the wall?
Elastic home pretension, and here's a video by
Admiral Richthofen . . .
Motel is in love and hoards it.
"Is his name Combat?"
"Well, he's gonna liquidate my sister-in-law."
He's on the Granitic Patrol in a limestone region.
"He'll never make it. Wanta get a *length* of pipe?"
or an order of "Itcher Waffles."
and thrown out of that cream pitcher of a motel.
"Chasin' the dead, and all for a look
she just got done getting out of prison
                        that one girl . . .
          a real set-up Indian . . ."
But motel maintains its raggedy-weak length of pipe
and did you know "K. Bob Motel"?
and did you see that commercial on the TV?
they locked the pet phone?

MAMMOTH NIGHT

The old hotel is gone, we sleep in the new brick,
Mammoth Cave Ridge, flat as a parking lot with trees
and deerlings nibble past our groundfloor window the night
I watch a single yellow incandescent hung to a pole in the
dark and think, surrounded by the caves

That streetlamp gathers all the darkness into forms
of cave, the whole night sky the Great Rotunda Dome
beneath our feet over there, near original entrance
I walked to down the cement former woodpath
heard all that drip drenching in, and the radium shrinking silence

Floyd inhabited his shackporch mostly, other than cave,
felt all the space in silence, learned to move away from walls
his padlock star still shackled here, over behind the Brain Brewery
a crude star, or spider, enforcing his fabric
But earth should bulge, dome up, I know so much cave down there

This pillow should grow ripe beneath my head asleep
and turned to the needle my body wants to make of limestone
I grow back to the report of silence on silence
a rubbed rough glacier played over the air, a snare
and porous determinant, held under ground by joist of the aching angles

All the vaults of dark are cavern 'round this point of lamp
they swirl here and connect, coincidence baffles
calcareous the limit ratios and nudging careless precise
I pass my hand over bones of ridge and gather all the cracks
                              to a switch of inks
I am here at the last to be born, take me in

THE SIXTH AND AFTER, NOTHING EASIER

So what did befall Bobby Dupea after
he left in lumberstruck "fine," leaving his
jacket, his wallet, his face in the mirror
and his Dipesto at the filling station wandering?
No one wants any time to be left on the quiet.
It's always cold to leave before things get bad
northwest or anywhere dangling. A life left
means little but *is* lots? Shifty as an American
he didn't even think to shrug.

But he'll have to get down, got off somewhere, and hire
himself out for a touch, test another spot, find
another unlike girl and set up another leave in the world.
Music. Eyebrows. What's going on?

All the little jobs with all the big emotions.
All the stares spent out of one into widening space
burned by elbow muscle of shock, a slowness.
Then a quick pickup and shuffle, avoiding one's
image, skipping the wonder. Rhapsody for backgrounds,
sunsets to light the hair, the backboard of the head.
He'll get up to something, then turn it
from him, stumbling, stammering, sent for you
yesterday and here you go today.

The night the day, what matter its scowl riders.
Afterward were the tenses left over, the
bicycle rider backwards, old rocking chair
wristed away, down there, back of the following days.

I live, he said, and rolled it over the next thing dead.
The arrow pointing to the back pocket, slim-throated, empty.
No neighborhood, no settle, no music that's not music.

Anyway, a lot. All the way, he's never gone
totally timbertruck filing out of sight, never out
of greyroad quite, a shoulder, seeming tight
never carom out of mind, a whim locked to
its following ray, Dipesto and Dupea . . .

HOMAGE TO BALLARD

I believe in solid ponderousness, and in the waking up from time.

I believe in sutures that pop like the bolts of a second stage booster.

I believe in tongues.

I believe in lace that won't retreat.

I believe that later there will be hunger.

I believe in the greater violence of soundlessness.

I believe in Delicate Arch, Machu Picchu, Sand Cave, Laura's Tower,
and Proctor's Arcade.

I believe in witness, careless, and total storm.

I believe that nothing left to be done tomorrow will remain the same.

I believe that dreams change the intent.

I believe in thresholds, faucet handles, and brads.

I believe that we are determined by broken spaces and broken times.

I believe in darkening pages and festered maps.

I believe in the opaque eye of the cat.

He walked around and couldn't think of anything.
Nothing had been put back. Later he would think
of all the names and they would bother him.
But right now everything was empty. The world
rose and fell, everything beating in regular
parentheses. Even the light, a pulsing grey.
He lifted a hand and then put it back, down.
By his side was a lift, which he entered and
shut the doors. He stood inside not moving
for a long time, listening to everything
without a thought.

Fragments are our wholes.

MOVEMENT ON A DREAM

She is going to remove her clothes and prove that her
breasts were not there, as I had thought.
I do dream of conditional bodies, horizontal
and hesitant. Under my hand is a lain thing,
the brain's sole coffer where things arise soft.
She turns and her face puffs into marking to make most overly
sure her eyes. I have left nothing to later, I
thought. Unexpectation in a ring of the same body,
are her breasts? She covers with so many
layers apertinent, strap, spokes. Why do I not
simply ask? I have so much doubt, the erotic
swarm sprung on doubt. In which position would
she be if I did ask? Today her breasts . . .
And tomorrow the strained thing surprises.
She removes everything hanging on and still hides.
Is expectation to blame? What if she shot
through the window frame, pane, hand rising in
careful and protect, and all the fending decimals spin.
Careful to take, nerves beneath and clothing slides.
My pen gives me fewer options than my thought,
as I had thought, expected, drawn on over me
like, stuttered when it was time to turn. And
the lengths one would go beneath clothing to ask.
And the sun has no part in this, afternoon
in the dark.

Then one morning, noon, I woke up, filtered out, and
she was, what was it?, the state of clothing her
mind as if breasts disarrayed? How to get
down to the thought through the layers of breast,

throat, loins connected to the, parts concealed?
She lifted her law, arm, and raised the thing
concealed. Revealed that there be further
conceptions, optional as where on the body.
I cleaved myself out of the numbers of myself,
I had thought. But she, her hair was as
blonde as a bird's nest in cartoon. And there
were sliding shelves behind her, satin coins, bell
ropes in friction, the turning of a space on her own
face dim. I should report this. I should
connect myself, correct myself.

But the dream was a cheat. She gained no
further position, stroked nothing, showed herself
just as the world would have it. Night shade in
blinking day, and the brick came off the toast, as
easily and as a cover with which stuck. I had
not even her arm to parry with, to make match
and hollowly worry, the sleeve out of the arm hole,
the head from its twist. At least I think she
prod threads, through which her blood, at which
my time, and the colors of all this spectral, no
decision. Who is somebody? And that particular
her that drills on the etching device, is hollowed
in the cup I cup to stare and think it. She
turns again and the material is black. Let my
shades of her whiteness be her concern. I would
contain at least the protectional arm, the cream
of underpinning weight and touch, a thread tendril
and loose tube, crevice at which the throat is
revealed, and the . . .

In the dream she befriends herself alarmingly.
And there is no drop to her guise. My face
and her fundamental, tones of lose and lucky to be me.
How can this all be seeming to think about her
backwards? And can this slip of heavy-collared
robe over flesh be thought? The nations
have raised a large enough rain against such
permissions. They think then they have saved the
day, but its bathing chamber is missing. I must
have missed her, that is the swelling that bulks
against, bolts in my hints, of what she could be
seeing when I am the dream. I have held
her up, must be. I have touched the wind
that does not vary her, not even her still departures.
The book on all this removed from my vice,
the way all of her body is heavier in mode
than my standing of it. The she it, that's the
rub. The thing that will not resolve into
own thought, face image, hers.

But there be tendencies. And all too much
time for the dreamed body's haste to reappear.
Why can she not just ask? Then I would have my
answers? This whole locked body dream a question.
And after the election of these dream shields, what
position of wetness her mouth appear? The classical
definitions are failures, and the dreamed binding of the hands,
the closing of the thoughts, the everything known in the
hugely tiny pressed breasts. That I move to
her window, that I move from the stir side, from
and to her further plans for marshalling of owner
face, face from which heavily the eyes plead

release. All depends where exit from this
circuit of the dream.

But I come no closer to the throat silk tamp
of my having brought her to this facing, who she
might after all systems wrought have to come to be.
And has she no rights in this felt side of the dream?
Penciling in the drape of liar's avenue, etc., the right
position from which to drill the window, and further.
I saw her standing there. Black underlying black
and then the white cancel that the beneath of the flesh
turns to hunger. I cannot remove in the way of
the mass of her, her tongue standing out in place
of the weightier matter this all turns to. What
would be your name if I could lie?

But the body of this dream in thought comes up
with nothing further. And after I have written
all will not recede. The thing to be stuck with,
the body in the throat. The other side of your life
canceling you at every blend. Stick to it, man,
and woman has no option. The pictures of the pictures
of the pictures, the lengths one would go to, the plan to
have the penis extend and all the rest of the dream recede.
To awake to find hand marks on myself? That
she has lifted the edge of this dream a little, but
the fundamental she will not fall. Nothing totters
like unsung weight. And the image I am afraid of
that will not revolve. I keep urging her to turn,
and she does but does not, nothing further is thought.
And the swim comes as the eye blares, the eye that

would stop if it could only reach, strokes branding
wall back as cereal of a charge, brads in drawn
condition, the flaming head of the woodpecker song.

She would do a little dance but is caught in my
flinch, my version of aim that dries a bit under
climbing duress. The avenue to her thighs seems little
of the answer. And keep your hand. Head up
and blanking out. Body then hidden still flares to the
touch, the fuck of still under clothes breaking the
mold of nude. And I would shiver my thought
as she could strain my body shaken. Her glance
at own pants a glimpse of story heaven.

But how bidden unbidden this glance of body dream,
with all its ray of unresolves, repetitious nodes and
additive subtractive clothing? Like the sentence that climbs
the body unbidden, as classically shaved as spine of loin.
Probably brought down to it I have shown her in.
And the no walls to any of this but her back if I
could shake it. I have been brought to lock it?
And she turns, I turn, the whole erotic is a
turning. Tends to the stillness of the obsessive,
never a blurring, however violent nondistortive, the
plates of the blends rising separable. That will I
defend myself against my own dreams? The girl caught in
the pool of thought covers whatever still of this
making own. This pearl in the skull never to be
exhausted. And I drape her more than
I bare her to me. All the movement still
my own.

from ROME NOTEBOOK

to dark Roma
   and the vast hall livingroom
  terrace mists la luna
and clang all doors their iron gating
        one star
          sta
guides and vocabularies and whistles
  and fusebox buzz
          an ape is scimmia
che ora? (no clock)

First Morning
awake to the light that glows from the stone
  dun, ochre, umber, burnt things
What to say?
  constant traffic beeps & rustles
birds, no bugs (no screens)
         no acqua caldo??!
How many numbers of things will we not know
    "What's *that* you're saying??!!"
Heavy scattered place of richness coated in light
  & yet this is a missing morning
         che ora?
        dove Alvin?
       dove anybody . . .
a huge lostness
the place for great rambling poems?
leaving the place you know & having to remember even more
Morning is the time of increase

•

on bus into Roma last night
    off to left, Dante's volcano forge fires
& around a park diamond blue point lights
                on aerial poles
the thundering blemish of everything
    & try to pay attention
        as the wheels . . .

•

              Gianicolo Walks
to St. Peters with the crowds
   pigeons, cats roam steps
   saints crust the crest
Bernini curves the posts with bees
          (vortex insecta)
the Christians are definitely *lodged*
             wherever
on walls, in walls, cupboards, alcovery
gold leaf band "Super Terram" a mile long
   Sixtus gets named at the apex
    couldn't they have risen a bit higher?
     Christianity is a *kingly* religion
         (the cops of man)
Walking terra cotta streets
   down the back side of the wall
climb steps to a cul-de-sac of cats
   black, blinking in the shrubbery

•

I puff on my cig & the dusk light glows up a notch
sun long set, these walls refuse to give up
   ghosts of daylight
   verspery serena in our lodgings
Mulls over a Serpentine Town
I could sit long & imagine I was . . .
   long after it's light to write
Improve on my hand & brush away the periods
& is that a bat flirting around
    between Academia roof & shrub top?
Now sky is wine in the blue glass
     star space priming
      & trees to stir the shallows

        •

Kronos play ferocity Bartok
   the way it should shake an audience
   & those groans that would tender files
    the chromium tire on velvet
& the interval bird
   pipes into Cage space
    as if cued

        •

Ashberyan rejoinder:
   We had a pretty good view
   but we couldn't see you.

        •

Italian sky thatch
  & a reary scumble
glowball down behind Academy fleshtone
They paint from buckets of the old soup
  combustibles not easily retired
& then thought, & thought big as it ages
a bat now, before the sky dims
  flies where a sparrow should be
in hive space, in made
& everything else is windows
  as if they marble
the in-shoots visible, edges
marling in, as if all
  edges, sills, jams should be
  marble, & your thumbs dip in
Is this place soft or hard?
  seems soft for so much stone
  but old stone, grain tired of hands

I sit before the wall of light
does not belong to us
but what will I snare here, so lit?
a dart, ranging at pagey things, untrimmed
  as some trees

Helped out of the Starling Havens into a
  brief crease of sky at hand

We watch each other more carefully here
this absconded family, creeping up on the Palatine
from a handful of windows, brain eaves, soundly politic
as if we clawed for the entrance of our own hands

•

Marble ball midst top of box hedge
no biting bugs, the bats *work*
today a midge approached the fruit &
    'jected away
bats have all flying bugs on the run here?
marble stills the centers

These high-top trees are for the birds
trunks trimmed all the way up to their nests

A guy over there out on the porch
we Americanos come out at dusk, watch
    all Rome

                    Say what
                    you wish but
                    keep an eye

                •

    Haiku
An ochre wall against the bush
    and plasterman's lamp
under sundown

            •

A rose guard sky
Christians hated
made mystics of them

They threw their towers &
held to their marks
    (elsewhere the marks)

          •

The sky stuff parades in mornings
all shunted back by dusk

Serena — serene — dimming light
Do we calm as the day goes, as the bees?

Sudden sundown "Whulp!"
a door bent out of a Mercedes

            bracket a small case
            means remove it

          •

Women shade the stone
as grass greens the hills
        —Dante, Canzone I

If over stone you would spin your worth
then let it take its side with love

And coil the man's hand stands
to a spear of shade
emptying over the wall
rest of day

light
on dark
a raid
      decimal pointing to zero

Place of the most finished thoughts on
  the planet
          (& the most obvious motors)

•

to *Cosa* (near Orbetello)
2 BC Roman town
  capitolium on hilltop commanding sea
  standing walls, foundations, rubble
  museo has Pan figure ("Martyras"?)
    hands crossed bound behind back
    prominent cloven hoof, erect penis
    : what rite?
Olive trees have *voices*
  whisper-breath, articulant moans
    in wind
    they *spoke*
          (I heard)
We inspect constructions on coast
water works, slots for fish prod.
gorge/slit-cave in cliff, follow
  through roofed spots to broken roof chambers
  with hoary dripstone & new green mosses
  way up, & large transparent-wing bats
            we woke

Place for Giant Acts
    pre-Roman/Etruscan, even pre-Aeneas
                            (Hesiod?)
cliff path ("copy" of Newport cliffwalk)
    with waves bounding
    beach with red & blue dorries, far rollers
      "LA STREGA" beach-stand ristorante
Then we go look at sites of turreted platform villas
    one contains an olive grove
      fields still cultivated
Long drive down Tuscan Coast, kept lapsing
    into reveries of 101 Cal to farm & St. Helena
      (hills similar)   (yellows)
near-Rome outskirts: BOOMERANG MOTEL
                  MIDAS PALACE (like a Holiday Inn)

We finally (4th day) come down off our hill
stepping through the Trastevere
across the Sisto (foot only) bridge over the
chalky green Tiber (Tevere) & into further
oldnesses, immediately to the Forum (after
a few natural enough off-twists & culs-de-sac)
the shades of ochre/brown are endless,
green drapes over restoration scaffolding at west
end of Forum giving a brutto shade of
modernity to the zone of antiquities, international
groups & tours widespread in the park atmosphere
& so an added gladness to be on our own
here, marble column barrels & capitals
thrown down at all sides in the green & sod,
the scale of the remaining upright columns showing
how impressive this city must have been to

the podunk country folks in from pee pond
flats, marble has honey tone & sugar surface
(the rains ate), fluted columns draw your
fingers to feel in & squeeze the flutes, Domus
Augustus on Palatine is garden plotted, cats
ranging for food, healthy tame cats (one ocelot
spotted Celia prefers), then Coliseum open
but overrun with scaffolding routes & white plastic
towering to (only way, now) reach upper galleries,
scale of the intimate grand, & back up to
the Forum, within a city a city, within
any time the ages, sun on stone nobody's
problem, & the cats . . .
                Piazza Venezia
by the Vittorio Monument fascist cakebox
(but cats here too) & up the Corso, Celia
looking for shoes finds none, off right through
the Via Frattina to Piazza de Spagna, the
steps & Keats House (closed today &
Caccitore's gone?), back west manage to grab
some orange to drink at tables in the street
but wait & halt (don't know the drill, never
mind the lingo!), eventually Piazza Navona,
Bernini fountains covered, through angled walls
every one a fascination, this the first city for me
since first NYC draws me to endlessly wander, walk
everywhere without plan, get lost no care,
but follow among the infinite leads, come
out through slit sidestreet onto a surprise
plaza as if from cave trunk passage into
big breakdown room unsuspected, an alien
lander without language, freeing me to see

& crank the backbrain by oddment angles
of wall & light, there's nothing for the mind
like the old mystery cities! The *layers* of
happen here, connect to the meaning-layers
of language strainless, but I lose my
language here, to find it again where?
after avenues of image-being immersement.
So mid-aft we cross back on the Sisto
& up the Garibaldi backstairs midst
litter of syringes (& their plastic packs)
& scooting lizards (fence variety) some
with emerald backs, puff to top & sit
by the fountain (just round corner from us here
& unsuspected till today), true that
thirsty body refreshed by *sight* of waters,
even with a syringe-dropper spinning in an eddy . . .
Home to a nap, & our first cooked dinner
here, now 10 PM a thunder rainstorm
blankets Roma . . .

:

L.A. IN TIME

Gerry Mulligan the spikey guy who booted the baritone
in L/A. afternoons of ash on the venetians.
And his Chet of length, white drape phrases and early
bop lyric intentions, as if Bix had lived to curl Bird.
In this last-minute music there was more space between
the chairs, the ashtrays, the stripes of light, the tiny
bandbox low tile ceiling stage for loony interruptions,
quotes of your mother's favorite hum, and abracadabras
of All The Things a physics without zones to plug.
High in a whiskey parturience they doodled on panes
of the early Horse, grew thin but standable,
dwelt elaborations on all heights to tune.
Mulligan heard it Lester to Monk, the pretty snake of
laze to the clear box of casement, where pounds
at the tips won't interfere. He angled for the
clearest blend of caught line and held fold,
arrangement in a cut moment, no blurs as the
knee rises. And Chet, he was so bent, his
voice sheared higher, his locks curled Deaner,
even a dogface part in a picture, he lullabyed the
orphan boy in barracks khaki, and Time After Time
the teengirls watched his T-shirt shrink, tumbled
at his bell, and I Get Along Without You Very Well
(an ultimate gloss on crewcut Hoagy?). Where now
his smile when last facture dried from his picture?
He found and stood at point of breath all melody
could circle.

These guys drew in a Renaissance sky.
The Densities came later.

Unclutterable provenance. Where vacuum of
the notes not hit outline the ones that are.

A ThinMan's Music. Every time see
where all the four limbs go.

And even the chaos
utter.

for David

ROME PASSAGE

Going down unknown by a seemly cafeteria
in line and strewn round by the honk places
intendant to fish forward but always struck back
the little lid of black over canceling fires, the moves
embolden by their swerve, smolder walls
of the stare brown
                              and the talk is out a ways
digits hidden but scarves slung out like planks
you walk up on your day from behind, arriving time
in broad space, spacing time in bold doubles
the bank from a facing bank, piazza, palazzo
merit paid out daffy in dancing the cars
                                        I've come here from years
arranged other, straws in the weather or lodged in the wall
the one you passed hiding lights ahead, or the brass bed
activity marred through a scrap of pane, full well
in stride and barely glimpsing, fish fry in there,
      the weltered hats
in the ribbons of stolen squares, gleam on a miter
the Egyptians would have sawn through
                                          A particular collar or belt
mixed off back of baffles by myself, extraining a fountain
imagining the mount of its stain, bare vugs, almost
the thought of the bellwether lighter clanging his pole on cue
and the lights all go up silent in penetrant avenue
                                                This is
the gog whole of city in close
banner tapping the marble marker, and on it all goes awhile
stamp as we wend on black iron paving stones, cubes in
woven arcs not quite grounded allow shaken blues

of aisling urchins in their bell cries, their woolen noses
snubbed by schools of day liars and the neat
hip young monk balancing his ruler in the vulgate duel
dreams of Jerome as he cuts along by the column barrels
in the popular nave and law of the Mercedes
as domes release and the bats come out

ROME ONCE ALONE

Stealing along in this eyelighter city
the trials are hidden, far behind the near wall
the views constructed full hewn and tap block
high away as shoe is settled the squares fill to static
the square where the magic hood is bronzed

The horned toad in a box is not brought here
its blood was hired here, mined from perimeter
vines reached to glass and lamp concocted violet
the sow caught in the stone part of the ambling language
and the Popeye held at the wire a high melancholic

Humour a rubber let loose in this backcourt reaction
times have so colored the river nothing greys
the center of all this marble a ruby prism
ashes tend by night a tongue by day
and the last time I pass will be by flashlight
and the last thing I rob will be a gong

GLANCE IN WHITE SPACE

No detail here, nothing but you. Unbroken gaze,
whole of the body, words cast away. It is level with
meaning, this white horizon. And when the air comes
together we bend.

Little strokes. The air has parted many. That the
perking lights all are you. And the time is a favor
presented to no one. Previously, whole.

Gone out like a wish, forgotten spoken. Dividing line
each touch. Novels could be ignored, or spent
in this chamber.

Little more than you telling me, with a brightness here
or now. Beneath skin, where the flesh begins.
Our clothing an imitation, a skin to remove.

Blush of red soak on the glass, into itself.
On the morning the unknown colors start, and the ones
we know imprisoned change.

Enclosing wind, air in lace chains. Torn flowers,
bronzed hedgerows, the moon as cut a sign.
The you I will be before you.

IN CELL

In the cell as lonely lover
in cell as if hell a longer
and bit tongue fighter, holder
of it all off till an inward
summer, the all that the cell
imposes encloses

In cell I hum the light
in cell the hum and light
increases, erases the mind
of swirling thing, rubbed
and paining possession to turn
its rules to chalk, its brine
to illumined ceiling

In cell short of hate
dart to the center of dress
this arming space, this whole
alone in stone, encased in
light the word increases
single in cell's total
a lining gaze

In cell nobody knows
in cell the pictures of light
remand to state the signing block
of held mind, trance
late as spark in splinter
dark contain as contain
the word does true, the beam

repeats but nothing holds
as my mind now held

Cell is mind stall, is
bone of brain illumined
in whole, at any point
the hall of curing time
of time's cells the light
in reaching each a whole
will lock and shine in tone

In cell you stop
stall and keep on stilling
the stare has you willing
the image to be the
one, the whole by self
in cell in light on
image air at rapture to
the nothing of

Done
before me is this thing I am
to become

SOMEHOW TO BE ABLE TO SAY

Here is a table
and here are some chairs
and here is the man who keeps
the truth, and there is something
you don't know here

I show you something
and it's ice or a drill
Nothing but things but a language of things
a hill with objects like dowels that roll
Whatever you haven't seen, or you have, and
I'll tell you about it

About all this talk
about what is written
a gesture as thin as that kitten
which is not what you thought
trades green eyes for blue
The words so plain, but not all names
Not all of the names are true

for M.P.

THE SAINTS

Saints of observance, saints of weighted pleasure
Saints are we when we see them?
Saints are we not?
Saints of fine avenues to flesh derision
Saints of long division
Saints who kneeling nod to beckon
Saints on whom we reckon

Saints in crevices, saints in hatches
Saints on whom the rhythm catches
Saints who merely time the battle
Saints who still commune with cattle

Saints who seek a higher window
Saints with whom the winds are kindred
Saints explained by a binding of thistle
Of which of the saints are we all a winner?

Saints in a bunch dial a single phone
Saints leave nothing when they're not at home
Saints whose pates are parted by cleavers
Saints whose thirst drains all the rivers
Saints who greet you never

For a certain saint you buy a kit
This one's for the saints who sit
Bow to him and the sky comes lighter
This one's brains grow ever tighter

And here are where the saints are beaten
Here where even saints are eaten

These have been the saints

after Ron Padgett

ASHBERY EXPLAINS

The people on the next block over from yours, you know?
Sounds transduced from ceiling to ceiling
to thought that won't admit of a washer replaced
without dousing all and sundry in sand and a mild solution
of pinks and reeds, hard sodium, the cap off the tube
he stood and he said, and he lay long and he thought
his mind encompassed, his perimeter taken in a bit
everybody talking at once but only one thread assorted
from it all a parrot reproduced on call

Out on a rooftop head down timing the sun
wishing it hadn't all come easy to such a rinse
living in a chipper vacuum of donuts chatting and jotting
and walking and salting the numbers coming up on the surface
of a silky phone, how can you store
all the bones of one time a leavening for
the canceled strikes in bridled strokes
I pick a pen from room of cobbled stacks
and head for Mars, Saturn

Add the epithet "farm," north and to the sum of that place
and you have the counting drama, away from which we reside but not
as anonymous kinds, drops of the goblin into the proper reservoir
it would be bogus continuing just to continue nonetheless
renders us very much against the day hell became a lover
of the spinal stanzas, he came, he didn't grow there
by the act of remaining there, mortal and hatless
strolled right down into the river the message takes
reason is plenty and we stake our obligations on it
but not our sayings, those tremble in a wind of

the reminding of focus, or a difficult shadow of
a pretty death, one's arm contrasts with any
of several reactive poems, ones taken up now but
not yet broken into, the clearest brush
will line the ledge with a conscious magic and absolve us
ink at an end and later on that day

Perhaps the he he is is
not explainable by the you you
have always mixed feelings with
the identity a gloomy and barren place for
a metaphor, the first field or last vice
or stanza containing dish or fish or sky
running with milk, or dots to the end
then dash and the initials responsible

A poem is larger than the situation
of one held longer than it actually is
though plenty would just continue
the salt charred under a lamp arm or
low sun the review couldn't be bothered with
one feeling ever borne out since its origin?
but close enough to the line if you are
the right person playing it or messenger
casting aside the bay leaf for death with a difference

Here and now Captain Specific is staring placidly
at an object
to an absolute halt, wrapping yard and sky
in needlework and frosting, binding energy
on the vastness of a stall
but he cannot reveal it

has not the language for it, is
unable to receive a thing

Gradually substances pall beyond the perimeter
the tin mine is rotting in honey
the strew of loam edges toward the oceans
the alleys echo themselves sour, clattering ink falls
toads clear the earth, it is perhaps
little enough that the fish of chalk is regained in light
that no thought is wasted on everything
everywhere and not at all in sole declension

But the poem prefers death and milk in contrasting stanzas
and now that I am here I feel it is all about
simply living, not looking for something else
the miles marked up on the trunks, or anything lucid
that anyone objectively drops, these or suitably ringing
others are mates to my nut's fattening, stated
the harmful chap pleasantly who just shared your most
recent and addling repast, he is the one to ask
the graduate who stands just outside the palace of remedies
and asks himself another for every one of yours
constant piecemeal and won't budge

CATS MOUNTED ON COTS

Stevens, his stuff so even, makes mine seem like
slipwash. Can you write in a box? Four-square
on a double dare and leave the whole rest of it
invisibly dangling. Eventually it would score you up.
Meet you back later and treadless. Thoughts, they don't
help on a dime. Saddle soap being the better emetic
on another planet. I am always tinged with
no-plan openness, figured by fingers relent at a fear.

The whole scowling school went up and down in
a syzygy. Even if it did close during the war.
When people knew it and just stood there.
The mile-hangers stood in for the box's magazine.
Whim loafs you couldn't imagine daring. Long enough
to write and you'll see the end parts fight.
We should all be thronged together and be mumbling.
Sides of day in blues of orange. And the night tider
strokes his bulking frays. Last avenue I caught
just a stretch of it.

How to go on? A mystery, but I always seem to
know just where to pause. A halt in back of the
baking soda magazine, the one with only its bridges
in braille. A whole long song nobody's tongue will
ever swim in. A California beyond the rationing of
clouds. My pen not this time to run out but
suck in. And the stammerings give way to
exact brackets, slides of deer meat, soundings
of the hull. Or little collateral timings like
needles in the pine. Waved at the cathedral

then landed by its subsidiary. The lights blacking
through, nine prongs to one stew.

But Stevens wins without a clue. All fell free
beyond his bargaining lessons. But to exact what
was he witness? Own poems. Maps without
alarms. Timings of the china to a frosty edge.
Later salivation and the numbers on the wine. Sent
to France for paintings never asked. Sat out alone
in a background in flower, needful of kilter power.
The cats avoid the starch in his cuffs. But he was
needful also of palladium of laughs. Coins around his
steering wheel he never clinked nor drove. Or
counted on leaving much. The world is a hand
closing on the decimal fan. And he did have harm
from attitudes. Closed them into a pure.
Not so pure, but with ready aisles and gates. Hid a
sock on his mate. She of the upstairs barriers
and an early cold town beauty. He would have given
up the law for a sternness of drawers. But they
all said he collected himself almost perfectly.
Laughed and handed on the answers over the oiled corner
globe. Kept a closet full of pictures of skin behind his
cowled and easeful desk. Subvocalized lines by the
gates to parks. And refused any rides but saddeningly.
He comes to pass. Habits won't notch his works,
the ones with adages blanked out on their backsides.
The ones with carparks featuring clams. Or claws in paper
rows, closed in the oils of a fishing camp. Poems
are an excuse for looking sure to the future backwards.
He never capped his pens. Gave them to grandchildren
with a joke like back of his hand. And they all tell

stories now on him. But his true weights
still organize the table. The one he left off
writing at and dried.

Each of his lines seem frills show an edge on
sanity. Removed in told thought and never quite
reaching the river. I see him clogging the room,
each tone etching the matter it grows. It is,
this style marking snow from straw. And those
reach your head nights the cold, just stare at the
double pane. Deeps and death laugh together,
but with or at? There are numbers on his
shoes, will never quite match no matter the
breeze on his sheen. A monkey reading a magazine
in the lemon light. A revolver purple on the hull.

Imagine that your each word would entail the rest.
And no matter the sametime nothing would cease.
The easing of a finger produce another letter than the
one, the one you had chosen in a less mindful ease
fractions before. The numbers to collect themselves,
you have construed at such length. And the statement
to blind you when you finally face it. Somebody else
did it. A loafing the subject of fine gems.
And the impossibilities stored chime firm in the wall.
He had another habit and I hear it tending now.

But even Borromini didn't tackle all the angles,
so Stevens in his blue gaze heightens all arcades
of the school whole. Seen is seeing after the last
of nights, so is not. Angles are only variation
on the matters of some less reasonable tone.

But still they craze. A light spoken in on them
from further lips. I read all the books to be
had, then cashed my class for overstuffed furniture.
Ones with rings, and ones with a patter of stars, and
ones with no sound at all. We agreed to manage
to meet to regress in that hall. But to speak
of that one would be to speak of the only, and
that is not. Nothing is lone.

Shots and beeps from beyond the locks disturb the
credulous. A crest of blocks that never strikes
to sink beyond the moon. These the pinnacles
of matters of thought losing balance. Then
gaining a hand from the crumpled brain.
These things are not the same. Words come in
in rows disjunct you with their regular
sonorous. You'll tie them in one limping strand
and think to see. But the falls are all the same
in bringing matter to itself. And risen thought
vulnerable regards only edges. Let us set the
tea a little closer.

Brawn man outshrugs his form. A chair,
surrounded by air surrounded by all the airs
surround that air. Same man outsets his
time, and sametime loafs in a delirium of stealth.
His wealth a tagging of the worths behind him.
Forms of gone, and the road edged in vacuums.
I have told you, Crystalled Master, once you
have form, to remain is to go. On, as if
further in a sightless dream. That part
of space erased by that man at his desk.
Then helpless to turn.

ATTENTION

Monk is alive, still
I saw him
coming out of a rent shop bent
at slow angles

Said nothing, the usual, the hat,
the moon dance, the opening
for a drummer's plot, building
edges still ringing, well

you had no need of thought
at a bridge presence of him
brought out and shaking up
ahead in the background flawing
in deedful
beauty

GODARD AND THE RHAPSODY OF MENTION

Color of rope, color of towels
colors of everything in the neartime dark
soft husks moving in central corners
she has half an answer for the cut-back question
as the radiance answers itself the questions
we had half as much luck we'd stop a car
part a wrap with a whip, another
thing numb, but coughingly clear
she sneaks another whisp of her breast and he
reposes the dart, the cold blank through a window
someone coming up to touching things as an introduction
he slaps the wall, both hands, turns and types "mal"
an introduction to running lessons around the car
and the thread of one's nipple is clear

Processional ice in a modified hallway, high angle
of the guy is just doing his work, clean on a ladder
no one's paid off until they tell the tale, plural
and he had nothing but to say that one thing, even
in no-ways Italian but what cut to her nation?
Robe colors juggled, temperatures forgotten, cigars
tapped into papercup drinks, the spine in torsion
under inspection, under a palm or inside bath cloth
she may have everything to say about her own angles
perhaps even looking, perhaps speech, and the sea rolls
the car sweep to an original violet line

can't you see back far enough to answer? Nodding
switching, nothing, pretending, half of acting, stopped
and taught, unschooled, unfriendly, in love, on a dime

in an action, unintended, untended, half tender
scowling one's shades through smoke, self-induced, partial
and trembling, showered and bending collapse and intend to
show, everything as if nothing, to it a connecting fluid
or line of traffic, business as a clue, she is
a tart in your view, is he a dancer?

Resultant of, even intention, image and sound
though all your accounting could end on a plastic
a barrier of hips too narrow for taste a bare half inch
or a thoughtful flick of the hair, turn of the brow, placed
eyes throttled back to a low hum, a tooth, a glass
more than you thought to find in a single room
drifted off hugging down on fucking the television she
passes him opens the following drapes frames her
self akimbo in laced light of the following day
he won't care but strokes a glass of blue

And her hair turns, her eyes won't wait, the table
is enough for a glance or an inch, or the wanting to
look down, not shave, save all your cellophanes, bright
in the singleman's dark, nobody knew everybody
didn't, half a smile, to the front, from the side
she's wandering in and out of, somebody else preoccupant
and this is all in no place, but a floor of the music

People not thinking of each other till called upon to
act up in the middle and see, hear, divide towel lengths
simple as no animals in a minute of the film
or lower or upper hallway, thing is break of a dream
into nothing that could be anything but rehearsed
people there doing when around them is nothing

but ending
            say it all again and still it is over

Does she know anything at all?
Pencil over words in book
I have to turn on lights or somebody
will, eager as a desk set to have me
stall here a moment, it is too
easy for her to have herself
all out and exchanged for the practice of music
stands on the floor, papers she won't touch
angles we won't hate, gunshots in the bank
and thoughts going on while the image is sounded
nothing after all interrupts the materials
Buster in the director's lap and what was that
book he was reading of hers?

Does he say her name to make it stop?
I think of something ceasing and he changes it
whose name is first, whose first name?
Cars seem to be let totally loose, completely useless
at certain points, then the sea overall remains
you first forget her name, and then her face
but could we all sit down and tell bodies?
Thoughts or shapes, or thoughts of shapes, of things
only to be standing by and watching, finally in the wash
nothing rhyming? Everything anyway going and
this a precise version, a learning
to see while hearing

Fucking in the place of no furniture
throwing things off anywhere, and little enough underwear

pillow or hook, love or work, bump and then
will find, will turn up the result that lasts
against the huge wall, music and no mind

And then to change something just stop and go
cutting on extreme motion, we will hold
no matter, and now the serious coffeecup
is cathode field no signal, and the meditation pop song

Able to hold himself the dunce in own frame
all the more slowed amidst terrorist shakes
and taken as what, whom in his age? The world is
big, bigger every frame-cut face
In any case I should show them something

Acknowledgments

All thanks to the editors of those magazines in which many of these poems first appeared and to the publishers who printed them in book form: Aram Saroyan (Lines Books), Lewis Warsh, Anne Waldman, Bernadette Mayer (Angel Hair Books), Fran McCullough (Harper & Row), Larry Fagin (Adventures in Poetry), Barrett Watten (This Press), Bill Berkson (Big Sky), Annabel Levitt (Vehicle Editions), Michael Wolfe (Tombouctou Books), Peter Ganick (Potes & Poets Press), Lyn Hejinian (Tuumba Press), Geoffrey Young (The Figures), Douglas Messerli (Sun & Moon Press), George & Chris Tysh (In Camera), Rebecca Wolff (Fence Books).

Station Hill thanks the following whose generosity made this volume possible: Peter Baker, Charles Bernstein and Susan Bee, Ron Brent, cris cheek, Nicholas Chiarella, Dennis Cooper, Johanna Drucker, Chris Funkhouser, Larkin Higgins, Steven Hirsch/Heaven Bone Press, Peter Janney, the Kelly Writers House, Grant Matthew Jenkins, Jack Kimball, Jon Klages, Katy Lederer, Andrew McCarron, Donald McWeeney, Kim Ding Pham, Archie Rand, Stephen Ratcliffe, Evelyn Reilly, Michael Ruby, Brent Sunderland, Andy Tang, Craig Watson, Anne Waldman/ The Jack Kerouac School of Disembodied Poetics, Kenneth Wapner, and Barrett Watten.

About the Author

Originally from Providence, Rhode Island, CLARK COOLIDGE now lives in Petaluma, California. He is the author of more than forty books, including *Space, Solution Passage, The Crystal Text, At Egypt, Now It's Jazz: Writings on Kerouac & The Sounds, The Act of Providence,* and most recently *88 Sonnets* and *A Book Beginning What And Ending Away.* In 2011 he edited a collection of Philip Guston's writings and talks for University of California Press. Initially a drummer, he was a member of David Meltzer's Serpent Power in 1967 and Mix group in 1993–94. Currently he has returned to active drumming with Thurston Moore and the free jazz band Ouroboros.